IDLE PURSUITS

IDLE PURSUITS

Literature and *Oisiveté*
in the French Renaissance

Virginia Krause

Newark: University of Delaware Press
London: Associated University Presses

© 2003 by Rosemont Publishing & Printing Corp.

All rights reserved. Authorization to photocopy items for internal or personal use, or the internal or personal use of specific clients, is granted by the copyright owner, provided that a base fee of $10.00, plus eight cents per page, per copy is paid directly to the Copyright Clearance Center, 222 Rosewood Drive, Danvers, Massachusetts 01923. [0-87413-835-3/03 $10.00 + 8¢ pp, pc.]

Other than as indicated in the foregoing, this book may not be reproduced, in whole or in part, in any form (except as permitted by Sections 107 and 108 of the U.S. Copyright Law, and except for brief quotes appearing in reviews in the public press).

Associated University Presses
2010 Eastpark Boulevard
Cranbury, NJ 08512

Associated University Presses
Unit 304
The Chandlery
50 Westminster Bridge Road
London SE1 7QY, England

Associated University Presses
P.O. Box 338, Port Credit
Mississauga, Ontario
Canada L5G 4L8

The paper used in this publication meets the requirements of the American National Standard for Permanence of Paper for Printed Library Materials Z39.48-1984.

Library of Congress Cataloging-in-Publication Data

Krause, Virginia, 1968–
    Idle pursuits : literature and oisiveté in the French Renaissance / Virginia Krause.
       p. cm.
    Includes bibliographical references and index.
    ISBN 0-87413-835-3 (alk. paper)
    1. French literature—16th century—History and criticism. 2. Leisure in literature. I. Title.

PQ239.K72 2003   2003047392

For my parents,
Helen D. Krause and George B. Krause

Contents

Acknowledgments	9
Textual Note	11
Introduction	15
1. Aristocratic Idleness: Claiming the Accursed Share	26
2. Work in Idleness in the Fourth Estate	56
3. Portrait of an Early Modern *Oiseuse: Les Angoysses douloureuses*	86
4. Leisure as Commodity: The *Amadis* Serial	121
5. *"en pleine oysiveté"*: Idleness in the *Essais*	143
Notes	171
Bibliography	212
Index	226

Acknowledgments

I HAVE RECEIVED FINANCIAL SUPPORT FROM THE NEWBERRY LIBRARY FOR a summer fellowship and from Brown University for a junior sabbatical and am grateful to both institutions. I would also like to thank the staff of the Houghton and Newberry Libraries as well as the staff of Interlibrary Loan at the Rockefeller Library at Brown University. Portions of chapters 4 and 5 appeared in very different form in *Viator* 31 (2000): 361–80. Permission to reprint in revised form is gratefully acknowledged.

It is my pleasure to acknowledge the support from friends and colleagues who have offered advice or commented most helpfully on portions of this manuscript. I wish to thank Marian Rothstein, Kathleen Wine, Scott Shershow, and Larry Kritzman. I am grateful to Gary Ferguson, a reader for the University of Delaware Press, whose suggestions for revisions have been invaluable. I also owe much to my colleagues in the Department of French Studies and in the Program of Renaissance and Early Modern Studies at Brown University as well as professors in the Department of French and Italian at the University of Wisconsin-Madison. One could not wish for a better scholarly model than Ullrich Langer, who with much patience offered guidance for this project at its inception and has since been extremely generous with his time in commenting on drafts and offering advice. For the many times when he has offered suggestions and guidance, I extend my warmest thanks to Lewis Seifert. I have had many occasions to be grateful to Pierre Saint-Amand for his support and friendly advice. My scholarly debt to George Hoffmann is visible throughout this study. I wish to add my personal thanks for his generous suggestions and comments on drafts, which have opened up new vistas on many occasions. Finally, I am grateful to Christian Martin, who has critiqued drafts and offered personal support during an arduous process.

Textual Note

IN QUOTING FROM EARLY PRINTED TEXTS I HAVE EXPANDED ABBREVIations and differentiated between u and v; i and j.

The following modern editions are frequently used and, unless otherwise indicated, are the sources for quotations.

Hélisenne de Crenne, *Les Angoysses douloureuses qui procedent d'amours*, ed. Christine de Buzon (Paris: Champion, 1997).
———. *The Torments of Love*, trans. Lisa Neal and Steven Rendall (Minneapolis: University of Minnesota Press, 1996).
———. *Les Epistres familières et invectives*, ed. Jerry Nash (Paris: Champion, 1996).
———. *A Renaissance Woman: Helisenne's Personal and Invective Letters*, trans. Marianna M. Mustacchi and Paul J. Archambault (Syracuse: Syracuse University Press, 1986).
Michel de Montaigne, *Les Essais*, 3 vols, ed. Pierre Villey and V.-L. Saulnier (Paris: Presses Universitaires de France, 1965).

> [I follow standard referencing in indicating the volume number, the essay number, the page number, and finally the strata: a (referring to writing mostly published in 1580); b (referring to material mostly published in 1588); c (mostly reserved for Montaigne's last revisions, made on his personal copy of the 1588 edition).]

———. *The Complete Essays of Montaigne*, trans. Donald Frame, (Stanford: Stanford University Press, 1958).
François Rabelais, *Gargantua*, ed. Gérard Defaux (Paris: Librairie Générale Française, 1994).
———. *Le Tiers Livre*, ed. Jean Céard (Paris: Librairie Générale Française, 1995).
———. *Gargantua and Pantagruel*, trans. J. M. Cohen (London: Penguin, 1955).

IDLE PURSUITS

Figure 1. Woodcut depicting Lady Idleness. Leaf a ii recto, in: Guillaume de Lorris, *Le rommant de la rose*. Paris: Clement Longis [150?]. TYP 515.00.532, Department of Printing and Graphic Arts, Houghton Library, Harvard College Library.

Introduction

On juge un cheval, non seulement à le voir manier sur une carriere, mais encore à le voir en repos à l'estable
—Montaigne

HISTORIANS AND LITERARY CRITICS HAVE EXAMINED THE NOBILITY'S military vocation, magistrates' professional ethos, and women's work in the domestic sphere.[1] In contrast to this focus on occupation, the present study explores the "idle pursuits" available to these same noblemen, magistrates, and women. What was the status of time left over from "serious" occupations? And why did this time become the locus of virulent polemic, including debates for or against nobiliary idleness, for or against women's right to leisure, as well as the more familiar debate for or against the superiority of the contemplative life over the active life? In short, what made idleness such a compelling notion for early modern writers, from Hélisenne de Crenne and Herberay des Essarts to Louise Labé, Ronsard, and Montaigne, to name only a few?[2]

Renaissance preoccupations with idleness have generally been explained in terms of a nascent subjectivity.[3] To be sure, idleness provided a fertile terrain for the development of *homo interior*. Yet its relationship to interiority should not obscure its social function: for during the Renaissance, idleness was also an instrument used to make a would-be interior disposition manifest to others. It served to *produce* the private, to make it public and visible. To "be idle" was to stage personal cultivation, noble status, or detachment. Only when "on display" could these qualities denote an ethical position or social posture: idleness had to be made conspicuous. The present study takes *oisiveté* to be as much an element of spectacle as of introspection, part of the quest to be known as well as to "know thy self."

Idleness, then, belonged as much to the realm of social practices as to the intimacy of being. One has only to think of the courtier's "leisurely" art of the self as one example of how closely notions of idleness were bound up with self-presentation. Castiglione's concept of *sprezzatura* put leisure at the center of the stage of court life. The perfect courtier had to appear nonchalant, he had to appear to excel *effortlessly* at horsemanship, dancing, or anything else he undertook. He produced a "leisure effect" in the public sphere before the admiring or jealous eyes of others. Far from being an alternative to the world of the court, idleness was enmeshed in the constant rivalries, machinations for social standing, and maneuvers for office that characterized court life. Just as material resources were the object of commercial exchanges, so too was idleness part of the sphere of social exchanges. As a prestigious condition, it was pursued for its symbolic capital (to borrow Pierre Bourdieu's important notion). Yet it could also become the object of commercial exchange. As the producers of romance soon discovered, there was an early modern market for idleness. Along with chivalric and amorous adventures, it was leisure itself that was consumed by the readers of the *Amadis* serial. At once a commodity and form of capital, idleness (*otium*) clearly belonged to the realm of social exchanges ostensibly reserved for affairs (*neg-otium*).

Thorstein Veblen first formulated the hypothesis that abstention from useful employment was the very index of prestige.[4] Although from very different angles, Georges Bataille and Pierre Bourdieu (along with Jean Baudrillard, to name only a few of the thinkers working in the wake of Veblen) each gave a new emphasis to this principle. From these theorists was derived one of this study's central postulates: how a class (or culture) treats idleness reveals as much about its ideology as its attitude toward material resources and social responsibility. The focal point for my discussions is not what Renaissance writers apparently deemed useful or even necessary, but rather the activities that transcended their ascribed occupation in society, be it spinning or public service. During the Renaissance, I argue, the *value* of idleness depended paradoxically upon its lack of any manifest worth. Useless, trivial, superfluous, ornamental, gratuitous, or autotelic, idleness was nevertheless a key pawn in the period's defining struggles. *Oisiveté* was thoroughly enmeshed in the cultural and political upheaval of the Renaissance. The sociopolitical order had been thrown into question by the rise of a new class of highly educated magistrates, members of the so-called "Fourth Estate," who challenged the values and lifestyle of the traditional nobility. Gender roles and ideals were also in dispute as women contested the monopoly men had long held on culture. In both cases, the notion of idleness was called into play. The officeholding "gentlemen" of the Fourth Estate struggled to reappropriate idleness from "lazy aristocrats." At the same time, women demanded the same right to idleness enjoyed by their male counterparts.

Why should a concept hailed for its lack of any real use be of such significance? Precisely because it was not classified among the "practical arts," idleness was free to assume a greater symbolic efficacy: did it not belong to the realm of *eros*, nobility, culture, and power? The pursuit of idleness was in reality an effective, if circuitous, means to status and even wealth. If writers struggled to appropriate idleness, it was because the concept had a covert utility, all the more potent for being elusive. I study how writers exploited rhetorical conventions and social codes in order to assume the posture of *oisifs*. Intimately bound up with self-presentation and social identity, idleness presents a fertile terrain for examining how the period's elites competed for the privileged role of arbiter of the social hierarchy. For to determine the meaning, value, and art of practicing idleness was to master a symbolic logic with high social stakes.

The corpus studied here spans a period ranging from Guillaume de Lorris's *Le Roman de la Rose* (ca. 1230) to Montaigne's *Essais* published at the end of the Renaissance. It includes some of the period's masterpieces as well as less familiar works, from the best-selling books of *Amadis de Gaule* to personal letters. I also study texts not literary in any traditional sense, including documents from the trial of Gilles de Rais (1440), treatises on nobility, hunting, and erotic melancholy as well as conduct books and annotations. These sources contain privileged insights into Renaissance notions of the uses and misuses of idleness, its pleasures and dangers, its capacity to confer prestige and unleash moral degeneracy. What were the allegories, myths, intertexts, and imagery of idleness? It is by an analysis of discourses and representations that I engage Renaissance notions of *oisiveté*.

The corpus of this study was chosen to include texts offering the most sustained reflections on *oisiveté*. At the same time, it accords a prominent place to genres associated with idleness. Hence the choice to privilege the essay and the romance genre, both deemed to be "idle" genres. This pairing may seem incongruous, especially given the heterogeneity of the early novel—a category that can, depending on its definition, include works ranging from Rabelais's novels to Hélisenne de Crenne's *Les Angoysses douloureuses* and Herberay des Essarts's adaptation of *Amadis de Gaule*. Notwithstanding, during the Renaissance these two genres were perceived to be read and composed by idlers. Indeed, the association of essay and novel with idleness persisted and even intensified into the seventeenth century. These two genres also offer microcosms of Renaissance transformations of leisure. More clearly than any other genres, they frame the birth of the modern contemplative (the *Essais*); a new commodification of leisure (the *Amadis* serial); and a definition of the novel as a sphere of women's autonomy in leisure (Hélisenne de Crenne's autobiographical novel and romance combined).

Navigating between rhetorical analysis and the early modern social reality, this study is indebted to the work of George Hoffmann and Philippe Desan, particularly in those sections devoted to Montaigne and his milieu.[5] The image of the essayist that emerges from the work of Hoffmann and Desan is far removed indeed from the picture of a "gentleman of leisure" residing in an ivory tower untroubled by mundane concerns. Their conclusions allow one to appreciate the full impact of work on Montaigne's daily life and literary imagination: not only did he effectively manage his literary career and family estate, but new economic paradigms penetrate the *Essais* despite his desire to reproduce traditional nobiliary values. My own study has been shaped by their findings and methods, but it also seeks to explain the enduring idealization of leisure by Montaigne and his peers. Despite the social reality and daily lives of these men, they nevertheless elaborated an "art of idleness" that became a cherished dimension of their identity. Idleness functioned as a potent myth for this class in full social ascension.

Although its focus is different from my own, Cathy Yandell's *Carpe Corpus: Time and Gender in Early Modern France* brings to the fore the meanings of time—and thus of wasting time. Her study reevaluates the category of temporality, too often understood by modern readers to be unidimensional. It offers a nuanced discussion of moralists' conceptions of how women should employ their time, and how women poets figured time and its passing. Her work also suggests that much can be learned by comparing how *religieuses* wrote about their leisure time to their secular counterparts.[6] At a time when monasticism was in decline, and with it the contemplative life, the convent nevertheless remained a particularly compelling alternative for many Renaissance women. Recent work emphasizes that religious life gave women the opportunity to participate in localized politics, cultural influence, and administrative power, not to mention *otium*—all forms of work or leisure from which women were generally excluded in the secular sphere.[7]

To be sure, theologians from the period often gave idleness a new polemical content. Max Weber's famous study *The Protestant Work Ethic*, as well as the critiques and reformulations that followed (including Tawney's), offer far-reaching analyses of notions of work and leisure in the wake of the Reformation.[8] Time itself assumed a new spiritual value in Calvin's writing and in Geneva.[9] I have chosen to emphasize changes taking place in the secular sphere in the analyses that follow. This choice reflects in part the necessity of limiting a subject that would have been impossibly large had it included religious doctrine and debates. But it also reflects the historical changes underway at the time. For the early modern world witnessed a redefinition of leisure as a *secular* ideal. Choosing a corpus of mostly secular writing allows me to explore the processes of secularization central to the transformation of leisure.

Scholarship on the history of leisure has been of great assistance throughout my study. French culture today is undergoing an extensive reevaluation of our civilization of work—witness the recent reduction of the workweek to thirty-five hours and the renewed interest in leisure among French economists, sociologists, and philosophers.[10] Dominique Méda in particular presents a genealogy of the modern notion of work. The contemporary sense of work as creativity—as an individual and collective freedom—was born only in the nineteenth century.[11] This point is capital. It corrects the misconception that it has only been attitudes toward work that have varied across the centuries, from the ancient Greek ethics of leisure to the modern work ethic. Only if we grasp that work's function as a social link and means of self-realization is the result of a particular moment in history can we then conceive of societies in which this notion of work was absent (as in ancient Greece) or only nascent (as in the early modern world).

From Commonplace to Dissensus

"I wrote the present work to avoid idleness." Although the Renaissance certainly did not invent it,[12] one finds variations on the idleness commonplace across all Renaissance genres and tendencies. The point of departure of this study is the rhetorical force of the topos, which reoccurs in a myriad of forms and contexts. By "rhetorical," I mean that authors write about idleness in a performative rather than a descriptive manner. Writers invoking idleness do not seek to describe the real so much as to situate themselves with respect to it. Rather than rehearsing a given "essence" of idleness, they position themselves with respect to a spectrum of its meanings on the one hand and social roles available to idlers on the other. My discussions follow a recurrent pattern, proceeding from the idleness commonplace to the agonistic social processes in which it was enmeshed.

Pour éviter oisiveté: for the most part, scholars have taken this topos at face value, understanding idleness in light of the moralists' condemnation. A general sense of moral depravity was indeed the most manifest of idleness's three meanings. Transmitted by Renaissance miscellanies, this vision of decadent idleness is condensed in its ritual epithet: *mère et nourrice de tous les vices*, a commonplace omnipresent in prefaces. The so-called *Diverses Leçons de Pierre Messie*, Claude Gruget's French translation of this immensely popular Spanish miscellany, is typical of such moralist discourse. In a rigorous polarization, the *excellence* of work is praised while the *dommages* engendered by idleness are enumerated in an insistently vituperative tone.[13]

Yet idleness carried a second meaning explicitly at odds with the former. *Oisiveté* conferred prestige on the privileged few able to master it—this notwithstanding its perceived degeneracy. Beyond its condemnation on moral grounds, idleness connoted a noble lifestyle, premised as it was on refraining from "debasing" activities such as commerce, working for another, and many forms of manual labor.[14] In other words, early modern conceptions of nobility gave idleness a veneer of grandeur. Hence the woodcut found in Renaissance editions of the *Roman de la Rose* (figure 1).[15] This image depicts Oiseuse (Idleness) in all her courtly majesty standing before a door and holding a key. She guards the threshold between the world of commoners and the courtly elite residing in aristocratic bliss within the garden; in other words, entrance into the Renaissance's social and cultural elite hinged upon idleness.

A third intertext contributed to the potential dignity of the concept. Idleness was elevated toward loftier meanings by Greek and Roman philosophical traditions: the contemplative ideal of *schole* on which Aristotle based his ethics; the utter peace embodied by the Epicurean divinities; the rigorous *otium* defended by Seneca; Ciceronian *otium cum dignitate* which reconciled civic values with the ideal of the speculative life. With such a wide spectrum of authorities taking its defense, idleness had a positive value that could not be ignored. Was it not at the basis of the good life, the bedrock of peace of mind, and the very condition of literary creation?[16] Closely bound up with humanist ideals, idleness was at the heart of the Fourth Estate's self-definition, for it was literally and conceptually *schole* that gave rise to *scholarly*.

Three conflicting versions of *oisiveté* thus shaped Renaissance conceptions: 1) the miscellanies' condemnation (*oisiveté*, a moral blight); 2) a normative code of nobility (*oisiveté*, a noble condition); 3) Greek and Roman authorities (*schole* and *otium*, concepts linked to knowledge and to ethics). This conceptual uncertainty had a defining impact on the fortunes of idleness in the Renaissance. Because it was elusively defined, idleness was open to manipulation. Competing interests thus sought to define the rules for practicing idleness properly, to lay claim to this concept endowed with high social stakes. As a result, the idleness commonplace becomes caught up in rhetorical labyrinths where stated intentions hide secret agendas. Even the seemingly most straightforward cases often conceal a highly complex rhetorical use of the concept. An example from "les plaisirs de la vie Rustique" by Guy du Faur de Pibrac, a prominent magistrate, serves as a case in point. He invokes the standard protest "I wrote the present work in order to avoid idleness."[17] The commonplace here figures as a variation on the modesty topos: in a depreciatory tone, the author presents his writing as a mere hobby devoid of any grandiose ambitions. Yet the topos assumes a subtle, even counterintuitive function when one recalls Pibrac's situation. The new class of *hauts fonctionnaires* to which he belonged was both critical of the traditional nobility and eager to usurp its place by becoming the new "leisure class." His milieu was marked by a hyperawareness of the proper use of idleness for a gentleman. Seen in this light, Pibrac's use of the topos resembles a performative contradiction: while appearing to dispel idleness (I avoid idleness), it subtly insinuates it (I know the true meaning of leisure). The idleness topos often serves a dual and contradictory function. On the one hand, it gestures toward the consecrated wisdom promulgated by commonplace books preaching that idleness should be avoided at all costs. Yet on the other hand, it allows writers to suggest their latent affinity for "the noble condition," what Madeleine Des Roches terms "ceste loüable paresse."[18]

Given the concept's polysemy and the commonplace's potential for antiphrasis, how is the interpreter to proceed? How is one to unravel the competing discourses interlaced and pitted against one another? Throughout the study, I offer a *situational* interpretation of idleness and its commonplace. I study how meaning and function are both inflected toward a specific social context. A "gentleman" with dubious aristocratic credentials and a woman writer may both write "to avoid idleness"; indeed, they may both employ the very same fixed syntagma ("pour éviter oisiveté"); yet it may have a different performative function in each case. Rather than simply reiterating a *doxa*, writers mobilized the commonplace to their own social or political ends.

Rhetoric always hinges on a specific public with specific assumptions. The method of literary analysis used here asserts this principle by bringing underlying sociocultural premises to the fore. The chapters that follow are thus indebted to the work of social and intellectual historians. In particular, studies by Arlette Jouanna and George Huppert have helped me evaluate how idleness was shaped by changing notions of nobility.[19] In exploring how women were excluded from idleness (and the pursuit of status that it entailed), I rely on Evelyne Berriot-Salvadore's analysis of the situation of Renaissance women.[20] Finally, Glending Olson's work on the medieval tradition of literature as recreation provides a general framework in which to situate Renaissance notions of reading as a "hobby." Although I interpret the romance phenomenon as a new paradigm that ultimately broke with this tradition, Olson's work allows me to better isolate the points of rupture.[21]

Winding from moral condemnation, through literary intertexts, to Renaissance social codes and ideals, the idleness topos was mobilized in complex rhetorical maneuvers. Less a vehicle for common wisdom than a notion dependent upon a specific situation, idleness and its commonplace partake of the profound disunity in Renaissance culture. As though passing through a particular lens, the meaning of idleness was refracted away from universals toward Renaissance debates and assumptions regarding the relative merits of work and idleness for readers and writers, for aristocrats, or for women. Even the most unambiguous prescriptions ("Aristocrats must not be idle"; "Women must keep busy") or the most seemingly disinterested musings ("How can one best reach mental serenity?"; "What role does idleness play in the good life?") ultimately obey an ideological logic that pits different discourses, and different agendas, against one another. Despite its rather poetic resonances, which suggest tranquility and detachment, idleness was in fact disputed terrain, the object of dissensus and social agonistics.

Leisure without Gods

The loss of a transcendent meaning for idleness is part of a larger process of secularization that shaped early modern culture. In his *Leisure: The Basis of Culture*, Josef Pieper argues that religious dimensions are inherent in leisure despite its current estrangement from its sacred origins. Festivals, monastic contemplation, not to mention the Sabbath, Sundays, or holidays, were all born as forms of humanity's participation in the sacred through leisure. The New Testament story of the two sisters, Martha and Mary, provides one illustration of this general principle. In contrast to her sister Martha, who was busy serving Christ and being useful, Mary sat at Christ's feet in an attitude of quiet adoration. Her withdrawal from productive activity to contemplation—the proverbial "best share" (Luke 10:42)—made Mary a symbol of the medieval ideal of contemplation. But when leisure ceased to possess a sacred origin and telos, it became simply a nonproductive category—what Georges Bataille has termed "the accursed share." Secular interests then struggled for control over the meaning and function of excess time and resources. The Renaissance notion of *oisiveté* was fiercely disputed precisely because of its nonutilitarian dimensions: achieving a monopoly on prestige, morality, and culture depended upon claiming the accursed share.

The gradual redefinition of leisure as a secular ideal constitutes the historical frame for the analyses I propose. Since this process began well before the Renaissance, my study opens with one of its central dramas in the early thirteenth century: the transfer of the ideal of leisure from religious institutions and ideals (monastic *otium*) to secular elites (the feudal aristocracy). *Le Roman de la Rose*, I argue, offers an allegorical representation of the nobility's newly defined identity as the "idle condition." Chapters 2 and 3 examine the next stages in this process. The nobility's monopoly on leisure was challenged first by a new class of officeholding "gentlemen" and later by Renaissance women. In contrast to a twentieth-century context in which work is a status-granting commodity, it was leisure that fulfilled a comparable function in the Renaissance. Thus, while the contemporary women's movement seeks "equal opportunity" for employment, Renaissance women writers struggled to conquer access to *otium* at a time when the leisure class had an exclusively male membership.

The second half of this study examines Renaissance precursors to modern leisure. Contemporary Western society has been described as a consumer culture with an ethos of work at its core. Work has become the basis for our social organization. Once synonymous with torture (*travail*: from *tripalium*, an instrument of torture), work is now commonly perceived as a means of self-realization. We seek fulfillment through our professional lives. In the nightmarish scenarios envisioned by some sociologists,[22] leisure is depicted as but a necessary cog in this wheel—an occasion for the worker-turned-consumer to spend the resources amassed by working. One person's leisure thus provides work for another. In 2000 the Chinese government created an additional holiday with the sole intention of stimulating consumer spending by giving the population extra free time to engage in shopping, tourism, entertainment—all expanding sectors of the economy. This example suggests the historical variability of what is deemed "leisure": for in the Renaissance, "shopping" could no more have been deemed "leisure" than *negotium* could have been considered a form of *otium*. At the same time, it conveys the extent to which any transcendent dimensions have been eroded in an ongoing process that threatens to reduce leisure to one commodity among many.

Yet despite this socioeconomic paradigm, we also cling to the idea that leisure is the affair of the private subject, the secret garden of our most intimate selves. The subject as complete master of its own leisure is a reassuring mythology; it offers symbolic compensation for the nearly unchallenged supremacy of the economic paradigm by promising that the private self maintains its autonomy, as though it were somehow protected from the purely "exterior" reality of total work.[23]

The Renaissance both laid the seeds for these developments and mounted an active resistance against them, as I argue in the last two chapters. Chapter 4 examines serialization, a new development in an ongoing desacralization of leisure. The literary serial transformed idleness into a commodity to be bought and sold like any other temporal merchandise. When humanists mounted a rearguard offensive against romance serials, it was thus in the name of the sacredness of time, and particularly leisure time. My study concludes with the figure of the autonomous contemplative. Montaigne's *Essais* dramatize the situation of the modern subject whose leisure no longer serves to know or celebrate God. Yet in the nascent age of *homo œconomicus,* the idea of leisure celebrated by the ancients was increasingly out of reach as well. Classical leisure proved to be as inaccessible as *contemplatio dei.* If Montaigne continued to cultivate leisure, in imitation of the Stoic sage and the Epicurean philosopher, his idle pursuits remained relegated to the essentially utopian space of his tower library. The essayist's idealization of leisure—his tower imagery and reiterated esteem for "full idleness"—was in fact belied by the very real commitment to *negotium* that characterized his daily life. Condemned to fulfill an essentially compensatory function, Montaigne's art of idleness announced the modern world of work.

The five chapters of this study chronicle transformations of leisure in the early modern world, from the initial detachment of the "idle condition" from religious contemplation in the thirteenth century to the birth of the modern contemplative at the end of the Renaissance. Examining discourses and representations of idleness provides a new frame for understanding Renaissance notions of social identity and how it could be manipulated. What was the function of idleness in the early modern social landscape? How did writers define their idle pursuits, and what made mastery of the "art of idleness" such a valuable asset in Renaissance France?

1
Aristocratic Idleness: Claiming the Accursed Share

> Pour moi l'homme n'existe véritablement que quand il ne fait rien. Dès qu'il agit, dès qu'il se prépare à faire quelque chose, il devient une pitoyable créature.
> —E. M. Cioran with Georg Caryat Focke, 1992.

"GENTLEMEN MUST NOT BE IDLE."[1] WITH THIS PHRASE, JEAN BOUCHET sums up the most familiar of Renaissance attitudes toward *oisiveté*. Discourse on idleness commonly targeted one social group (aristocrats) and privileged one discursive mode (prescription). Scores of variations on this theme run through moralist literature. In his *Œuvres morales et diversifiées* (1575), Jean Des Caurres attacks "degenerate" nobles for being "lazy, useless and decadent."[2] Louis Le Roy similarly cautions that a long period of peace may make noblemen "insolent, and by opulence and illicit idleness, superfluous and effeminate."[3] As though to join the campaign to end aristocratic idleness, even romance prologues exhort their chivalric readers to "avoid idleness, the mother of vice."[4]

Treatises on nobility, pamphlets, and commonplace books present ample testimony to a moral castigation of idleness. Yet the sheer abundance of these condemnations suggests that the idea of nobiliary idleness was a matter of contention. The intensity of the debate further suggests that it had high stakes: idleness had to be attacked all the more fiercely because it was a central element in the definition of aristocratic identity. For idleness was not simply a state of inaction to be denounced, but also a social practice rewarded with distinction. In sum, idleness was both explicitly denounced and implicitly valued. By juxtaposing two antithetical prescriptions ("aristocrats must not be idle" / "to be noble one must be idle"), Renaissance discourse on idleness bears witness to a defining ambiguity.

1: ARISTOCRATIC IDLENESS: CLAIMING THE ACCURSED SHARE

The following passage from Jean de Caumont's treatise entitled *De la vertu de noblesse* is representative of the Renaissance's ambivalence toward the nobility's *oisiveté*. This excerpt functions as a prime example of the broader phenomenon that this chapter seeks to elucidate: in condemning nobiliary idleness, Jean de Caumont's vituperative rhetoric betrays a "social unconscious." Negated but not effaced, the positive value of idleness remains discernible. Reading against the author's explicit intention, we can glimpse the aristocratic ideology of leisure under attack:

> Car le nom de Noblesse n'est pas un nom d'arbre sterile, *ce n'est pas un nom de licence*, un nom de vaine jactance, *un nom d'oisive splendeur*, comme *s'ils n'estoyent nez qu'à leurs plaisirs*: *C'est un nom de fonction & de charge*, un nom de vertu . . . un nom plein d'acte, plein de substance, plein de divine puissance. (emphasis added)[5]

> [For the name Nobility is not a name of a sterile tree, *it is not a name of license*, a name of vain boasting, *a name of idle splendor*, as though *they were born only for their pleasures*: *it is a name of function and office*, a name of virtue . . . a name full of action, full of substance, full of divine power.]

Its peremptory tone coupled with extensive denegations calls for a reading attentive to what this passage might seek to repress. Negating the affirmations and affirming the negations thus reveals idleness to be part of a social ideal. Reformulating the italicized passages, nobility becomes defined as follows:

Explicit Definition of Nobility	*Implicit Conception of Nobiliary Identity*
the name Nobility is not a name of license	nobility is a "license"
[or] a name of idle splendor	[and] an idle splendor
as though aristocrats were born only for their pleasure	aristocrats do indeed have an innate right to cultivate pleasure
it is a name of function and office	nobility is in fact an essence, not a function or office

What was nobility if not a "license," a freedom from the common condition of labor? If labor was the degrading condition of peasants, was not idleness a source of splendor? Was it not the nobility's privilege—or even obligation—to cultivate pleasant things?[6] And finally, was it not by virtue of its very essence that nobility transcended the realm of mere function in order to partake of a timeless essence of all things beautiful and worthy? The vision of nobiliary identity targeted by Jean de Caumont is surprisingly coherent: at its core is a mysterious essence rather than a given activity, just as a symbolic order of "idle splendor" takes precedence over useful occupations. I want to argue that these traits constituted an ideology of aristocratic idleness. It is of course present here only in an implicit and inverted form. During the Renaissance, nobiliary idleness was represented mostly in an ironic, inverted, or masked form. But a positive formulation of this aristocratic ideology can be traced back to *Le Roman de la Rose*. Since she played a key role in defining the aristocracy as a "leisure class," Oiseuse (Idleness) and the ideal she represents will be given close scrutiny.

The following pages study transformations of nobiliary idleness. They chronicle the struggle of secular elites competing to determine the meaning and function of leisure. This struggle began in the early thirteenth century with the elaboration of the founding myth of nobiliary idleness in the *Roman de la Rose*. Examining subsequent literary representations will reveal attempts to negate, revise, and ultimately dismantle this ideology. These attempts were carried out first by clerics and increasingly by the rising elite of early modern *fonctionnaires* who made up the *noblesse de robe*. But my aim is to first understand on its own terms the aristocratic ideology they so fiercely opposed. How was idleness used to fabricate a mythic nobiliary identity? What ideological *use* was served by this ostensibly *useless* state of being? As a point of departure, the life of Gilles de Rais presents a vivid portrait of the "idle splendor" denounced by its Renaissance critics.

Gilles de Rais

Gilles de Rais (1404–40), *Maréchal de France*, is best known today as the infamous *Barbe Bleue*. While the extent to which he may have inspired the story of Bluebeard is difficult to determine,[7] he is undoubtedly worthy of the role of such a villain. His crimes culminated in the rape and murder of children, crimes to which he confessed before being executed in 1440. In this confession, or *amende honorable*, he characterized his life by a defining lack of work. Looking back on his life, he linked the some 140 rapes and murders as well as numerous acts of heresy and apostasy committed in ten years of debauchery to idleness.⁸

> hortans insuper quosquam patresfamilias ut caverent ne liberos suos delicate vestiri occioseque vivere tollerarent, innuens et asserens quod ex occiositate et ediis superfluis mala plurima generantur, et declarans expressius de se ipso quod occiositas et nimia curiosaque ciborum delicatorum vinorumque calidorum frequens assumptio sibi incentiva principaliter prebuerunt, unde tot peccata et scelera perpetravit.

> [he exhorted fathers to take care that their children not be dressed in delicate clothing and to refuse that they live in idleness, observing and insisting that from idleness and excessive pleasures of the table are born many evils, and declaring explicitly that primarily this idleness, an excessive craving for delicate foods, and the frequent absorption of warm wine induced a state of excitation in him, which led him to perpetrate so many sins and crimes.]⁹

It seems ironic that Gilles de Rais should account for his unprecedented crimes with a rhetorical commonplace from the moralist tradition. Yet a moralist rhetoric replete with all of the conventional topoi shapes the confession of one of history's most infamous figures. His assertion that many evils are "born" from idleness ("ex occiositate . . . mala plurima generantur") echoes *oisiveté*'s ritual epithet as "the mother" of vice. He also associates idleness with wine and refined pleasures of the table, explaining that this combination induces sexual appetite. Unchecked and unfettered by work, the school of discipline, his "appetite" became uncontrollable.¹⁰ In a sense, his excessive leisure was a kind of free rein or "license" that in turn led to an unbridled licentiousness. The affinity of these three concepts is confirmed by their common etymology: for *loisir* (leisure), license, and licentiousness all come from the same Latin verb *licere* (to be permitted).¹¹

On the eve of his execution, the *Maréchal* retroactively placed his own story into a moralist framework. He could have taken the terms of his self-incrimination directly from a moralist such as Valerius Maximus. Indeed, the latter's popular *Factorum dictorumque memorabilium* was among the manuscripts in Gilles de Rais's library.¹² One chapter, entitled "De luxuria et libidine" (IX, I), explicitly associates luxury, desire, and crime. It includes a litany of negative examples, infamous men whose decadence led directly to criminality. Each case recounts a tragic fall. Hence the life of Metellus Pius, once the "first citizen of his time," an austere man of high moral virtue who was corrupted by banquets, feasting, and luxury. Also included in this list are military heroes, as glorious in their own time as Gilles de Rais was in his. Hannibal himself was "conquered" by no enemy army. Rather, this hardened soldier was defeated by feasting, exquisite wines, delicate perfume, and voluptuousness.[13] With his confession, Gilles de Rais adapts his own story to a ready-made narrative mold. Idleness precipitated the downfall of the *Maréchal de France*, just as it had led to the ruin of so many great men before him.

Moralist discourse thus provides one explanatory system with which to interpret nobiliary idleness. But the life of Gilles de Rais also points to the limitations of moralist rhetoric. Before becoming a condemned criminal "guilty" of idleness as well as of his evil deeds, he led a life of leisure and splendor that made him one of the last great feudal lords. The moralist paradigm cannot account for the extravagant leisure he cultivated in the years leading up to his trial. Clearly, idleness had a social function beyond its moral meaning. A second look at the case of Gilles de Rais will elucidate the symbolic order in which idleness conferred prestige.

Before becoming a condemned criminal, Gilles de Rais was a national hero. Known for the military exploits he performed with Joan of Arc at his side, he went on to stage a form of idleness that was ultimately no less spectacular than his war exploits. With each annual celebration to commemorate the deliverance of Orléans, he spent vast sums of gold on processions, mystery plays, sumptuous clothing used only once, wine served generously to the crowd—all to celebrate his personal glory. When he traveled, he transported his personal library, chapel, and several organs. A military suite of more than two hundred mounted men, a *collège* consisting of fifty members (all mounted), and an ecclesiastical service accompanied him in a spectacle of "idle splendor."[14] As a result of this lifestyle, he squandered perhaps the largest fortune in all of France, making him the very personification of conspicuous leisure and expenditure.[15]

In war and in idleness, Gilles de Rais preserved the same disdain for the preservation of life and resources. What defined heroism if not a willingness to sacrifice life itself for the sake of honor? Idleness transposed this same logic to times of peace: willing to sacrifice both time and resources, the idle aristocrat placed honor before all else. In both cases, immoderation—heroic *démesure*—conferred prestige.[16] Seen in this light, his *idle* exploits appear no less glorious than his war exploits. Gilles de Rais was a champion of aristocratic idleness just as he was a heroic warrior.

This picture of the idle aristocrat in all his glory reveals its debt to the work of Georges Bataille. Revising Veblen's notion of "conspicuous expenditure," Bataille adopted a broad anthropological perspective. He suggested that what Veblen had interpreted as a class-defined gesture was in fact the result of the drive to dissipate excess. The paradoxical focal point of Bataille's thought was not humanity's positive constructions—its reasonable endeavors, its works and days—but rather its relationship to its own excess, material, symbolic, and sexual. Given this project, most clearly formulated in *La Part maudite* (1949) and *L'Erotisme* (1957),[17] his interest in Gilles de Rais seems perfectly consonant if not inevitable. For Bataille, material expenditure, idleness, and sexual crime go hand in hand, all three being tributary to the same cultural framework.[18] It is in no small measure thanks to Bataille's work (published along with Klossowski's translation of the documents of the trial) that Gilles de Rais has drawn critical attention. Bataille saw in Gilles de Rais an icon of the "accursed share," the fascinating "other" of morality, of rationality, and of utilitarian work, which together define the modern world. In his fifteenth-century world, bureaucratic and technological changes were making aristocratic chivalry less and less relevant, the crown was gaining ground against feudal lords, and the ascending bourgeoisie was laying the basis for a new kind of hero (the entrepreneur) possessing a new morality (the work ethic).[19] Bataille's Gilles de Rais was the tragic hero of feudalism, a desperate figure unwilling to accommodate the emerging era of *homo œconomicus*.[20]

The conceptual framework elaborated by Bataille has broad implications for anything that, like idleness, falls outside the narrow scope of usefulness. Reassessing classical utility is indeed a defining thrust of Bataille's thought.[21] But his determination to think outside of bourgeois values and the cult of usefulness risks imposing an overly rigorous polarization. For Bataille, the bourgeois ideology of work (based on a reflex to seek out the maximum utility, to pursue gain and profit) is strictly opposed to an aristocratic paradigm based on loss (idleness and other forms of expenditure). But the differences between these two ideologies are perhaps not as irreconcilable as Bataille suggests. Pierre Bourdieu's notion of "symbolic capital" may ultimately be more fruitfully applied to nobiliary idleness than Bataille's concept of the accursed share.

Activities that appear to be the most disinterested can nevertheless generate prestige—a kind of capital, as Bourdieu insists.[22] This point casts an entirely different light on the imaginary of *oisiveté*: idleness generated prestige only insofar as it appeared to depart from the logic of interested calculation; that is to say, its very real utility hinged on a facade of uselessness. Precisely because it was not overtly useful in any traditional sense, idleness had a specific utility of its own, for it was by virtue of its ostensible "uselessness" that idleness assumed an honorific function.[23] In short, by squandering time and resources, the idle aristocrat generated what remained a valuable resource, prestige—a "symbolic capital" that nevertheless functioned as a kind of currency in human exchanges. The usefulness of idleness was thus not lacking, but rather part of the social unconscious.

In sum, expenditure (producing honor) and profit (producing wealth) are not as ontologically different as Bataille suggests. As proof of their compatibility, both terms possess a large measure of interconvertibility. Bourdieu makes this observation, central to my purposes here, in stating that symbolic capital can be converted into material capital, and vice versa.[24] Medieval and early modern societies present ample testimony to this postulate. As an example, one has only to think of old-regime marriage practices. It was common for one family's prestige to be exchanged against another family's wealth: or, parallel formulation, a family could convert its symbolic resources into material resources through a marriage alliance. Prestige, then, belonged to a family's patrimony just as material wealth did. The *covert* function of idleness was thus firmly integrated into a system of exchange and social rivalry—provided this usefulness remained camouflaged, unspoken, and seemingly unrecognized.[25]

From Bellum to Otium: Redefining Aristocratic Identity

In the portrait of Gilles de Rais outlined above, war and idleness emerged as two privileged modes of an aristocratic existence. But did theory follow practice? Did the *bellum/otium* dialectic inform how medieval writers and theorists defined the aristocracy's place within the social order?

Beginning in the early eleventh century, political discourse commonly envisioned a tripartite social order based on function. From Gérard de Cambrai's initial formulation in 1024 (recorded in 1025) to Charles Loyseau's *Traité des Ordres et Simples Dignitez* in 1610, the social order was divided into three groups (clergy, aristocracy, and Third Estate), defined by their specialized functions (prayer, war, and labor, respectively).[26] Each estate had its role in society, its purpose in the larger order.

But on top of the three orders were juxtaposed two conditions: on the one hand, nobles; and on the other hand, *ignobles*. Georges Duby observes that by the end of the twelfth century, in reaction to widespread social mobility, a new category implicitly established the nobility's status as a hereditary caste. As a result of this redefinition, birth, not military specialization, determined nobility.[27] With the notion of *dérogeance,* the prejudice against work took the form of a legal injunction: idleness was no less of an imperative for aristocrats than was work for peasants. Each destined to its condition by birth, the nobility commanded and enjoyed leisure while the Third Estate obeyed and suffered labor.[28] Thus, all nobles, regardless of their specific social role (prayer or warfare), belonged to a "leisure class," just as all commoners *worked*, be it in traditional agriculture *(labor)* or—increasingly—in commerce *(negotium)*.[29] Only the Third Estate toiled in the "sweat from its face"; only the Third Estate engaged in "vulgar" material production.

"Knights and clerics, without exception, / are sustained by peasants' production."[30] To illustrate this general rule, one has only to recall the literary figure of the knight-errant in twelfth-century romance. He obtains sustenance almost exclusively through the tradition of hospitality; only under extreme circumstances is he seen to produce (even through hunting) the food that he consumes. The case of Yvain, described at one point as eating animals caught with his bare hands (*Yvain*, 2825–75), proves revealing. Chrétien de Troyes's hero engages in this activity during an episode of madness—during a period of temporary alienation from civilized society and from humanity itself. Indeed, the fact that he should hunt and forage (and eat raw meat) serves to confirm his madness: such shocking behavior illustrates for the reader the extent to which the hero has completely forgotten who he is (a member of the aristocracy) and what it means to be civilized (to abstain from food production).

In summary, two competing systems offered two very different ways of dividing—and explaining—the social order. On the one hand, a trifunctional model defined society in terms of three estates corresponding to three complementary functions. According to this model, to be noble was to wage war. Occupation determined social identity. Yet on the other hand, a binary logic divided the social order into two conditions, the first noble (and leisured) and the second non-noble (and laboring). This second model shifted the emphasis from the aristocracy's military specialization to its idle condition, from what it *did* to what it *was*. In other words, the concept of idleness privileged an understanding of nobility as something that had to be ontologically transmitted, something that could not be acquired, something beyond social role and beyond any useful occupation.

Placed within this struggle to determine social identity, the centrality of idleness and its capacity to elicit polemic become apparent. The notion of *oisiveté* allowed the feudal nobility to transcend its ascribed social function *(bellum)* while reducing commoners to their function *(labor* or *negotium)*. Only by laying claim to a mysterious essence beyond any real occupation could the nobility truly set itself apart. This symbolic act has manifest advantages for any ruling elite. For the feudal aristocracy, it both rationalized seigneurial privileges and restricted social promotion for non-nobles—an important function in a time of social mobility. Idleness, that is, contributed to the naturalization of the social order: it made nobility an autonomous state of being divorced from any specific occupation. Nobility was a matter of (social) "grace" rather than (useful) "works."

Allegories of Idleness in the *Roman de la Rose* and the *Pèlerinage de vie humaine*

This context informs the role Guillaume de Lorris gives Oiseuse (Idleness) in *Le Roman de la Rose* (1225–30).[31] She is charged with elevating nobility to the status of a charmed and elusive essence, an "idle condition" beyond "works" of any kind. Her role is to define aristocratic identity outside the sphere of social function. Indeed, the nobility's military function (initially the basis for its identity) is entirely evacuated from the allegory, along with its other responsibilities such as rulership and justice. The *Roman de la Rose* thus contains an allegorical representation of Idleness, along with other courtly ideals including *Courtoisie, Amour, Franchise, Beauté*. However, it completely effaces *Proesce* from the aristocratic ideal it celebrates. Aristocratic identity is an enclosed garden from which all *vilains* are excluded; and it is the figure of Idleness (not prowess, or even chivalry, courage, or prudence) that stands at the gate.[32]

The *Roman de la Rose* recounts a dream, which the author claims to have had at the age of twenty. The sleeping man dreams that he gets up one morning and sets out in search of adventure. Drawn by the sound of birds singing in a garden, his first reaction is to look for a door into the enclosed *locus amœnus*. The narrator lingers on the problem of an opening into the garden or a ladder over its walls, both of which at first elude him (vv. 496–505). The symbol of exclusivity, the walls reinforce the primary sense of *jardin* (enclosed)[33] with ten images depicting the excluded categories. Several of these pictures prefigure the courtly nature of the garden by announcing the exclusion of *Vilanie, Felonie*, and *Pauvreté*.

When he finally locates the door, he notes that it is small, narrow, and of course, locked.[34] But he does not attempt to force an entry, which one might imagine a chivalric hero doing. Instead the narrator simply knocks and waits, as though to signal that no effort, however great, can grant access into the garden. Activity does not open the door to the courtly ideal contained within; nor does a given occupation define the elite it represents; only Lady Idleness, who resides within the garden, can open the door. Renaissance editions of the *Roman de la Rose* thus depict her standing before the door and holding a key (figure 1). But before Oiseuse opens the door, and even before her name is revealed, the narrator describes the lovely maiden in detail.[35]

The first term invoked to describe her physical appearance is "gente" or "noble": "adonc m'ovri une pucele, / qui estoit assez gente et bele" (vv. 523–24). The narrator then describes her physical traits, emphasizing the whiteness and softness of her skin—part of the canon of female beauty, but also signs of the life of ease she leads (*face blanche*, v. 534; *sa gorge estoit autresi blanche*, v. 543; *la char plus tendre que poucins*, v. 526). Lovely *white* gloves further confirm her existence of nonwork (v. 561). They also offer a delicate veil for her hands as though to shield her from this part of the body, the most compromised of all, being the potential agent of *manual* labor. This primary and functional sense of the hands has thus been discreetly covered over. White gloves insure that her hands make an aesthetic statement rather than effecting real changes directly on matter. Meticulous grooming has indeed perfected her natural beauty—even her breath is sweetly perfumed (v. 533). The narrator concludes the description by observing that she has no care or worries aside from adorning and grooming herself nobly:

> Mout avoit bon tens et bon mai,
> qu'el n'avoit sousi ne esmai
> de nule rien fors seulement
> de soi atorner noblement
>
> (vv. 569–72)

[As she did nothing besides dressing herself nobly, she had much more time and pleasure than worries or troubles] (my translation)

These verses are no doubt the most ambiguous, given their latent suggestion of narcissism. Oiseuse spends all of her time preening and admiring herself. The mirror she holds might be taken as the very symbol of Narcissus. However, as though to acquit her in advance of this shade of moral reprehension, the narrator describes the care he took in performing his own *toilette* (vv. 89–94).[36] Whether it belongs to a garden or an aristocrat, is a carefully cultivated aesthetic perfection not a worthy pursuit?

But insisting on the time devoted to self-adornment also obeys a social logic distinct from any aesthetic motivation. Careful grooming offers a solution to what Thorstein Veblen identifies as the central problem for any leisure class: prestige is granted only on evidence; but leisure tends to be elusive, to leave no tangible signs. How then can one testify to a life of idleness? For unlike work, idleness does not (indeed, should not) result in a material product that could serve as evidence; nor does it necessarily take place under the gaze of subordinates or rivals. This is particularly true for idle women. Traditionally having highly restricted access to the public sphere, they are by the same token kept out of the public gaze.[37] Oiseuse resolves this problem by an elaborate *toilette*: "proof" of the extended idleness she enjoys. Soft skin, white gloves, sweet breath, combed hair, impeccable and carefully arranged clothing, these elements constitute so many tangible vestiges of idleness, effectively transforming personal adornment into "conspicuous leisure." The narrator makes this function manifest. He notes that Oiseuse's refined personal adornment is evidence of her idleness, stating categorically that she has nothing else to do besides adorning herself nobly (vv. 571–72).

Oiseuse then introduces herself to the young man, beginning with her name, which has been carefully withheld until after her description:

> "Je me faz, fet ele, Oiseuse
> apeler a mes conoissanz.
> Rice fame sui et poissanz,
> s'ai d'une chose mout bon tens
> que a nule rien je n'entens
> qu'a moi jouer et solacier
> et a moi pigner et trecier."
>
> (vv. 580–86)

["Those who know me call me Idleness," she said. "I am a rich and powerful lady, happy especially in one thing, that I have no care but to enjoy and amuse myself, and to comb and braid my hair."] (p. 11)

Wealthy and powerful, Oiseuse nevertheless has no function to exert, no concrete occupation by which she exercises her power, apparently *doing* nothing besides combing and braiding her hair. Any puissance she claims to possess is not turned outward to act upon the world; rather, it is devoted solely to play and adornment. Her world excludes instruments (the scepter, the sword, or—for a woman—the spindle) in favor of ornament and autotelic play. She celebrates an aristocratic existence turned inward as though an exterior telos would be demeaning. The mirror functions as the symbol of this autotelic existence, the cultivation of self coinciding with the effacement of an external object.

Roughly one century later, Guillaume de Deguilleville, a Cistercian monk, rewrote the *Roman de la Rose*, transposing its images and motifs into a new moral context.[38] He proclaimed the beautiful *Roman de la Rose* to be his inspiration.[39] However, it is clear that his primary objective was to mount an attack on the mostly secular values of the court.[40] With its condemnation of aristocratic ideals, the *Pèlerinage de vie humaine* (1330–31) is in reality a *Roman de la Rose moralisé*.[41]

Lady Idleness in particular is singled out for critique and revision. No longer the porteress to courtly society as in the *Roman de la Rose*, she is redefined as a moral peril in the *Pèlerinage de vie humaine*. If this human life is a journey or "pilgrimage" toward the Creator, idleness is a treacherous trap set along the way:

> Pour nient marrastre de vertu
> Saint Bernart pas ne l'apella,
> Quant la connut et l'avisa.
> Plus est marrastre aus pelerins
> Que l'escoufle n'est aus poucins.
>
> (vv. 6918–22)

[It is not for nothing that when Saint Bernard encountered idleness and recognized her, he called her the stepmother of virtue. She is more of a stepmother toward pilgrims than is the hawk for chicks.]

Lady Idleness is here defined in relation to a moral rather than social context: she is "virtue's stepmother" *(marrastre de vertu)*. This transformation is a careful reworking of the notion of idleness from what was a traditional moral perspective.

In the course of his journey, the "pilgrim" encounters Huiseuse, a lovely young maiden who promptly attempts to lure him off the path to God into the lap of idleness. Here, Lady Idleness does not reside in a beautiful garden, but rather at a crossroads where she is *seated* at the head of the left path (bearing all of the moral connotations commonly attributed to the *voie a senestre*). The narrator describes her as noble *(gentile)*, which was also the first adjective used to describe Oiseuse in the *Roman de la Rose*. He further observes that she has placed her left hand under her right arm, while her right hand holds a glove that she twirls nonchalantly (vv. 6525–28)—an idle gesture that reinforces her lack of occupation while suggesting tedium.[42] Finally, the narrator states that he could see by her expression that she had few worries and cared little for spinning or other forms of labor:

> A sa contenance bien vi
> Que n'estoit pas de grant souci,
> Que pou li chaloit de filer
> Et d'autre labour labourer.
>
> (vv. 6529–32)

[By her expression I saw that she clearly had few worries, that she cared little for spinning or for laboring at other labors.]

Although she remains an essentially aristocratic figure, Idleness is here revealed to be the daughter of Sloth *(Paresse)*. Her beauty makes her more seductive than her mother (an ugly old woman), and thus all the more dangerous for naive pilgrims. When Idleness introduces herself, her words recall Oiseuse's words in the *Roman de la Rose*. She states:

> "Miex aime mes gans enformer
> Et moi pignier et moi graver,
> Moy regarder en un mirour
> Que je ne fais autre labour."
>
> (vv. 6847–50)

["I like putting on my gloves, combing and parting my hair, and looking at myself in a mirror better than I like doing other labor."]

Her petulant expression of personal preference ("Miex aime . . .") culminates in a fully assumed narcissism. In contrast, in the *Roman de la Rose*, when Oiseuse uttered her aristocratic manifesto, she celebrated idleness as a cultivated art of existence that made all else irrelevant, an existence that privileged the ornament (the emblem of conspicuous leisure) over the tool (an instrument of degradation). It is not that Guillaume de Lorris's Oiseuse *chose* idleness over work; she simply did not understand work because it was foreign to her very being: ". . . a nule rien je n'entens / qu'a moi jouer et solacier / et a moi pigner et trecier" (vv. 584–86).

Guillaume de Deguilleville's narrative represents an ecclesiastical attempt to reconquer hermeneutic control of idleness. Effecting an assumed transvalorization of Idleness, he retains her defining traits from the *Roman de la Rose*, but subjects them to another interpretative context (see table below).

Trait:	Meaning in Roman de la Rose	In Pèlerinage
absence of occupation	idleness as noble "essence"	"oisiveté, mère des vices"
youthful beauty	beauty itself	appeal to the flesh
gloves	refined abstention from manual labor	unwillingness to work
mirror/*toilette*	conspicuous leisure, primacy of aesthetics	narcissism

These two allegories make manifest the competition between the Church and the aristocracy as each of these two rival elites attempted to lay claim to idleness. A struggle to define values accompanied the growing secularization of culture, as ideals such as *otium* were subject to reinterpretation. Seen within this broader context, Guillaume de Deguilleville's enterprise was an act of resistance: at a time when leisure was beginning to assume a secular orientation, he reaffirmed its place within religious institutions. Several centuries later, humanists would perpetuate the same struggle, as commodification pushed the secularization of leisure one step further. But for this fourteenth-century context, it was not yet the new economic model that represented the greatest threat to the sacredness of leisure. Rather, it was the secular values of the court that constituted Deguilleville's implicit target. Indeed, the particular synthesis of leisure, the feminine, and sensuality points to court life, newly defined by precisely these traits. That is, at the time of the *Pèlerinage de vie humaine*, court life was characterized by the presence of women, leisured aristocrats, and an atmosphere of luxury and sensuality. Guillaume de Deguilleville's allegory attacked these elements, the ingredients of the modern court.[43] Yet despite his attack on aristocratic values, his allegory ultimately remained within the very paradigm he sought to contest. His conscious moral reworking of Oiseuse was in fact shaped by unconscious similarities with nobiliary idleness, as will be argued below.

On "the right path," the pilgrim finds Occupation, predictably hard at work. Surprised, he observes that Occupation weaves bed mats only to unweave them afterward, over and over again:

> Au chemin destre un refaiseur
> De nates et reparelleur
> Vy sëoir qui rapareilloit
> Ses viez nates et refaisoit
> Et encor plus dont esbahy
> Fu, ce, qu'avoit fait, ly vy
> Du tout en tout redespecier
> Et puis apres rapareillier.
>
> (vv. 6533–40)

[On the right path, I saw a seated remaker and a repairer of bed mats who repaired and remade his old mats. What surprised me even more was that I saw that when he had finished, he undid all of it, breaking it apart, and then afterward began repairing it.]

The pilgrim first manifests aristocratic scorn for such a "vulgar and poor trade." Addressing Occupation, he states, "'Je voy que t'ez mis a natier / Qui est vil et povre mestier'" (vv. 6567–68), concluding that since the activity is so manifestly futile, Occupation must be mad:

> "Et voy que souvent tu deffaiz
> Ce qu'as bien fait et le refaiz.
> N'est pas, ce me semble, grant sens,
> Se la cause ne m'en aprens."
>
> (vv. 6569–72)

["I see that you often undo what you have already done well and redo it. There is not much sense to this, it seems to me, unless you can explain the reason to me."]

Occupation replies with a kind of maxim: "better a poor trade that is loyal [legitimate] than Idleness in court royal" ("Miex vaut povre mestier loial / Quë Huiseuse de court royal," vv. 6593–94). He thus substitutes a moral perspective on idleness and work for the social meaning these terms had in the *Roman de la Rose*. He later reveals himself to be "he who produces bread": "Quar savoir doiz que sui celui / Qui a la gent donne du pain . . ." (vv. 6668–69). As for the pilgrim's accusation that weaving and unweaving mats is utterly unproductive and thus "mad," Occupation responds that any work, even unproductive labor, is preferable to idleness:

> "Se je depiece et je refas,
> A fin que je ne soie pas

> Huiseus, ne m'en doiz pas blasmer,
> Quar s'autre chose a labourer
> Eusse, je m'i occupasse,
> Et point ne redespecasse
> Ce qu(e j)'ai fait pour le refaire;
> Mes tu voiz (bien) que rien a faire
> N'aroie, se ne (re)binoie
> Mon ouvraige et refaisoye."
>
> (vv. 6595–6604)

["If I break apart and redo (my mats) in order to repudiate idleness, you must not blame me, for if I had something else to do, I would work on it and not break apart what I have done in order to redo it; but you can see well enough that I would have nothing to do if I did not break apart and redo my work."]

The pilgrim and Occupation continue to debate the value of work and idleness: the former, defending idleness and condemning work in the name of aristocratic values; the latter, defending work and condemning idleness in the name of sacred truths. Occupation eventually persuades the pilgrim, who nevertheless chooses to take the path of Idleness based on the (bad) advice of his body *(le corps)*. This allows the author to show that Occupation is ultimately right while also depicting the moral dangers of idleness, thereby exploiting both logical argument (Occupation wins the debate) and negative *exemplum* (the reader witnesses the terrifying consequences of idleness). For shortly after the pilgrim embarks upon the path of idleness, he is assaulted by the Seven Deadly Sins, beginning with Sloth, bearing ropes and a butcher's knife to capture and lead her prey to slaughter.[44]

The *Pèlerinage de vie humaine* presents an unequivocal lesson: better occupation—any occupation at all, even senseless busy-work—than idleness. Work serves an unproductive, but essential function: avoiding idleness. Occupation's futile labor recalls Abbot Paul, one of the desert fathers (the cenobites and anchorites whose early communities became the foundation of monasticism). Just as Occupation made mats, Paul assiduously wove baskets. Living in such a remote part of the desert, Paul could not sell the fruits of his labor and give the profits to charity, as did many others. At the end of the year, he thus burned all the baskets he had woven, demonstrating that the value of work was not to be found in its product, but rather in the moral value of the activity itself.[45] This stands as a reminder of the defining rift separating medieval and early modern *moral* discourse on work from economic discourse: if it is the moral value of the activity that counts, then it matters little if one's labor is productive.

Yet despite the heavy didacticism and the avowed intentions, it also testifies to the stigma attached to productive work, a bias that the *Pèlerinage* ultimately shares with the *Roman de la Rose*. Although Deguilleville has Occupation defend (food) production, the degrading responsibility of the Third Estate, he refrains from representing him engaged in such productive labor. Of course, Occupation claims that he weaves and unweaves mats simply because he has no other more useful activity to perform. Nevertheless, a de facto unwillingness to represent such activity suggests the disgrace it still carried. If Deguilleville chose to portray a busy but unproductive Occupation as an explicit model for the reader, was it not because productive labor remained too distasteful? Occupation embraces the *humility* of labor while implicitly disdaining any real productive dimensions. For in the end, Occupation's "labor" (weaving and unweaving mats) bears a close resemblance to Huiseuse's "idleness" (idly twirling her gloves). Just as Occupation undoes and redoes mats, so Idleness is described as turning her glove first one way and then another: "Entour son doi le [le gant] demenoit / Et le tournoit et retournoit" (vv. 6527–28). Both activities are circular and equally (and conspicuously) unproductive. This conceptual affinity suggests the difficulty of divorcing the concepts of leisure and work from their social context, a difficulty Guillaume de Deguilleville confronted head-on, but did not completely overcome.[46] It also established a discursive mode that would govern *oisiveté* into the Renaissance, a mode characterized by a conscious moral message (work is morally necessary) masking a social unconscious (work is degrading).

Oiseuse's Posterity in the Renaissance

Both widely read during the Renaissance,[47] the *Roman de la Rose* and the *Pèlerinage* elucidate the *différend* between moralist discourse on idleness and the nobiliary ideal it censured. It was clearly Guillaume de Deguilleville's duplicitous idleness that informed the plethora of attacks on "idle gentlemen" during the Renaissance. Josse Clichtove, an early humanist defender of "nobility of virtue," mounted one of the most sustained and influential attacks on aristocratic idleness. He devoted an entire chapter to "why nobles should avoid idleness" in *De vera nobilitate* (1512), a treatise that was translated into French and had an enduring influence on Renaissance debates.[48]

In some formulations, profession determined noble status as it had in the eleventh-century definition of nobility outlined above. Ellery Schalk studies the proponents of a functional definition of nobility, a nobility based solely on the profession of arms.[49] Montaigne's definition of the nobility is often cited to this effect: "La forme propre, et seule, et essencielle, de noblesse en France, c'est la vacation militaire" [The proper, the only, the essential, form of nobility in France is the military profession].[50]

Yet the military profession was clearly not a satisfying basis for nobility with universal appeal. In the first place, members of the new corps of *hauts fonctionnaires* known as the *noblesse de robe* disputed the equation of the military profession with nobility. The relative merits of "arms versus letters" were subject to virulent debate, as James Supple demonstrates.[51] Moreover, even outside of this polemic, the functional view does not account for actual practices: only a minority of so-called "sword nobles" fulfilled regular military service.[52] Finally, Montaigne's oft-cited definition of the nobility as "the military profession" presents only part of the picture. Elsewhere in the *Essais*, Montaigne defines the nobility not in terms of social function (military service), but rather in relation to idleness. Laconic and deliberately neutral, Montaigne describes the nobility as an "idle condition," without hazarding a moral judgment of any kind. "The nobility is an idle condition," he states matter-of-factly, "which lives, as they say, only on its private income" [(La noblesse . . . est d'une condition oisive qui ne vit, comme on dit, que de ses rentes (II, 8, 389–90a?)].[53] He thus shifts the focus from what noblemen *did* (wage war) to what they *did not do* (work for a living) or even to what they *were* (idle).[54] The choice of the term "condition" reinforces his equation of the nobility's inner disposition with its idle status. Frequently used interchangeably with *qualité*, the word *condition* had the double meaning of moral disposition and social position.[55]

Often a traditionalist on such matters, Montaigne thus returns to the *bellum/otium* dialectic long associated with nobles. Referring first to the nobility's military profession (II, 7) and later to its idle condition (II, 8), he adopts a position in keeping with the standards

1: ARISTOCRATIC IDLENESS: CLAIMING THE ACCURSED SHARE 45

of his time. As Arlette Jouanna has argued, social role was thought to be merely the visible manifestation of an interior quality: the sword itself was understood to reflect a virtue and not a profession.[56] By privileging idleness in addition to arms, Montaigne both indicates an appropriate arena to exercise nobility (the battlefield) while carefully situating nobility itself above and beyond function of any kind.[57] Better to be accused of "uselessness" than to make noble status so vulnerable as to depend on a specific occupation. Thus, nobility was a "human excellence," a virtue, a quality, but not a function. To borrow Arlette Jouanna's phrase, nobility was a matter of *being* rather than *doing*.[58]

An ambiguous legacy from medieval debates thus informed the Renaissance notion of idleness. *Oisiveté* was shaped by the preceding centuries' struggle that pitted the version of idleness promoted by religious elites against a version embraced by secular elites, each one attempting to claim for itself the category of leisure. For writers, using the idleness topos thus carried with it both latent social value and moral sanctions. This made the position of *oisif* a delicate one to maintain, but a potentially valuable source of social identity. The opening to Montaigne's essay "De la vanité" presents one example. Used as a subtle strategy of self-presentation, idleness allows the essayist to affirm his noble status while pretending to condemn his century's useless idlers.

"*DE LA VANITÉ*": TRYING IDLENESS

Near the beginning of "De la vanité," Montaigne stages what appears to be a formal trial and condemnation of idleness and idlers. The essayist theatrically and hyperbolically confirms the lessons conveyed by *compendia*, providing a vivid example of the blame moralists showered on *oisiveté*:

> On accusoit un Galba du temps passé de ce qu'il vivoit oiseusement; il respondit que chacun devoit rendre raison de ses actions, non pas de son sejour. Il se trompoit: car la justice a cognoissance et animadvertion aussi sur ceux qui chaument. Mais il y devroit avoir quelque coërction des loix contre les escrivains ineptes et inutiles, comme il y a contre les vagabons et faineants. On banniroit des mains de nostre peuple et moy et cent autres. (III, 9, 946b)

[One Galba was blamed in the past for living idly. He replied that each man should give account of his actions, not of his leisure. He was wrong; for justice has cognizance and corrective power also over those who are on holiday. But there should be some legal restraint aimed against inept and useless writers, as there is against vagabonds and idlers. Both I and a hundred others would be banished from the hands of our people.] (721)

The passage rehearses the three defining stages of a criminal trial: accusation (a Galba [Otho] is accused of idleness); defense (he argues that one can be held responsible only for one's actions, therefore one cannot be "guilty" of idleness); and verdict (Montaigne finds him guilty: idleness falls under the jurisdiction of the courts since there are laws against it, as he points out by recalling his own century's anti-idleness legislation).[59] Then, in a final ironic twist, Montaigne puts himself in the category of *oisifs* ("On banniroit des mains de nostre peuple et moy et cent autres"). Pleading guilty to the charges he brings against himself, he recommends banishment as an appropriate punishment, albeit hardly a severe condemnation in an essay partly devoted to Montaigne's passion for traveling. The entire demonstration appears to illustrate the "criminality" of idleness preached by Renaissance *compendia* such as the *Diverses Leçons de Pierre Messie*, which associate idleness with malice and moral corruption.

Yet the essayist's trial of idleness is not a reiteration of the moral depravity of idleness. As is often the case in the *Essais*, such dogmatism is the sign of the essayist's irony. In this particular case, Montaigne's assertion later in the same essay that idleness is in fact one of his "favorite qualities" adds further evidence for an irony beneath the adamant tone. Another intertext at work in the passage, this time from one of Montaigne's favorite books—Plutarch's *Lives*—further undermines the ostensible moral lesson conveyed by Montaigne's condemnation of all idlers, including himself.

In the chapter on Lycurgus, the Spartan lawgiver, Plutarch presents two antithetical attitudes toward idleness. Condemned in Athens, idleness was in fact valorized in Sparta. He recounts a visit to Athens made by an anonymous Spartan (elsewhere identified as Herondas) who witnessed the trial of an idler like the one Montaigne recreates in "De la vanité." As in Montaigne's version, the Athenian was found guilty of the "crime" of idleness. But upon hearing the verdict, the Spartan turned to those around him and asked them to show him "the man who had been condemned for living nobly and as it befits a gentleman" ("qu'ilz luy monstrassent celuy qui avoit esté condemné pour vivre noblement & en gentilhomme").[60] Appropriately laconic, the Spartan's request is then glossed by Plutarch: this reaction, he explains, reflects the aristocratic scorn for work shared by all members of the Spartan elite. "Criminal" idleness is thus revealed to be the only condition appropriate for a gentleman. Aristocrats should, after all, refrain from engaging in a slavish or common activity such as exercising a mechanical trade or doing manual labor for profit:

> Ce que j'ai allégué pour monstrer combien il estimait estre chose roturière & servile, que d'exercer aucun mestier mechanique, ou faire aucun ouvrage de main pour gaigner de l'argent. Quant aux procez, on peult bien penser qu'ilz furent bannis de Lacaedomone avec l'argent . . .[61]

> [I cited this example to illustrate how much he (the Spartan) deemed exercising any mechanical trade or doing any manual labor in order to earn money to be a slavish and vulgar common attitude. As for trials, one would be justified in thinking that they must have been banished from Sparta along with money.]

We know that in the *Essais* "sword nobles" are often figured as Spartans, both being the bearers of true nobility. Their disdain for "trials and money" make them the mirror opposites of bourgeois and *parlementaires*. Beyond this parallel, the Spartan's reaction had a compelling actuality for Montaigne, for it embodied his century's own legal definition of "derogeance"—the laws that governed aristocratic behavior. Significantly, in his translation, Amyot borrows a fixed syntagma from legal treatises which dictate that *to be* a gentleman, one has to live nobly and as befits a gentleman: *vivre noblement & en gentilhomme*.[62] Amyot's translation thus absorbs his own century's code of derogeance, assimilating idleness to nobility. He makes Plutarch's Spartan the laconic spokesman for Renaissance notions of nobiliary idleness.

In light of this intertext, the mock trial's true function becomes apparent. By finding himself guilty of the crime of idleness, Montaigne simultaneously finds himself "guilty" of "living nobly and as a gentleman." His overstated condemnation of idleness is in fact a subtle defense of his own nobility. Reiterating the depravity of idleness does not prevent him from exploiting the concept's potential to generate prestige. The ironic rhetorical mode only reinforces the social dynamic at work in this passage. A "naive" reader would take Montaigne's indictment of idleness at face value; this reader would be appropriately excluded from deciphering the passage's irony. Only the happy few would interpret beyond the literal meaning (idlers are criminal), recognizing an incrimination of Montaigne's own century which, like the Athenian courts, condemned people guilty only of "living nobly." Reading through the Plutarch intertext and the Renaissance's own code of nobility, one discovers an encrypted defense of nobiliary idleness and Montaigne's own identification with the venerable Spartans, the very personification of an aristocratic existence based exclusively on *bellum* and *otium*.

In a 1583 letter addressed to Abel l'Angelier, Madeleine des Roches comments on the same passage from the *Lives*. She refers to the Spartan attitude toward what she aptly terms "this praiseworthy laziness,"[63] a formulation that conveys the Renaissance's ambivalence toward idleness. This ambiguity was precisely what put idleness at the center of the social stage. In "De la vanité," Montaigne turned the concept's ambivalence to his own advantage, using it as a strategy of self-presentation, slyly implying that he was a member of the idle elite. This was indeed the strategy of Montaigne's milieu, eager to reappropriate the category of leisure for its own purposes, redefining it in accordance with a new social and cultural agenda. A careful examination of the last chapters of Rabelais's *Gargantua* will further reveal the machinations of a new Renaissance elite aspiring to determine social identity through leisure.

Thélème: A Utopia of Aristocratic Idleness?

It is tempting to see a Renaissance version of the aristocratic Garden of Delight in Thélème, the utopian "abbey" described in the final chapters of *Gargantua*. This would certainly have been in keeping with the times, for the editorial success of the *Roman de la Rose* in the first part of the French Renaissance suggests that its ideals were still compelling. Humanists of unquestionable standing adapted and interpreted the allegory in light of mystical and evangelical theology.[64] Yet it was also found on the bookshelves of many country manors and was one the favorite books of François I. The *Roman de la Rose* apparently still spoke to aristocratic values.[65]

At first glance, Rabelais's utopia appears as the mirror reflection of Guillaume de Lorris's allegory: Thélème is an (anti-) abbey that borrows its values from courtly society while the Garden of Delight is a courtly society that borrows the ideals underlying an abbey.[66] Both spaces admit only the aristocratic ("nobles chevaliers" and "dames de hault parage," *Gargantua*, 457; 459) and the beautiful ("les belles femmes, bien formées et bien naturées, & les beaux, bien formés, et bien naturés," *Gargantua*, 443).[67] Both spaces exclude the social function normally reserved for elites, bringing aristocratic leisure to the fore instead. Rabelais provided for every aristocratic pastime imaginable within Thélème, including the obligatory *jardin de plaisance* (*Gargantua* 463) and tennis courts, along with a theater and three-level baths.

Most of all, though, the hunt dominates Thélème. Hunting trophies from a broad range of real and imaginary wild animals adorn the interior of the manor, prompting one critic to compare Thélème to a "museum of the hunt."[68] Outside Thélème, one finds all the necessary equipment and fauna. Rabelais persistently draws the reader's attention to the horses, wild game, hawks, and trainers as though they were but so many ropes and pulleys in what was in fact an underlying technical apparatus of the hunt. Exhaustive in his enumeration, he describes the "great park, which teemed with all kinds of wild game." He names the weapons used in the hunt: "the arquebus, bow, and cross-bow." He gives the precise location of the stables and the falconry, praising the qualifications of their staff: "the stables were beyond the offices; and in front of them was the falconry, managed by falconers most expert in their art." The varieties of birds of prey are delineated, each specimen the "finest" of its breed: "eagles, gerfalcons, goshawks, great falcons, lanners, falcons, sparrow-hawks, merlins, and others." So well trained were these creatures that no prey escaped them. They swept through the fields like highly efficient machines: "When they flew from the castle to disport themselves over the fields, they would capture all the game they met."[69]

This nuance of efficiency given to the hunt becomes more apparent in light of another humanist's reflections on the matter. Guillaume Budé's *De Venatione* (the second book of *De Philologia*) was published only one year after *Gargantua*. Budé's treatise praises the hunt as a distinctly inefficient—and thus noble—pastime.

The Hunt as Aristocratic *Loisir*

In its privileging of play, spectacle, and nonutilitarian activity, the hunt offers an elaborate model for an aristocratic ethos of leisure. The hunt was, after all, the quintessential aristocratic *loisir*. As Guillaume Budé observes, the aristocracy was devoted to hawking and hunting. Because it is both a hunting manual and a meditation on the hunt, this short text, written in the form of a dialogue between François I and Budé, provides important insights into the hunt as aristocratic leisure or *passetemps*, a term that reoccurs throughout Louis Le Roy's French translation of Budé's treatise. Like Oiseuse's elaborate *toilette*, the hunt emerges as both a form of conspicuous leisure and a rejection of an instrumental relationship with the world.

Budé begins with a long preamble, praising François for having elevated the hunt to a degree of magnificence unprecedented even by the ancients. In a playful tone, Budé also emphasizes the ludicrousness of a humanist composing a discourse on the hunt, pretending to sidestep some questions and double back on his tracks, thereby engaging in the same evasive maneuvers the stag supposedly uses in the course of the hunt. The sinuous detours of Budé's presentation not only mime the very movement of the hunt but also announce his thesis:

> Donques, pour entrer en propos, ceste coustume et maniere se trouve en la venerie, entre ceux qui en font parfaittement profession non afin de fournir la cuysine, ains pour retirer avec plaisir le profit de l'exercice du corps, a sçavoir d'elire pour courir un grand cerf portant pour le moins dix cornettes, que j'appelle beau et eminent.[70]
>
> [Thus, to get to the heart of the matter, in hunting there exists a particular custom and manner among those who make it their profession, not in order to stock the kitchen, but rather to get, with pleasure, the profit of physical exercise: namely, to choose to chase a big stag (whom I call beautiful and eminent) bearing at least a ten-point rack.]

Because of the physical exercise the hunt provides aristocrats *(le profit de l'exercice du corps)*, it offers useful training for war, the nobility's traditional occupation. But the hunt also possesses a strong element of play. Before all else, Budé emphasizes that the purpose of the hunt is not subsistence *(non afin de fournir la cuysine)*. This point is capital, since food production remained the vocation of the Third Estate. If this utilitarian motivation were the purpose of the hunt, then it would make sense to choose the slowest stag—the one least likely to offer resistance. Instead, aristocratic hunters choose the biggest, strongest stag (whose rack has at least ten points) in order to emphasize the means (the chase) over the end (the kill). Budé devotes the vast majority of the treatise itself to praise for the stag, whose many ruses earn it the epithet of *courageux* and *sage*—a worthy foe indeed, and not simply meat for slaughter.

Budé later has François confirm the nonfunctional dimensions of the hunt. The king says that he enjoys both falconry and the hunt more for the pursuit (and pleasure) than for the kill:

> . . . maintenant par recreation seulement regarde volontier les oiseaux de proie voler es campagnes et es marez, qui me semble estre plutost quelque chasse haulte et volante qu'oiselerie ou prise d'oiseaux. Si est ce qu'en l'un et l'autre passetemps nous ne regardons tant a la prise et proie, que'au plaisir des oreilles et des yeux . . . (27–28)

> [Now, only for recreation do I willingly watch birds of prey flying in the countryside and marshes, which seems more like a lofty and airborne pursuit than hawking or capturing birds. In both pastimes we do not focus so much on the capture and the prey as on the pleasure for the ears and eyes . . .]

The spectacular elements of the hunt *(plaisir des oreilles et des yeux)* take precedence over the *telos (la prise et proie)*. In Thélème it is precisely the opposite, for hawking is strictly a teleological endeavor: only the *prise* counts.

François continues to emphasize the spirit of play that animates falconry and hunting. This explains the element of contingency purposefully introduced into the hunt insofar as aristocrats provide the hunted stag ample means to escape ("nous donnons aux cerfs tous les moyens de fuyr librement . . ."[28]). An elusive object is crucial to the hunt's status as an aristocratic pursuit: it prevents it from being merely a function, and the hunters the instrument of this function. The stag's potential escape lends honor to this aristocratic hobby. And this limited measure of programmed loss, of squandering what could be a resource (food), is precisely the "inefficiency" that Rabelais carefully eradicates.[71] For it is the contingency of the kill, the potential for loss, that makes the hunt all the more beautiful in Budé's treatise. If a utilitarian purpose were to take precedence, if, for instance, the purpose were to kill as many stags as possible in the most efficient way possible, then the hunt would cease to embody idleness—and nobility.

The full implications of Rabelais's choice to emphasize efficiency now become apparent. In effect, this gesture sacrifices honor (potential loss) to efficacy (insured gain). It makes the hunt a technique rather than a form of nobiliary idleness. A final look at the mechanics of leisure in Thélème will confirm this voluntary de-gradation of nobiliary idleness.

Oisiveté, arts et métiers: The Technicity of Leisure in Thélème

Rabelais continues to display all the signs of nobiliary idleness in Thélème. But the effect is to transform rather than replicate the aristocratic ideal. As in the Garden of Delight, the mirror is thus present, but in a new and improved packaging: full-length mirrors with ornate frames are mounted in all the quarters (463). The Thélémites are apparently no less concerned with the aesthetics of aristocratic life than were Oiseuse and her companions. Both Thélème and the Garden of Delight similarly celebrate—indeed require—sumptuous clothing and careful grooming. Yet while Guillaume de Lorris gave no thought to how luxury products would be supplied to the inhabitants of the Garden of Delight (is it not the very essence of the aristocratic mentality to give no thought to such matters?), Rabelais meticulously attends to this detail, the prosaic basis for his aristocratic wonderland. A locus of intense labor thus exists just outside Thélème in order to satisfy the need for luxury goods—and this spatial proximity signals the interdependence of idle aristocrats and industrious artisans:

> autour du bois de Theleme était un grand corps de maison long de demie lieue, bien clair et assorti, en laquelle demeuraient les orfèvres, lapidaires, brodeurs, tailleurs, tireurs d'or, veloutiers, tapissiers, et aultelissiers, et là œuvraient chacun de son métier, et le tout pour les susdits religieux et religieuses. (469)

Here, in a "great block of houses," the technicians of leisure are hard at work. Goldsmiths, jewelers, embroiderers, tailors, wireworkers, velvet-weavers, tapestry makers, and upholsterers produce the various paraphernalia required by idle aristocrats. Further, the Thélémites import other precious goods from the Perlas and Cannibal Islands. They rely on a nascent "global" (colonial) economy, as Michel Beaujour observes.[72]

In short, Rabelais attends less to aristocratic leisure itself than to the productive activity and material conditions on which it depends. Thélème is announced as the locus of the aristocracy's idle bliss, yet it is encumbered by endless and prosaic details and is ultimately monotonously "lovely," as François Rigolot observes.[73] Rabelais's exactitude has a decisive effect on the aristocratic ideal of idleness. The *Roman de la Rose* makes clear the nature of "representing" aristocratic idleness: it must appear to be magically "given" at birth, not laboriously produced for an arbitrary elite. Guillaume de Lorris does not describe the peasants laboring to produce Lady Idleness's lovely clothing; nor does he tell us *where* this work takes place or *how* their production is delivered to the Garden. Like any spectacle, aristocratic idleness requires that the theatrical machinery underlying the illusion be concealed.

Rabelais, in contrast, scrupulously enumerates its underlying costumes, props, and scenery—the stables, the baths, the gardens, the staff of dressers, the location of the artisan complex, the delivery system, the location and size of the mirrors. In explaining its underlying conditions and processes, he effectively disenchants aristocratic leisure, no longer based on a perpetually elusive—and thus inimitable—essence. In Thélème the idle condition is revealed to be merely the effect of a leisure infrastructure. If the *Roman de la Rose* elaborated the founding myth of nobiliary idleness, Thélème is its demystification. It is no doubt to *L'Astrée* more than to *Gargantua* that one should look for a renaissance of Guillaume's courtly *otium* in the early modern world.[74]

Present outside its doors in a narthex of productive labor, work also exists in the hallowed space within Thélème. With all its trappings present, aristocratic idleness itself remains mysteriously absent. Instead, the Thélémites apparently use their leisure in order to work. If no clocks impose a work schedule (443), it is not because they engage only in leisure, but rather because these devices would be simply unnecessary since the Thélémites *choose* to work of their own volition. They have no need for clocks to measure—

and enforce—work time, being *naturally* prone to work. In Thélème, work is not a form of discipline, a prudent bridle on free will (inevitably drawn to sin, as for Luther and Calvin); nor is it a strategic defense against desire (a tool used in curbing the licentiousness of leisure, as for the moralists); rather their labor apparently flows freely from their intimate being, as though work were the natural consequence of free will and desire:

> Toute leur vie était employée non par loix, statuts, ou règles, mais selon leur vouloir et franc arbitre. Se levaient du lit quand bon leur semblait, beuvaient, mangeaient, *travaillaient*, dormaient, *quand le désir leur venait*. Nul ne les éveillait, nul ne les parforçait ni à boire, ni à manger, ni à faire chose autre quelconque. Ainsi l'avait établi Gargantua. En leur règle n'était que cette clause: FAIS CE QUE VOUDRAS . . . (473; emphasis added)

> [All their life was regulated not by laws, statutes, or rules, but according to their free will and pleasure. They rose from bed when they pleased, and drank, ate, worked, and slept when the fancy seized them. Nobody woke them; nobody compelled them either to eat or to drink, or to do anything else whatever. So it was that Gargantua had established it. In their rules there was only one clause: *Do what you will.*][75]

The reader later learns that the women are skilled at needlework (*doctes à l'aiguille*, 475), although what form the men's work might take remains a mystery. Nevertheless, innately noble and (thus) virtuous, the Thélémites are also innately bound to work. Their very essence is industrious. Rabelais's humanist utopia synthesizes *otium* and *neg-otium*, as though to suggest that ideally work would simply be one possible form of leisure, not its antithesis.

Although there are no clocks to measure time, Rabelais clearly cannot imagine the Thélémites *wasting* time. He thus specifies that a highly trained staff performs their careful grooming and dressing:

> En ces vêtements tant propres et accoutrements tant riches, ne pensez que eux ni elles perdissent temps aucun. Car les maîtres des garde-robes avaient toute la vêture tant prête par chacun matin, et les dames de chambre tant bien étaient apprises, que en un moment elles étaient prêtes & habillées de pied en cap. (469)

> [Do not suppose, however, that any time was wasted by either men or women over these handsome clothes and rich accoutrements. For the

masters of the wardrobe had all the clothing so neatly laid out each morning, and the chambermaids were so skilful, that in a minute they were all ready and dressed from head to foot.]⁷⁶

The Thélémites delegate the *oisiveté* of dressing and grooming to their wardrobe staff. But the "masters of the wardrobe" in Thélème are not like their equivalent in nineteenth-century bourgeois households in which a corps of sometimes one hundred servants dressed in livery was employed more to display the wealth of the master than to fulfill any precise duties. Veblen analyzed the function of such unoccupied servants as "vicarious leisure." They signified to the world that their master was not only idle himself, but even employed others to be idle on his behalf.⁷⁷ But in Thélème, the wardrobe staff wastes no time, expediting the entire procedure in only a moment. They make grooming and dressing into a task to be performed in the most efficient manner possible, thereby transforming conspicuous idleness into vicarious work. To appreciate this detail, one has only to compare the Thélémites to Oiseuse, whose sole "concern" was leisurely adornment: "Mout avoit bon tens et bon mai, / qu'el n'avoit sousi ne esmai / de nule rien fors seulement / de soi atorner noblement" (vv. 569–72).

Having followed the fortunes of Oiseuse from her appearance in the *Roman de la Rose* to her revision in the *Pèlerinage* and on to her synthesis with *neg-otium* in the Abbey of Thélème, my discussion points to the new social playing field of the Renaissance. Questions of work and leisure were inevitably subject to reevaluation in accordance with the cultural and social project of the so-called Fourth Estate. For Thélème announced the ideals of this new elite, composed of hard-working humanists nevertheless eager to master idleness. This new context explains Rabelais's hyperawareness of the conditions of possibility of idleness: for a meticulous exposition of how nobiliary idleness was in fact produced undercut its mythic dimensions. It thus cleared the way for the rival elite to reinvent an ethics of idleness in its own image.

2
Work in Idleness in the Fourth Estate

> ... quelques grands et sages personnages se conformans à mon dire, disoyent qu'ils n'estoyent jamais moins seuls que quand ils estoyent seuls, ny moins entachez de l'oisiveté que quand ils estoient oisifs.
> —Etienne Pasquier, Lettre IV, "A Monsieur de Marillac"

F EW INDEED ARE THOSE WHO CAN CLAIM TO WORK AS HARD AS RENAISsance humanists. Their renowned diligence earned them Montaigne's scorn. A self-proclaimed *oisif*, Montaigne mocks the humanist work ethic with his portrait of the scholar-philologist emerging from his study well after midnight, dirty, with running nose and eyes, completely exhausted by his lifelong quest to discover the meter of a single verse from Plautus and the true spelling of a Latin word.[1] Beyond denouncing strictly bookish knowledge, a favorite theme in the *Essais*, this portrait fulfills a clear social function: reducing the humanist cult of effort to absurdity is Montaigne's way of distancing himself from the notion of labor. It belongs to a studied presentation of the *Essais* as a leisurely hobby, not a work of careful erudition, composition, and revision, lest the essayist himself be taken for an intellectual worker.

A broad survey of the reputations of his contemporaries and humanist predecessors reveals an attitude toward work very different from Montaigne's scornful posture. It is said, for instance, that Budé spent part of his wedding day studying his favorite authors.[2] In his *Vie de Ronsard*, Claude Binet portrays the young poet burning the midnight oil studying Greek letters and "other good sciences."[3] The humanist's labors may indeed have been Herculean, as a portrait of Erasmus holding a book with the title *Herakleou Ponoi (The Labors of Hercules)* suggests.[4] Pibrac chose the bee, the symbol of industriousness, for his personal emblem, just as Ramus adopted as a motto the proverbial *labor omnia vincit*.[5] There existed a widely shared conviction that strenuous effort was the very condition of knowledge and that the steps leading up Parnassus were steep indeed. The elaborate *(ex-labore)* correspondence that took place among humanists is sufficient proof that their "leisure" was not wasted. As artifacts, their personal letters give an account of their time, time clearly not spent in indolence.

Yet given their solid background in the humanities, citizens of the republic of letters also knew that work could not be the purpose of existence. Aristotle himself defined humanity's highest calling as the contemplative idleness he termed *schole*. Even Cicero, the very personification of the active life, recognized that *otium* was sometimes legitimate. He composed his own treatise on work and moral duty during a period of idleness, as he states in the preface to the third book of *De Officiis*, a text that often framed Renaissance discourse on idleness.[6] Despite their conviction that work could indeed conquer all, most of Montaigne's contemporaries did not wish to be themselves conquered by work, becoming what Montaigne terms slaves to work *(serf de mes négoces)*; they were not eager to make contemplation into work, and work itself into the purpose of existence. Their attempt to reconcile an esteem for work with the ideal of Classical leisure will be my focus here. Such a reconciliation was made all the more difficult by the simple fact that the Renaissance already had a constituted leisure class—"idle aristocrats"—as we saw in the previous chapter.

Any discussion of idleness in this milieu must confront the contradictions arising from a compelling imaginary of idleness at odds with the ever-pressing reality of work, complete with schedules, political responsibilities, and economic concerns.[7] In short, idleness was idealized yet increasingly subject to a de facto marginalization—a situation not unfamiliar to us today. This chapter explores an early paradigm of the modern professional—someone who both works long hours and is affluent enough to enjoy leisure. For the writers studied here are the forebears of today's professionals, including, of course, professors. At the same time, the sociologists, philosophers, and economists who today militate for a reform of our contemporary civilization of work are no less their cultural heirs than is the "workaholic" professional.[8] This dual and conflicting inheritance brings to the fore the contradictions within the Fourth Estate itself. The Renaissance's busy writers and proto-professionals laid the seeds for our society of total work; at the same time, they launched an active resistance against the very society that they were building.

While Montaigne's *Essais* are central to the questions examined in this chapter, I also focus on contemplative moments, however fleeting, found in less familiar texts, from personal letters and handbooks of idleness to a rewriting of Montaigne's essay "De l'oisiveté." It is not altogether inappropriate that these reflections on idleness should be found in shadowy places. But before examining the rhetoric of idleness in detail, let us begin with a brief outline of the Fourth Estate, a class in full ascension.

EX LABORE HONOR: THE FOURTH ESTATE'S RISE TO NOBILITY

The preeminence of the officeholding *robe* milieu during the Renaissance confused traditional conceptions of the three estates. This prompted some to speak in terms of four estates[9] and others to recognize in the nobility two varieties: *la noblesse de race* (genealogical or "sword" nobles) and *la noblesse de robe* (an elite corps of bureaucrats of recent ennoblement). Historical evidence suggests that in reality both *robe* and *sword* belonged to the same reasonably cohesive landed elite that constituted the ruling class.[10] Notwithstanding, contemporaries seemed to regard the two milieux as incommensurable: hence the virulent arms versus letters polemic studied by James Supple.[11] Generations of historians have struggled to account for these perceived differences with reference to occupation. But explicit occupation or "profession" alone cannot fully account for the lines contemporaries seemed to draw between the so-called Fourth Estate and the "old" nobility or, more generally, between nobles and non-nobles.[12] The category of leisure may provide a new opening into this famously thorny question. Can the perceived difference between the two rival elites be explained, not through a given occupation, but rather through how they conceived of the time they spent away from their explicit occupations? How can the ethos of idleness adopted by the Fourth Estate shed new light onto Renaissance conceptions of nobility? But first, to address questions in their logical order, how did the Fourth Estate come by idleness in the first place?

Fourth Estate families made their social ascension thanks to hard work, by passing from commerce on to officeholding and a noble lifestyle. After three generations had successfully "lived nobly," successive generations could lay claim to nobility, sometimes dropping the family name, as did Montaigne, the first to drop "Eyquem." The eminently useful work they performed allowed them to amass and maintain their fortunes, secure prestigious offices, and thus achieve high social standing. In other words, work led to nobility *(ex labore honor)*.[13]

However, the next stage in the process of becoming noble was to take distance with respect to any commercial origins since nobles were barred from engaging in most kinds of commerce.[14] As the jurist and specialist of nobility André Tiraqueau put it succinctly in 1549: *"mercatura deroget nobilitati"* ["commerce derogates nobility"].[15] The true nature of the noble estate required abstention from *negotium*—or rather, parallel proposition, it instituted a mandatory *otium*.[16] To recall Montaigne's phrase, the nobility was "an idle condition" *(d'une condition oisive)*; its existence was assured by private income *(rentes)*.[17]

The final stage in becoming what George Huppert terms a *"bourgeois gentilhomme"* was to redefine idleness in keeping with the Fourth Estate's own ideals, to make idleness conform to its own particular brand of "living nobly," all the more since "a noble life makes a nobleman."[18] It is my contention that a distinctive way of using idleness played no small role in the Fourth Estate's self-definition. But in order to redeem *oisiveté*, long the privilege of nobles, members of the Fourth Estate had to differentiate their practice of leisure from the perceived uselessness—and laziness—associated with "idle" aristocrats. Not only was this newly defined art of idleness active, it was in a sense performed. And in keeping with this competitive spirit, complex criteria were elaborated in order to measure the success or failure of a given performance. The leisured gentleman of the Fourth Estate did not associate idleness with an intimate self and personal gratification. Instead, *oisiveté* was a code to be mastered—a code that fulfilled the dual, and contradictory, function of both reflecting and establishing membership in an elite. Idleness, then, had a social function well beyond the moralist terms that nevertheless continued to provide a rhetorical framework for Renaissance discourse.

Leisure's ideological imperative is nowhere more apparent than in Antoine de Laval's treatise on leisure. As one of the most comprehensive treatments of work and leisure, his chapter entitled "Du Loysir et comme on le peut employer honnestement" in *Des-*

seins des professions nobles et publiques (1605) makes an appropriate point of departure.

Antoine de Laval: The Stigma of Un-Leisure

In many ways, Antoine de Laval embodied the aspirations of his milieu by virtue of his successful professional life combined with personal cultivation. Although he boasted familiarity with gentlemen whose nobility and prestige were more firmly established, including Michel de Montaigne, Laval's own noble status was rather recent for the standards of the time.[19] His hasty social promotion may partly explain his investment in the question of idleness.

Laval mobilizes precepts and *sententiae* in a thoroughly predictable way, revisiting the topoi established by the moralists. However, when it comes to his choice of exemplars, he breaks with tradition. Aside from Scipio, invoked near the beginning of the chapter, none of his exemplars come from conventional storehouses. He does not, in other words, cite famous ancients as examples of how to—or how *not* to—practice idleness. Even Montaigne, who *essays* idleness, selects his exemplars from literary sources.[20] Instead, the reader is invited to emulate *Monsieur Rapin, Monsieur de Pybrac, Monsieur le President de Thou, feu Monsieur de Bosbecq*. All contemporaries of Laval, these men are all illustrious members of the Fourth Estate. Laval, in other words, looks for *exempla* of how to practice idleness among his peers. Why stray from bookish wisdom when it comes to *otium*, which after all, is a highly conventional topic? The art of idleness, it would appear, was so rooted in the social practices of his peers that it escaped the common language of exemplarity. As for negative *exempla*, Laval asks readers to recall anonymous figures from their memories of social encounters:

> Que je plains ces pauvres gens quelques grands & riches qu'ils soient, qui transissent d'ennuy & de chagrin aussi tost qu'ils perdent le train de leur vie ordinaire: vous les voyez baailler, resver & suer d'ahan de ne rien faire.[21]

> [How I pity those poor people, no matter how great and wealthy they may be, who die from ennui and chagrin as soon as they lose the rhythm of their customary activities: you see them yawn, daydream, and sweat from the strain of doing nothing.]

Laval addresses his reader who has certainly encountered people unable to achieve idleness, people who pathetically succumb to boredom rather than assuming with dignity the role of idler: "vous les voyez baailler, resver & suer d'ahan de ne rien faire" [you see them yawn, daydream, and sweat from the strain of doing nothing]. He ridicules this spectacle of boredom in a condescending tone: "que je plains ces pauvres gens . . ." [how I pity those poor people . . .]. The aristocratic afflictions of *ennui* and *chagrin* inspire only contempt, as though they were the result of a personal defect. Indeed, Laval seems to consider *ennui* to be not a medical condition to which one falls prey (as in medieval and Renaissance medical discourse on melancholy), but rather the sign of a moral weakness and inability to resist boredom. In this sense, his scorn for weak-willed aristocrats prefigures an eighteenth-century understanding of boredom as a moral failure.[22]

This gesture further reveals an attempt to establish complicity based on a new class morality. Together, author and reader form an implicit consensus against those unable to achieve idleness "no matter how great and wealthy they may be . . ." *(quelques grands & riches qu'ils soient)*. This clause, added almost as an afterthought, suggests that mastery of the art of idleness transcends not only material wealth, but also noble birth: one may be both *riche* and *grand*, yet still unable to master the art of idleness. In other words, neither wealth nor noble ancestry—nor even a combination of both— confers the mysterious quality necessary in order to practice leisure well. This savoir faire is a distinctive excellence, one that transcends genealogy and cannot be purchased. It was precisely this art of idleness that allowed the Fourth Estate to set itself apart from both its roots in *négoces* and from "genealogical nobles."[23]

Far from being an alternative to public life, mastery of the art of idleness was part of a contest for distinction. The test required to establish membership in this elite was very simple, for one did not have to demonstrate prowess on the battlefield (like the chivalric hero) or conquer markets (like the successful merchant). Even a distinguished career of public service did not guarantee membership.[24] A temporary respite in an ordinarily busy life was sufficient to distinguish those noble beings who possessed the true art of idleness from everyone else. In Laval's symbolic economy of prestige, proficiency in the art of idleness was tautological: it both reflected and determined social rank. To be idle, one had to be noble; yet to be truly noble, one had to know how to be idle.

In the margins of work, the Fourth Estate's *homo otiosus* nevertheless functioned as a profoundly social being as he vied for standing with rivals. He did not pursue the intimacy of being through leisure. Rather, staged under the gaze of others, the art of idleness offered another medium for the diverse *commerces* assuring human interconnections. This logic of distinction informed the Fourth Estate's reinvention of idleness; it gave a manifest social function to seemingly disinterested musings on how best to be at leisure. What, then, was the nature of this art of idleness, the basis of *quality* of life in the Fourth Estate?

Guidelines for Practicing Idleness

The first concern was to situate *oisiveté* with respect to the active life, to make idleness not the antithesis of work, but rather its complement. The ideal was to be alone without being alone, to quote the second half of Pasquier's phrase cited in epigraph. To this effect, Erasmus's adage *nemo sibi nascitur* [no one is born for himself][25] became a virtual mantra in Fourth Estate discourse on idleness. It was also used to attack idle aristocrats, accused of retiring to a life of self-indulgence and of using their leisure to benefit only themselves: in other words, it was used to castigate what was perceived to be a close association of nobiliary idleness with personal gratification and privacy.[26] The courtier's reputation for leading a life of ease and plenty at the expense of the vast majority made him a common target.[27] But even country gentlemen fell under attack.

Barthélemy Aneau, for one, denounces their status as a non-working class of noble landlords in the poem and emblem entitled "Nez sommes nous: Et non pour nous" (a translation and amplification of *nemo sibi nascitur*) from *L'Imagination poétique* (1552). Aneau mounts a wholesale attack on rural landlords—idle aristocrats who live off the income generated by their property—terms that anticipate Montaigne's definition of the nobility based on its *oisiveté* (idleness) and *rentes* (private income). An aristocratic existence of *oisiveté* and *rentes*, Aneau insists, amounts to theft, for the noble landlord is a "a private thief" who steals the fruits of another's labor: ". . . et ce privé robeur / Ravit en peu de temps le fruyct, d'un grand labeur." [. . . and this private thief / Seizes in little time the fruit of a great labor.][28] The emblem depicts a gentleman carrying off a plate with honey and wax that, Aneau adds, should be reserved for all of humanity and for God, respectively.[29] In other words, idleness should not be a privilege, a class-defined license with which aristocrats alone are born: it is not their "private" prerogative to "eat honey"; aristocratic idleness plagues all of society. The moralist Jean Des Caurres makes the same point: idleness is a cesspool that infects the air *everyone* breathes; idlers harm not just themselves, but "the entire state and Republic."[30] As Montaigne notes ironically, we are held accountable not only for our actions, but also for our leisure.[31]

How, then, did the Fourth Estate realign its art of idleness with civic ideals? How was idleness to be reconciled with the axiom that "no one is born for himself"? Antiquity provided ample exemplars—worthy men who used their leisure as an alternative form of public service or at least as a dignified way to spend the time left over from *officia*. Etienne Pasquier speaks wistfully of a "belle et honorable retraicte" (his translation of Ciceronian *otium cum dignitate*). Nothing, he observes, is more beautiful than retiring after having long devoted oneself to the public: "après avoir longuement vacqué au public."[32]

Leisure comes "*after* having long devoted oneself to the public": achieving a "beautiful and honorable retirement" was thus partly a question of timing. Yet this problem had no simple quantitative solution, as it does today. Leisure time was not simply calculated in function of work time (in the United States, retirement is legitimate at the age of sixty-five; we are generally entitled to two weeks of vacation per year of work; a weekend break follows a forty-hour workweek). How, then, can it be determined when retirement to idleness is legitimate? When, in other words, has one worked long *enough*? Montaigne, for instance, resigned from the Bordeaux Parlement at the age of thirty-seven, already "weary" from his years of public service. Would his idleness qualify as *otium cum dignitate*?

Pierre de La Place (1520–72) supplies clear answers to such questions in his treatise *Discours politiques sur la voye d'entrer deuëmment aux estats, & maniere de constamment s'y maintenir & gouverner* (1561).[33] Significantly, he composed this treatise during a brief "retirement" in the midst of a distinguished career in law.[34] The last pages of his practical treatise discuss what he calls "honneste contemplation" and "tranquillité d'esprit." To help his reader navigate in a sea of particulars, he situates leisure within a clear hierarchy, at the summit of which lies the common good. It thus follows that leisure becomes legitimate only if one cannot serve the public. Then, and only then, can one "withdraw" to leisure.[35] The absolute priority of the *commun profit* is reiterated throughout his treatise. Inspired by Cicero's *De Officiis*, La Place then gives several examples of legitimate motivations for retiring to *otium*: these include physical infirmity (blindness, for instance) and corrupt regimes that make it impossible to practice virtue.[36]

Despite his reputation as the century's most famous idler, Montaigne often respects these criteria in justifying his own idleness. Near the beginning of "De la vanité" he admits to being idle while obliquely reminding his readers of the corruption of the times and of his own powerlessness:

> La corruption du siecle se faict par la contribution particuliere de chacun de nous: les uns y conferent la trahison, les autres l'injustice, l'irreligion, la tyrannie, l'avarice, la cruauté, selon qu'ils sont plus puissans; les plus foibles y apportent la sottise, la vanité, l'oisiveté, desquels je suis. (III, 9, 946b)

> [The corruption of the age is produced by the individual contribution of each one of us; some contribute treachery, others injustice, irreligion, tyranny, avarice, cruelty, in accordance with their greater power; the weaker ones bring stupidity, vanity, idleness, and I am one of them.] (722)

In confessing to "stupidity," "vanity," and "idleness," Montaigne appears to assume a cynical persona, laughing ruefully at his own idleness and impotence. But in reality he offers a sly rationalization of his retreat to *otium*. The passage begins with a denunciation of the corruption of the times *(la corruption du siecle . . .)* and ends with Montaigne's self-professed impotence to effect any change *(les plus faibles . . . dont je suis)*. With these two givens, is Montaigne's idleness not exonerated? Cicero justified his own *otium* in much the same terms, although without the cynical twist Montaigne gives the formulation.

Another passage reveals a less ambiguous acquiescence to the absolute priority of the *commun profit*. Despite its polemical beginning, "De la solitude" is not an unequivocal defense of the private, leisured self. Although he opens the essay with a rhetorical pirouette refuting Erasmus's adage *nemo sibi nascitur*, Montaigne goes on to align his art of idleness with the civic-minded criteria of a La

Place. "C'est assez vescu pour autruy, vivons pour nous au moins ce bout de vie" (I, 39, 242a) [We have lived enough for others, let us live at least this remaining bit of life for ourselves] (178), begins one maxim. But he later adds a qualifying clause, specifying that "untying" ourselves from society is permissible *since we can no longer contribute*: "Il est temps de nous desnoüer de la societé, puis que nous n'y pouvons rien apporter" (I, 39, 242c; emphasis added).[37]

Alone without being alone, the ideal leisured gentleman also endeavored to be idle without being idle; he did not seek to *be* at leisure, but rather to *do* leisure. Members of the Fourth Estate engaged in elaborate correspondence, poetry, translation, and other forms of what we might today call "personal cultivation." Beyond supervising their country estates,[38] they actively pursued hobbies or *loisirs*—a term coined only in the mid-eighteenth century. Michel de L'Hospital's letters give a sense of how these men occupied their leisure, dividing their time between reading, writing, and conducting (domestic) business. George Hoffmann's important study of Montaigne's daily life spent managing both the family estate and his literary career reveals how busy his so-called "retirement" really was.[39] And as Montaigne often complained, everyday business *(menage)* could be as demanding as public office.[40] Instead of trading business for idleness, members of the Fourth Estate traded an incredibly busy "active life" for a life of *otium* that was ultimately no less active.

Idle but never "lazy," members of the Fourth Estate believed one had to paradoxically *work* at achieving leisure. The gentlemen of the Fourth Estate embraced effort which sword nobles disdained—except on the battlefield. Effort had of course long been an aristocratic value, but only when applied to its most traditional occupation: warfare. When engaged in combat, the chivalric hero may appear drenched in sweat (and all the more worthy as a result). It was the particular contribution of the Fourth Estate to make effort the condition of *leisure* as well as of work. And among the most virulent spokesmen for the importance of effort in achieving leisure was Nicolas Pasquier. His *Le Gentilhomme* (1611) mounts a defense of the Fourth Estate's conception of ennobling leisure—or rather the particular kind of "work" that was designated "leisure." After a series of chapters on the virtues in the second book, he turns to the problem of idleness, to the physical and moral threat posed by aristocratic leisure as *license*, and to the importance of learned leisure in the civilizing process.[41] How can one be a gentleman, he asks, if one squanders one's leisure living a life of pleasure and ignorance? How can one enjoy leisure if one does not know how to work?

Underlying Nicolas Pasquier's vehemence is a struggle to reappropriate idleness, but in a new form stripped of the age-old bias against "vulgar" work. The traditional aristocratic scorn for labor had been reaffirmed and nuanced during the Renaissance by Baldesar Castiglione's *Cortegiano* (first published in 1528). Castiglione gave a new sense of mystery to the nobiliary ideal of nonwork with the neologism *"sprezzatura."* The perfect courtier was truly an artist, but one who concealed his art by effacing all traces of effort. An underlying imperative that work appear as leisure informed this elegant negligence. As Eduardo Saccone argues, this artless art functions much like irony—no doubt one of the most aristocratic of all modes, based as it is on the implicit exclusion of a real or virtual public.[42]

In the place of this aesthetics of nonchalance, Fourth Estate writers substituted an ethics of work—the new, and paradoxical, basis of leisure. Effort assumed a pragmatic, moral, and sometimes even epistemological value: as though survival, morality, and even knowledge were all somehow earned in the sweat of one's brow. "The paternal roof," writes Michel de L'Hospital in a passage that subtly attacks *sprezzatura* and its avatars, "is a place of exile only for he who allows his idleness to be spoiled by wine and sleep and who finds work distasteful."[43] With this highly charged phrase, L'Hospital castigates the nobiliary attitude par excellence. For the terms he chooses to characterize improper leisure combine a veneer of nonchalance, of *laisser aller* (he "allows" his idleness to be spoiled), and a posture of scorn—of finding work "distasteful." Scorn and nonchalance, *mépris et nonchalance*, were precisely the terms chosen by Gabriel Chappuis to translate Castiglione's *sprezzatura*.[44] Michel de L'Hospital attacks this courtly ideal of nonwork in the name of a new ideal that encompasses—indeed, requires—effort. If *sprezzatura* is a kind of "negligent diligence," the new ideal becomes a *diligent* negligence.

Busy *doing* leisure and being useful, the idle gentleman of the Fourth Estate reconciled idleness with his conception of the common good and the merit of work. Du Bellay reinforces both these values in defending the humanist's new culture of learned leisure in his *Deffence et Illustration de la langue francoyse*:

Les allechementz de Venus, la gueule & les ocieuses plumes ont chassé d'entre les hommes tout desir d'immortalité; mais encores est ce chose plus indigne, que ceux qui d'ignorance & toutes especes de vices font leur plus grande gloire, se moquent de ceux qui en ce tant louable labeur poëtique employent les heures que les autres consument aux jeuz, aux baings, aux banquez, & autres telz menuz plaisirs.[45]

[The pleasures of Venus, gluttony, and idle quills have chased from the society of men any desire for immortality: but what's worse is that those who gloat about their ignorance and all sorts of vices waste their time (literally: "consume their hours") on games, baths, banquets, and other little pleasures while making fun of others who use this so praiseworthy poetic labor to employ the hours.]

Du Bellay puts the two distinct ways of practicing idleness into sharp relief, following a clear moral polarization and enlisting the moral foundation of work in defense of humanist learned leisure. In the first place, the humanist *works*; his poetry *employs* time (*employent les heures*); it is a labor (*tant louable labeur poëtique*). In contrast, stereotypical idle aristocrats apparently exert no effort at all: they obey the flesh, not the will, engaging in gluttony (*la gueule*) and carnal love (*les allechementz de Venus*), in the same association of aristocratic leisure with licentiousness discussed in the previous chapter. Effort thus redeems learned leisure while idle aristocrats apparently wallow in the sins of the flesh. Du Bellay all but reduces the value of leisure to the effort put into achieving it.

He further targets the very core of a traditional aristocratic ethos of idleness: the pastime. Frivolous pastimes, gambling, baths, banquets and "other little pleasures" are all targeted in the name of the expenditure they entail: these forms of play serve only to make time pass—to "consume" time. Barthélemy Aneau makes a similar point in criticizing tennis, the epitome of the aristocratic pastime. In "Grand et vain labeur" he disparages tennis because it accomplishes no other purpose besides hastening the passage of time:

> Et brief il [the tennis player] prend grande sueur, & peine
> A un Esteuf chose petite, & vaine.
> Pour, à la fin de s'estre tant lassé;
> N'avoir rien faict, sinon le temps passé.[46]

[In short he (the tennis player) breaks out into a great sweat and strains / Over a ball, a small and vain thing, / And ends up wearing himself out so much / In order to do nothing besides pass the time.]

Gratuitous pastimes are, for Antoine de Laval, a sacrilege. "Mais j'ay tousjour creu que la perte & prostitution du temps à chose vaine, & sans fruict, estoit une espece de sacrilege"[47] [But I have always believed that the loss and prostitution of time for a useless cause, without fruit, was a kind of sacrilege]. One has only to contrast this attack on the aristocratic pastime to Budé's defense of the hunt discussed in chapter 1. Laval, Aneau, and Du Bellay single out its spirit of play as among the most pernicious elements in the old spirit of leisure still animating stereotypical "genealogical" nobles. In *De Venatione*, it was precisely this nonutilitarian dimension—this element of programmed loss, of "wasting" what could be used as a resource—that made the hunt a pastime worthy of noblemen.

At stake, then, are two competing attitudes toward effort, time, and utility in idleness. Learned leisure is a useful *employment* of time (humanists *"employent les heures,"* writes Du Bellay) while old-guard aristocrats *consume* time *("les autres consument [les heures]")*. Making abstraction of the moral dimensions, the opposition of the use*less* versus the use*ful* reveals a fundamental conceptual rift. The suffixes themselves oppose dissipation (-less) to accumulation (-ful). For a defining function of leisure for members of the Fourth Estate was not to dissipate time, but rather to use it to collect and conserve the works of their leisure.

(Ful)filling Leisure

Montaigne's rhetoric of *pleine oisiveté* studied in chapter 5 presents one example of a desire for plenitude through idleness. The private collection presents another common example. A ubiquitous hobby in the Fourth Estate, it reflects an attempt to give a material form to the plenitude associated with idleness. The collector is driven by the need to accumulate and preserve (an atavism from a past in *négoces*?). Part of a desire for encyclopedic fullness, the collection drew a sharp line between the civic gentleman's employment of leisure and mere pastimes such as tennis. The collection served to reify leisure, to leave a monument that withstood time, and thus mortality.[48] As such it was the precise antithesis of the pastime, which hastened the passage of time, requiring great *labeur,* but leaving no *ouvrage.*

The most common examples of Fourth Estate collections include personal libraries and coin collections. More spectacular was the menagerie constituted by Augier de Bosbecq, or Ogier Ghislain de Busbecq (1522–92), a Flemish ambassador sent regularly to France beginning in 1574. Busbecq's public service provided him with a means to pursue his hobby. As ambassador to Turkey under Ferdinand from 1555 to 1562, he was able to make detailed annotations on the fauna and assemble a veritable zoo in the German embassy in Constantinople, both to amuse his staff and observe firsthand the fauna discussed by Pliny and other ancients.[49] The exhaustive nature of his collection prompted one friend to label it "Noah's Ark."[50]

Busbecq's hobby of collecting animals also points to an underlying symbiosis between work and leisure in the Fourth Estate. Because of his official functions as ambassador to Turkey, Busbecq was able to engage in his hobby. His friend, Antoine de Laval, also bridged work and leisure with his collection. At his estate, Laval assembled a collection of maps and books—a logical interest given his position as royal geographer.[51] In both cases, work and leisure were intermingled and mutually dependent.

But of all of the hobbies pursued by members of the Fourth Estate, the most important was writing, the key to living well in leisure and the gay science of an elite. Literary works of art and humanist scholarship had a clear honorific function.[52] But even the less ambitious practice of letters as a simple hobby belonged to a logic of social distinction.

"LA VRAYE OISIVETÉ": LITERATURE AS LOISIR

As a common strategy of *captatio benevolentiae* during the Renaissance, writers often claimed for their writing the modest status of a hobby—a way to fill *loisir* with *loisirs*. When the magistrate-poet Guy du Faur de Pibrac published his defense of "les plaisirs de la vie rustique" he invoked this commonplace:

> S'efforce qui voudra le laurier meriter,
> Quant à moy, ie n'escris sinon pour eviter
> Les trompeuses douceurs d'une langueur oisive.[53]

[Whomever so desires may struggle to earn the laurel / As for me, I write only in order to avoid / The deceptive sweetness of a languorous idleness.]

Pibrac used writing (and also translating and paraphrasing Latin verse, here Horace's *Epode II*) to improve the quality of his leisure. He was thus able to convert potentially bad leisure ("langueur oisive") into *otium litteratum*. Even Ronsard first composed poetry as a simple hobby, maintains du Perron in his funeral oration. Initially, the future Prince of Poets composed verse *"en se jouant."*[54] If he soon chose to devote himself solely to poetry, du Perron continues, it was partly because of a physical infirmity (deafness).[55] In this version of Ronsard's life, the Prince of Poets chose to become a poet because he was unfit for a more traditional career. As we have seen, physical infirmity is one of the valid reasons for withdrawing from public service in Pierre de La Place's *Discours politiques*.

Members of this milieu made a dogma out of Seneca's maxim "idleness without letters is death" *(otium sine litteris mors est)*. Without exception, all of the handbooks on leisure cite or gloss Seneca's phrase. "Ce n'est pas ouvrage de tout le monde de scavoir vivre seul," begins Laval, "il faut porter sa compagnie quant & soy: ce sont les lettres *vita sine litteris mors est & vivi hominis sepultura*." [Not everyone knows how to live alone, one must bring company along with oneself: this company is to be found in letters *life without letters is man's death and burial*.][56] Des Caurres paraphrases the maxim and Messie cites Seneca to conclude that literary idleness is the only true idleness *(vraie oisiveté)*.[57] The famous inscription Montaigne had carved on the walls of his *cabinet* presents another exaltation of *otium litteratum*—of literary idleness. This Latin inscription proclaimed his desire to retire to *otium* and the muses.[58]

At the end of the period, Charles Loyseau, a prominent jurist, commented on the ascension of the Fourth Estate during the Renaissance. According to Loyseau, sword nobles had lost their monopoly on power because they had "scorned letters and embraced idleness" [la noblesse a méprisé les lettres et embrassé l'oisiveté].[59] In their wisdom, members of the Fourth Estate knew to unite idleness with letters in the tradition of *otium litteratum*.[60]

"DE L'OISIVETÉ": REDEEMING IDLENESS

Montaigne's "De l'oisiveté" (I, 8) presents the Fourth Estate's reappropriation of nobiliary idleness in microcosm. This short but

2: WORK IN IDLENESS IN THE FOURTH ESTATE 71

suggestive essay stages the presentation, crisis, and resolution of nobiliary idleness. "Of Idleness" is not about aristocratic idleness per se. Yet even though the literal meaning raises essentially moral questions, a social intertext permeates the choice of words and themes. These two levels (a conscious morality and a social unconscious) remain perfectly coherent but are never articulated together. In effect, the play between these two levels suggests aristocratic idleness without representing it, beginning with the title itself.

The title announces the aristocratic condition according to Montaigne's own definition of nobility, mentioned above: "la noblesse . . . est d'une condition oisifve et . . . ne vit, comme on dit que de ses rentes" (II, 8, 389–90a). An alternative translation for "Of Idleness" might thus be "Of the aristocratic condition."

According to the terms of this same definition, aristocratic idleness was made possible by *rentes*, i.e., the income generated from property. The first words of the essay condense this cause and effect relationship: "comme nous avons des terres oisives . . ." Strictly speaking, land makes idleness possible: Montaigne can enjoy idleness *because (comme)* he has (idle) land.[61] The essay's opening line directs our attention to a simple sociological factor. It was nearly impossible to divorce the idea of nobility from land during the Renaissance, since aristocratic identity was intimately connected to land ownership.[62] Beyond the income it generated, the noble estate had a strong symbolic value. Hence its presence in titles of nobility, as in Michel *de* Montaigne. Land was also the crucial factor in crossing the threshold between being a successful commoner and a noble. At some point in a family's rise to nobility, someone retired from *négoces* to the country estate, forsaking commercial activities, at least ostensibly.[63] In the case of the Eyquem family, this step was taken by Montaigne's father, Pierre, the first to "live as a gentleman" on his country estate.[64]

The metaphor of the mind as horse constitutes a third element of nobiliary idleness. Montaigne first presents minds as something that must be "bridled and controlled" in order to prevent them from running wild in "the vague field of imagination." He returns to this metaphor several sentences later to explain that in reaction to his state of idleness his own mind had indeed turned into "a runaway horse." This extended metaphor condenses two figurative meanings: the notion of *license* (idle minds should be reined in and bridled) and sexual appetite (the runaway horse commonly represents the victory of sensuality over reason in allegorical imagery).⁶⁵ Montaigne's idle mind as runaway horse thus triggers the association leisure-license-licentiousness, (all from the Latin *licere*) studied in chapter 1. Finally, the image of the horse refers obliquely to the aristocratic condition, for the horse is the very emblem of the chivalric ethos.

The quintessential components of nobiliary identity are thus scattered through the essay, from idleness, land, license (and sexual appetite) to the horse.

Yet, beginning with the initial metaphor of idle fields producing only useless weeds, Montaigne signals an overarching moral problem: the inutility of idleness. Idle (or "fallow") fields produce only useless weeds ("cent mille sortes d'herbes sauvages et inutiles" [32a]); only through labor are they able to be harvested and *used*.⁶⁶

The rhetoric of uselessness in "De l'oisiveté" projects the imagery of aristocratic idleness into crisis, as idle fields generate "wild and useless plants" and idle minds "throw themselves in disorder hither and yon in the vague field of imagination" (21). And in reaction to the inutility of idleness, Montaigne concludes, he turned to writing. His famous writing cure not only brought order to disorder, it also redeemed idleness. Out of nobiliary *otium*, Montaigne thus fashioned *otium litteratum*—literary idleness. The difference between nobiliary idleness and the art of idleness is culture, mostly *literary* culture, as we have seen. As a form of cultivation, idleness works and reworks a mental and cultural terrain. This *culture* of idleness was at the foundation of the Fourth Estate's project.

Conquering idleness was the final stage of this class's rise to nobility. Yet in reforming the concept of leisure in keeping with its own values (merit, effort, public service, utility, letters), the specificity of leisure as an ideal was thrown into question. In the end, it is perhaps the personal device fashioned by Etienne Jodelle that best speaks of the true nature of leisure in the Fourth Estate: *in ocio negotium*, i.e., work in idleness.⁶⁷

The sword nobility—the traditional "leisure class"—had a different conception. For sword nobles, leisure was the prerogative, not prerequisite, of nobility. It remained close to its etymology: leisure—from *licere*, or license. Nobles did not have to "work" in order to achieve leisure; it was their privilege by virtue of being noble. One was born in and for idleness as in Ovid's phrase quoted by Montaigne: *"fugax rerum, securaque in otia natus"* (III, 10, 1003b) [Fleeing affairs, and born in idle ease] (767). Thus in *Le Roman de la Rose*, Oiseuse allows the courtly lover into the garden simply by virtue of his *condition oisive*: he does not have to *do* anything in order to get into the garden: entrance into the garden is effortless; he simply has to *be* noble.

For members of the Fourth Estate, one was not blessed with the "idle condition" at birth. Idleness was no longer either a birthright or self-evident. It had become a question of merit and work—of self-improvement through leisure. Like a profession, it was something one had to strive for, something one had to study and practice. In other words, leisure as an aristocratic *license* was rejected in favor of a new, active culture of leisure. This new savoir faire amounted to privileging leisure as work (doing), instead of leisure as privilege (license) and as essence (being). A time of intense activity, leisure was a culture of the mind and of the self, and knowledge of this culture was a quality that eluded the traditional "leisure class." Returning to the metaphor of idle fields, the Fourth Estate sought to use effort and art in elaborating a literary culture of idleness out of the copious but useless weeds generated by aristocratic fields of idleness.

OTIUM LITTERATUM: BEYOND USEFULNESS

> Now there can be no unused space in the total world of work,
> neither an unused area of ground nor an unused time.
> —Josef Pieper, *Leisure: The Basis of Culture*

Newly integrated into a single continuum with work, carefully situated within a paradigm based on the absolute priority of public service, closely allied with letters, and, finally, defined in opposition to inutility, idleness in the Fourth Estate was clearly distinguished from the perceived laziness and uselessness associated with the old nobility. Yet there was a curious resistance to taking the next logical step by defining *otium* as a useful art for useful men. A close examination of passages where the usefulness of *otium litteratum* is at stake will reveal that members of the Fourth Estate posited idleness as a third term: neither useless nor useful. Arriving at this third term required intricate and ambiguous rhetorical play.

Montaigne's essay "De l'oisiveté" leaves the question of the usefulness of his *otium litteratum* hanging in suspense. After elaborating on the uselessness of idleness and confessing that his own idle mind produced "monsters and chimeras," Montaigne then posits his literary venture as a reaction to this inutility: "j'ay commancé de les mettre en rolle . . ." (I, 8, 33a) [I have begun to put them in writing] (21). However, he avoids taking the next logical step by describing writing as useful. *Otium litteratum* is apparently in reaction to uselessness without being, itself, useful.

Laval will practice the same studied ambiguity when it comes to the usefulness of his *otium litteratum*. Literary idleness is first described as an "honest use" of the time left over from work. But, like Montaigne, Laval carefully abstains from concluding that it is thus "useful." Instead, he obscures the issue with understatement. Had he not recklessly composed these poems (poetry is a kind of extravagance for Laval), he would have spent this time "more vainly," he explains. He describes a period during his youth when he used to compose verse, most of which he claims to have later burned:

> Je n'ay pas trouvé à propos de les laisser vivre plus long temps puis que j'en avois le fruict esperé, qui estoit l'honneste employ du temps que mes affaires avoient de reste, & lequel j'eusse peu dependre plus vainement. (307v)

> [I did not find it suitable to let them (his poems) live any longer since I had the desired fruit, which was an honest use of the time left over from my business, time I could have spent more vainly.]

More vainly: is *otium litteratum* simply a way of spending one's time *less vainly*? The construction suggests that his art of *otium* is not entirely devoid of "vanity" itself. As an indirect construction, based on the negation of an opposite, his understatement makes it impossible to arrive at a clear understanding of how to interpret the adverbial phrase "more vainly." In other words, his youthful poetry was neither entirely useless nor entirely useful, but somehow occupied a space in between the two terms.

Etienne Pasquier situates his *otium litteratum* in an equally ambiguous zone. In a personal letter, he playfully points out that he is perfectly capable of engaging in idleness in addition to fulfilling his professional duties. He recounts a journey to Blois, where he had some legal business. But upon his arrival, he realized that the court was in recess. He explains that he then mobilized his literary culture in order to transform simple *otium* into *otium litteratum*. So far, the anecdote presents nothing unexpected. However, his next remark comes as a surprise, for he declares that his journey culminated in idleness:

> . . . trouvant que les vacations estoient donnees aux procez, je ne les voulus octroyer à ma plume; *ou pour mieux dire*, pendant que j'estois oiseux, je voulus parachever mon voyage en une autre oisiveté, qui fut de tracer une Pastorale du Vieillard Amoureux . . . (emphasis added)[68]

> [. . . upon learning that court was in recess, I did not want to accord it (recess) to my quill: *or to put it better*, while I was idle, I wanted to consummate my voyage in another idleness, which was to compose the pastoral of an old man in love . . .]

The rhetorical term for this gesture (*ou pour mieux dire* [or to put it better]) is the *correctio*. It allows Pasquier to theatrically stage an initial rejection of idleness, with its implied sense of uselessness, only to then overcome this reflex and embrace idleness: "in order to avoid idleness—no, in order to embrace idleness," he writes to his friend. Of course, this gesture poses no problem for the golden rule that gives precedence to the public over the private: serving the public interest, had, after all, been his intention; he turned to frivolous idleness only when the courts were closed. Nonetheless, Pasquier is perfectly able to indulge in gratuitous idleness *(une autre oisiveté)*, his dedication to *negotium* does not exclude a tentative, carefully circumscribed gratuitousness.

Yet he is also joking. And like the *correctio*, the joke offers a way of saying both one thing and its opposite, for the literal meaning (I was idle) is negated by the discursive mode (I am joking). These ruses leave the reader in a zone of indecision, unable to resolve Pasquier's situation by a simple idleness/work dichotomy.

Rabelais clouds the issue to the same effect in the preface to the *Tiers Livre*. Invoking the Diogenes anecdote, he asks: If one cannot work efficiently (in Pasquier's case, the court was in recess), is idleness, then, legitimate? Faced with his inability to contribute to his country's defense, but unwilling to stand by idly watching, Diogenes poses the age-old question of the usefulness of the intellectual's *otium*. In parody of the silent contemplative, Rabelais has Diogenes first "contemplate" the work of his compatriots: "Diogenes, les voyant en telle ferveur mesnaige remuer, et n'estant par les magistratz employé à chose aulcune faire, contempla par quelques jours leur contenence sans mot dire"[69] [Now when Diogenes saw them all so warm at work and himself assigned no duties by the magistrates, he watched their behaviour for some days in complete silence.[70]] Then, in a burst of martial zeal, he rids himself of his intellectual's paraphernalia[71] and proceeds to mime the actions of the Corinthians, to great comic effect:

> y roulla le tonneau fictil qui pour maison luy estoit contre les injures du ciel, et, en grande vehemence d'esprit desployant ses braz, le tournoit, viroit, brouilloit, barbouilloit, hersoit, versoit, renversoit . . . (17–19)
>
> [hither he rolled his earthen tub, which served him as a shelter against the inclemencies of the weather; and putting out all his strength, in a tremendous outburst of spirits, he twirled it, whirled it, scrambled it, bungled it, frisked it, jumbled it, tumbled it . . .] (282–83)

When one of his friends questions what possible use his frantic tub-rolling could possibly serve, the philosopher explains that since he had no other task to perform for the republic, he decided to devote all of his energies to moving his tub around, so that he would not be seen as the only sluggard and idler *(cessateur et ocieux)*.[72] Notice, however, that the motivation Rabelais gives Diogenes appears blatantly at odds with the philosopher's mores. Diogenes claims that he began "working" because he did not wish to *appear* idle: "pour . . . n'estre *veu* seul cessateur." This concern with what people think and with how he might appear seems entirely out of character. For Diogenes the Cynic is known for having led his life with utter disdain for both *doxa* and image. His categorical rejection of idleness thus assumes a latent irony. Moreover, this a priori rejection of idleness is further belied by the uselessness of the "work" he is able to contribute.[73] Far more reasonable was the reaction of Solon: once faced with a very similar situation, he simply gave up and went home, as Pierre de La Place recounts.[74] Montaigne, too, recommends idleness if one cannot really contribute to society: "il est temps de nous desnoüer de la societé, puis que nous n'y pouvons rien apporter . . ." (I, 39, 242c).

Having established the two alternatives available to Diogenes as idleness or pointless work, both ultimately unsatisfactory, Rabelais proceeds to place Diogenes's frenzy of a-telic activity on a par with his own activity as a writer. He, too, was apparently eager not to *appear* idle ("Je pareillement" [19]):

Par doncques n'estre adscript et en ranc mis des nostres en partie offensive, qui me ont estimé trop imbecille et impotent, de l'autre qui est defensive n'estre employé auculnement, feust ce portant hotte, cachant crotte, ployant rotte ou cassant motte, tout m'estoit indifférent: *ay imputé à honte plus que mediocre estre veu spectateur ocieux* de tant vaillans, disers et chevalereux personnaiges, qui en veue et spectacle de toute Europe jouent ceste insigne fable et tragicque comedie, ne me esvertuer de moy mesmes et non y consommer ce rien, mon tout, qui me restoit. (21–23; my italics)

[I have been considered too weak and impotent to be enrolled in our country's attacking force, and have not been employed by its other, defensive army, even as a carrier of hods, a bender of rods, or a cutter of sods—I should not have cared which. But *I have felt it to be most disgraceful to [appear to] stand idly watching* all these valorous, eloquent, and warlike persons who are performing their noble interlude and tragicomedy before the watching eyes of all Europe. I have been ashamed not to exert myself, not to contribute that nothing, which is all that I have left, my all.] (283–84)

Paradoxically, however, Rabelais compares his own intellectual activities (composing the *Tiers Livre*) to Diogenes who, after all, decided to abandon intellectual pursuits in favor of a hands-on participation in (mock) work. It is thus by writing that Rabelais resembles Diogenes-Sisyphus—the intellectual-turned-worker. Despite repeated claims that his own writing is not "useless," Rabelais nevertheless heralds the *Tiers Livre* as a Diogenic pursuit—work with no manifest or stable *telos*.[75]

To further complicate matters, Rabelais combines a deliberately overstated zeal for work with no small irony when it comes to the true value of the martial labors he enumerates. Rejecting idleness, he nevertheless puts into question the "useful work" of his compatriots, who are ultimately only "vaillans, disers et chevalereux personnaiges" just as the war for which they are working so hard to prepare has an element of absurdity: "ceste insigne fable et tragicque comedie." Is it truly better to be an *actor* in a tragic farce than an "idle spectator"? The critical distance with which Rabelais describes "public works" belies his overstated willingness to participate; the rhetorical mode undermines the ostensible lesson just as Rabelais's writing remains self-consciously "Diogenic"—of dubious utility.

Finally, in Montaigne's imagery of *oisiveté*, idleness connotes unused space as well as unused time. The space he selected for his *librairie*, he tells us, had previously been the most useless part of his chateau:

> Elle [la librairie] est au troisiesme estage d'une tour . . . C'estoit au temps passé le lieu plus inutile de ma maison. Je passe là et la plus part des jours de ma vie, et la plus part des heures du jour. (III, 3, 828c)
>
> [It is on the third floor of a tower. . . . In the past it was the most useless place in my house. In my library I spend most of the days of my life, and most of the hours of the day. (629)]

He thus exploits a cultivated ambiguity in this construction that leaves the reader wondering: Did Montaigne choose to convert this useless space into a library in order to make it useful? Or did he choose it precisely because its gratuitous quality made it the perfect theater for his idleness? As in the examples from Pasquier, Laval, and Rabelais, Montaigne's formulation is deliberately ambivalent—it makes two antithetical statements at once, situating the *librairie* somewhere between used and unused space.

The rhetorical strategies observed so far—*correctio*, understatement, irony, suspension, exaggeration, ambiguity, humor—all serve not to state, but rather to understate, overstate, or even avoid stating. Their effect is to insist that *otium litteratum* is *not* useless without stating that it *is* useful. The rhetoric of idleness is thus a rhetoric of evasion. It projects idleness into an indeterminate zone between the useful and useless, a zone of indecision and ambivalence. Clearly there was something not quite satisfying about importing utility to the realm of idleness. Why this reluctance to make idleness into something categorically useful?

Toward an Ethics of Idleness

In the first place, expediency alone runs counter to an ethical framework. In his synthesis and commentary of Aristotle's moral and political philosophy, Louis Le Roy explains that for Aristotle, idleness (*la vie ocieuse*) is ethically superior to work (*la vie negocieuse*):

> . . . la contemplation [est] quelque action voire tresexcellente, pour avoir sa perfection interieure & estre desiree pour soy. Aristote qui es-

toit fort studieux maintient au dixieme des Ethiques, & au premier de la Methaphysique, la contemplation estre plus noble [que la vie negocieuse].[76]

[... contemplation is an action, indeed an excellent action, because it has its interior perfection and is desired for its own sake. Aristotle who was very studious maintained in the tenth book of the *Ethics* and the first book of the *Metaphysics* that contemplation is more noble (than work)]

Making idleness manifestly useful would deprive it of its ethical potential—its capacity to transcend and question expediency. As Le Roy reminds his reader, contemplative *otium* is not inactivity, but rather autotelic activity ("quelque action voire tresexcellente pour avoir sa perfection interieure, & estre desiree pour soy"). The highest ethical ideal must be absolute, something worthy in and of itself, and not simply useful in accomplishing some other end. Thus, for Aristotle, *schole* (contemplative idleness) is superior precisely because it is not useful (telic), just as Cicero defined *honestum* as an autotelic category.[77] In accordance with Aristotelian ethics, work (*ascholia*) is to be endured only insofar as it leads to idleness (*schole*)—the locus of happiness. To quote Aristotle: "[h]appiness seems to be found in leisure [*schole*], since we accept trouble so that we can be at leisure ..." (X, 1177b, 5–7).[78]

On this respect, humanist translations of and commentaries on this crucial passage are revealing. In translating this passage, humanists began to invoke the *otium/negotium* dialectic, resituating the debate of work *versus* idleness on a properly ethical plane. "Videtur que felicitas in *ocio* esse, *negociamur* enim ut *ociemur*," writes Leonardo Bruni.[79] Likewise, Victorius: "[v]idetur autem beatitudo in *otio* manere. Suscipus enim *negotia*, ut *otio* fruamur ..."[80] And, finally, Joachim Périon's 1540 translation, praised for its elegance: "[b]eatitudo etiam in tranquillo quodam *otio* videtur consistere. *Negotia* enim suscipimus ut in *otio* simus ..."[81] These Renaissance translations attest to the connection perceived between *otium* and the per se (autotelic); to the renewed interest in Roman *otium* and its perceived relation to Aristotelian *schole*; and finally to the primacy of *otium* over *negotium*. Montaigne's *Essais* render a personal, at times lyrical, version of these conclusions reached by humanist scholars. And while his elegy of *oisiveté* is something of an anomaly in the literature of the sixteenth century, it was to have an important posterity in the seventeenth century, as Bernard Beugnot has shown with respect to writers from Honoré d'Urfé to Guez de Balzac.[82]

From Classical leisure, Montaigne borrowed the importance of finality in distinguishing work from idleness. His posture as an idler becomes, in this light, an ethical stance, part of his resistance against the tyranny of utility. The problem with work, Montaigne insists, is precisely that its end is external: "[t]oute magistrature, comme toute art, jette sa fin hors d'elle: *'nulla ars in se versatur'* "(III, 6, 903c) [All authority, like all art, has its end outside of itself: *no art is directed to itself]* (689). The epitome of the telic nature of work is commerce, which assigns profit as the purpose of activity. The "enslavement" of work invoked in the inscription in his *cabinet* reflects the simple fact that work is, by definition, telic: for the worker must submit to an exterior telos.[83]

Near the end of the *Essais*, he will thus insist that his actions are performed for their own sake and not as an end to something else. Montaigne does not dance in order to become more elegant or athletic; nor does he sleep in order to rejuvenate:

> Quand je dance, je dance; quand je dors, je dors; voyre et quand je me promeine solitairement en un beau vergier, si mes pensées se sont entretenues des occurences estrangieres quelque partie du temps, quelque autre partie je les rameine à la promenade, au vergier, à la douceur de cette solitude et à moy. (III, 13, 1107b)

> [When I dance, I dance; when I sleep, I sleep; yes, and when I walk alone in the beautiful orchard, if my thoughts have been dwelling on extraneous incidents for some part of the time, for some other part I bring them back to the walk, to the orchard, to the sweetness of this solitude, and to me.] (850)

This passage will thus culminate in praise of idleness, the emblem of an art of life:

> Nous sommes de grands fols: Il a passé sa vie en oisiveté, disons nous: je n'ay rien faict d'aujourd'huy. —Quoy, avez vous pas vescu? C'est non seulement la fondamentale mais la plus illustre de vos occupations. (III, 13, 1108c)

> [We are great fools. "He has spent his life in idleness," we say; "I have done nothing today." What, have you not lived? That is not only the fundamental but the most illustrious of your occupations.] (850)

Here, then, is Montaigne, *philosophe* of idleness and of *l'art de vivre*.

RECUPERATING THE ACCURSED SHARE: ORNAMENTAL IDLENESS

At the same time, for members of the Fourth Estate, mandating *utilitas* would be a symbolic regression to a commercial mentality. Is the common merchant not the most devoted disciple of the *utile*? Who else governs his life according to what is most profitable and expedient? These, in any case, are among the connotations of the *utile* at the end of the Renaissance, as Philippe Desan observes.[84] Transcending the *utile*—if only for a short time—was thus necessary in order to preserve the honorific function that idleness had long served. In order for idleness to confer nobility, it could not be useful in the same way that work was; or rather, its usefulness had to remain covert.

The desire to maintain the prestige of idleness is reflected in the evasiveness of Fourth Estate writers when it comes to the usefulness of their idle pursuits. It is also reflected in the Ciceronian epithet *honestum* that one finds attached to a variety of terms for leisure common in Fourth Estate terminology, including idleness, leisure, contemplation, and retirement. Thus Pierre de La Place speaks of "honneste contemplation"; of "l'honneste contentement des lettres pleines de repos & tranquillité," and of "l'honneste repos de la vieillesse." Laval entitles his chapter on idleness "Du Loysir et comme on le peut employer *honnestement*" (emphasis added). Montaigne terms reading an "honneste amusement" (II, 10, 409a). After having playfully defended his "Pastoral du Vieillard Amoureux" in the name of idleness, Pasquier refers to his *otium litteratum* as "quelques honnestes jeux d'esprit."[85]

Only when differentiated from overtly practical arts can the art of idleness assume an honorific function, becoming what Laval (quoting Busbecq) terms a "zero"—it adds value, but has no intrinsic use value:

> elle [poetry composed while idle] ne pouvoit non plus valoir que le zero au chiffre: elle adjouste à la lettre qui la precede: ainsi faict la Poësie à un homme qui sçait quelque chose d'utile, elle luy sert d'ornement, & le faict priser, cherir, & bien venir aux compaignies.[86]

[Poetry composed while idle could be worth no more than the zero added onto a figure: it augments the letter which precedes it: so, too, does poetry for the man who knows something useful, it serves as an ornament for him, and makes him valued, cherished, and a welcome presence at gatherings.]

Poetry as *loisirs* constitutes a temporary and complementary abstention from work and from the *utile*, for only as a form of nonwork with no manifest use can it confer prestige. It becomes not a "tool," the epitome of *utilitas*, but rather an ornament: "elle luy sert d'ornement." Letters may have been the catalyst initially used to magically transform nobiliary *otium* into *otium litteratum*. In the end, though, they bring perfect idleness in the Fourth Estate closer to nobiliary idleness by situating literary idleness somehow "beyond" *utilitas*. It is a beautiful *(belle)* and conspicuous *(evidente)* mark of distinction because it is removed from the prosaic realm of functionality: "aussi est-elle, (certes) une des plus belles & evidentes marques d'un esprit vif, & courageux . . ." The choice of the term "evident" emphasizes the social function of *otium litteratum*, situating it beyond a simple public-private distinction. The need to make the fruits of idleness "evident" was of course a driving impulse behind publishing one's writing.

In his commentary on Busbecq's maxim, Laval defends the extravagant hobby of poetry in the name of autotelic play—with the caveat that it not replace a useful profession:

". . . à celuy qui est appellé à une autre profession . . . je ne tiens point qu'il y ait un plus beau jeu au monde, lors qu'il n'est prins que pour jouër . . ."[87]

[for he who is called to another profession . . . I think there is no more beautiful game in the world, when it is taken only as play]

He thus reasserts the importance of nonutilitarian play in defining idleness. The aristocratic universe was governed by *bellum* and *otium*; Laval merely shifts the terms to *officium* and *otium litteratum*. The non-telic dimensions inherent in perfect idleness ultimately allow it to transcend the realm of the necessary in order to cautiously partake of the accursed share.

These discreet claims for a certain nonfunctionality are not without some strategic bad faith. For *otium litteratum* remained indirectly or directly connected to *negotium*, despite protestations to the contrary like the ones studied above. Certainly, literature could function as a medium conveying useful information when it came to the erudite conversation expected of diplomats, courtiers, and learned magistrates, but it also presented an occasion to study and ideally master for use in one's daily life different literary voices and performative modes (the request, the plea, or the demand, for instance).[88] Most obviously, it could of course also be used to flatter important personages. But even the seemingly most *disinterested* of all literary pursuits with no direct applications in the professional sphere could serve the most prosaic uses: for it generated prestige, a kind of currency that could be converted into material resources. This "interconvertibility" (to recall Pierre Bourdieu's important point discussed in chapter 1) insured that idle hobbies maintained a certain covert functionality. Michel de L'Hospital's Latin verse presents a clear example. His ostensibly disinterested hobby turned out to be a very sound investment in property and profession: it was instrumental not only in enlarging his patrimony (through a marriage alliance), but also in securing the highest office.[89] In short, he very adeptly "converted" his symbolic resources (*otium litteratum*) into material ones (*negotium*, wealth). Perversely, literary idleness could be made all the more useful by repressing any visible traces of its *utilitas*.

One final example, taken from a student of the *Essais* who obviously made a careful study of Montaigne's rhetoric of idleness, will complete the picture. In 1606, Florentin de Thierriat relies on Montaigne's "De l'oisiveté" in his spirited defense of a gentleman's right to idleness. In his *Trois Traictez,* a treatise on nobility, he first states:

> Je sçay bien que l'oysiveté comme les terres fertiles qu'on laisse à repos, nous produit des choses nuisibles, & nous apporte, plus de travail que ne fait l'exercice, car l'ame qui n'a point de but, se pert parmi le vague champ des imaginations . . .[90]

> [I am very aware of the fact that idleness, like fallow fields which one does not cultivate, produces pernicious things for us, and brings us more travail than does occupation, for the mind without some definite objective becomes lost in the vague field of imagination.]

Thierriat quotes "De l'oisiveté" almost *verbatim*: from the *terres oysives . . . grasses et fertilles* and the *âme qui n'a point de but* to the *vague champ des imaginations*. Given the moral dangers of idleness, he asks, is it not better to have a trade than to be idle?: "Mais quoy? vaut il pas mieux que le Gentil-homme s'applique à un mestier que d'estre oysif toute sa vie?" He categorically rejects this proposition, maintaining that a gentleman needs idleness as part of the self-reflective, philosophical attitude toward life embodied by the ancients:

> Je respons qu'Aristote n'a point dit sans cause que l'oysiveté est necessaire pour l'entretien de la Vertu. Et Platon respondant à aucuns qui blasmoyent la vie des Philosophes, de ce qu'elle estoit trop reposée, & trop oysive, disoit que telle oysiveté estoit plus serieuse que toute autre occupation. La Noblesse de toutes les Nations defendoit l'exercice des mestiers à ceux de son ordre, parce que les Grands ont estimé que le moyen de rendre une personne vertueuse estoit de luy donner beaucoup de loysir de Philosopher, songer à soy-mesme, & remplir de pensements graves la partie raisonnable de nostre ame. . . .[91]

> [I reply that Aristotle did not say without good reason that idleness is necessary for the cultivation of Virtue. And Plato, replying to some people who were accusing the life of philosophers of being too restful and idle, said that this idleness was more serious than any other occupation. The Nobility of all nations prohibited the exercise of trades for members of its order, because the Great believed that the way to make someone virtuous was to give this person a lot of leisure to Philosophize, to ponder oneself, and to fill the reasonable part of our mind with serious thoughts.]

Mustering the authority of Plato and Aristotle, Thierriat defends idleness in the name of Classical leisure.

But the philosophical immediately becomes social. Thierriat concludes his elegy of *oisiveté* with a defense of aristocratic *otium* as idleness becomes a class privilege: nobles of all nations are "given" leisure ("luy *donner* beaucoup de loysir . . ."). Thierriat then goes on to oppose philosophy, idleness, and warfare—all proper occupations for a social elite—to degrading mechanical arts. "Entre nous vivre Ignoblement & Roturierement, c'est vivre artistement & mecaniquement: c'est taisiblement renoncer aux privileges de noblesse." [Among us, to live commonly and crudely is to implicitly renounce the privileges of nobility].

Refusing to reduce perfect idleness to the prosaic realm of useful arts, he defends idleness as an aristocratic prerogative, thereby enacting a return to the definition of idleness as an aristocratic license. Thierriat's defense of a gentleman's right to idleness reflects both a nostalgia for the aristocracy of days-gone-by and a defensive position with regard to the modern age, the beginning of the reign of *homo œconomicus*. It thus puts into sharp relief the dual vocation of idleness as both an ethical category (a refuge from the *utile*) and a social ideal (the emblem of a vanishing nobility).

The Fourth Estate's project to redeem leisure had at its heart a profound duplicity. It aspired to being the only leisure class able to practice idleness without being idle, to disdain uselessness without placing *utilitas* above *honestum*, to achieve perfect idleness through hard work without degrading leisure by work. Leisure was not a birthright, yet they were the only elite blessed with this elusive savoir faire. The Fourth Estate's art of idleness replied to what the ancients defined as humanity's highest calling, giving them privileged access to the ethical ideal underlying Classical leisure. Ethically superior to nobiliary *oisiveté*, the art of idleness in the Fourth Estate nevertheless served the same honorific function. What better ornament to adorn the useful lives of useful men than idleness that defied usefulness? All the more since the most disinterested forms of idleness could paradoxically yield the best returns.

3

Portrait of an Early Modern *Oiseuse*: *Les Angoysses douloureuses*

Idleness passed from religious ideals and institutions (monastic *otium*), to first one secular elite (the feudal aristocracy), and later another (a new class of officeholding "gentlemen"). It followed broader societal changes, lending an air of nonchalance to the elites currently holding power. But as this *translatio otii* played out, what role did it leave Renaissance women, the wives and daughters of the "leisured gentlemen" studied in chapter 2? Excluded from the realm of public acts, were Renaissance women also excluded from private—and public—idleness?

This chapter studies the ideological forces restricting women's access to what Madeleine Des Roches terms "ceste loüable paresse."[1] To be sure, triviality, uselessness, and frivolity—all central to shaping Renaissance meanings of idleness—were closely related to the construction of "the feminine" during the Renaissance. Yet the social order prevented the dubious honor of displaying these qualities from benefiting women. An idle woman was a form of currency in a male economy of honor; she mediated between male rivals but did not participate on her own behalf. On this respect, the role given to Oiseuse in *Le Roman de la Rose* proves instructive. For Lady Idleness serves essentially as an emblem, not of women or even of idle women, but rather of the ruling male elites who employ her delicate idleness to their own ends.

Hélisenne de Crenne stages this dynamic, and reflects on it, in her *Angoysses douloureuses qui procedent d'amours* (1538) and *Epistres familières et invectives* (1539).[2] Her heroine, Hélisenne,[3] breaks all of the rules for uxorial conduct by her conspicuous idleness. A brief survey of conduct books pretending to dictate women's behavior at work and leisure will reveal the heroine of *Les Angoysses douloureuses* to be precisely the sort of "idle woman" denounced by moralists. Far from being a paragon of humble industriousness, Hélisenne resides in a universe governed by idleness, love, elegant clothing, games, and beauty—a universe that would resemble *le jardin de déduit* were it not for the tragic coloration given to her story. Shifting the focus from representation to discursivity, the second part of this chapter argues that Crenne attributed a new mode of *otium litteratum* to her fictional persona Hélisenne, a learned woman and masterful writer. This *otium* offered an important third term to the *occupation/oiseuse* alternative that ultimately constituted an impasse for early modern women writers. In so doing, she forged a new discursive mode that made public the most private state and intimate truths, a properly secular paradigm of confessional speech that has since been baptized "sentimental discourse."

The Feminine Condition

From Juan Luis Vives's influential *De institutio fœminae christianae* to the plethora of conduct books composed by Symphorien Champier, Jean Bouchet, and others emerges what appears to have been an unchallenged injunction: women must not be idle. These figures elaborated a system of moral values governing domestic life, not for princesses and ladies of the court, but for the wives and daughters of successful bourgeois. Along with Louise Labé, Madeleine and Catherine des Roches, and indeed many women writers of the period, Hélisenne de Crenne belonged to this milieu. Since she will be my focus below, the following discussion highlights how conduct books intended for such women treat the question of idleness. Crenne proves to be acutely aware of the feminine ideal these treatises championed, for she presents her heroine as the exact inverse.

In *Les Triumphes de la noble et amoureuse dame* (1530), Jean Bouchet prescribes spinning, embroidery, and "other work belonging to women's station" as a necessary part of avoiding idleness. He defines this *negotium* as one of the conditions "que doit avoir une pucelle":

> La troisiesme condition est que une fille ne doit estre oyseuse mais tousjours filler, tistre, broder, couldre ou faire autres ouvrages appartenans à leur estat ès jours ouvrables. . . .[4]

[The third condition for a girl is that she must not be idle on workdays, but rather always spin, weave, embroider, sew, or do other work belonging to their station. . . .]

Bouchet's phrase proves revealing of the status of women's work. He does not present it as an activity good in and of itself, or even as a vocation, but rather as a *condition* ("la troisième condition"). He thus posits women's relationship to idleness as the exact inverse of the nobility's *condition oisive*: a woman's being must equal a perpetual doing, and this doing is, itself, an exercise in humility.[5]

Following in Xenophon's footsteps, Bouchet and other moralists elevate the figure of the housewife to the status of a feminine ideal. Although spinning emerges as the quintessential form of women's work, other housewifely arts such as cooking are also lauded. To better instill a sense of the value of housework, some treatises even recommend that young girls be given miniature household utensils as toys.[6] Conduct books give a strong moral value to women's work, often invoking biblical injunctions to this effect such as "if any will not work, let him not eat" (2 Thess. 3:10) and "in the sweat of your face you will eat bread" (Gen. 3:19).[7]

The moral value attributed to housework belonged to a broader trend, which critics have described as the birth of a veritable "morality" of the domestic sphere and its roles.[8] Yet when it comes to women's work and leisure, this prototype was in fact grafted onto a much older one. In defining a new feminine exemplar, moralists drew from the ideals long associated with the contemplative life. The novelty thus lies perhaps less in the ideals themselves than in their transposition onto a different sphere (the home) and social category (women). The Renaissance ideal of the good housewife as contemplative represents no doubt one of the more surprising chapters in the history of leisure's secularization. Nevertheless, a semantic field of contemplation permeates conduct books dictating the rules for women's conduct at work and at leisure.

The underlying opposition is a familiar one, with the moral dissolution of idleness on one extreme and humble labor on the other. This strict moral polarization (spinning is good and idleness is bad) recalls the *Pèlerinage de vie humaine*. Guillaume de Deguilleville figures the moral dichotomy of occupation and idleness with the motif of the crossroads. On the left path, the pilgrim encounters the seductive Lady Idleness, who seeks to lure unwary souls into the arms of the Seven Deadly Sins. The narrator notes that she clearly exhibits her disdain for spinning.[9] On the right path he finds Occupation, who embraces the humility of manual labor, ceaselessly weaving mats, only to undo and redo the same mats over and over. As Occupation then explains, his primary goal in this futile enterprise is repudiating idleness: ". . . je depiece et je refas, / A fin que je ne soie pas / Huiseus . . ." [I take apart and redo (my mats), / so that I might avoid / idleness].[10]

Conduct books similarly place women at a crossroads with Occupation on the right path and Idleness beckoning from the treacherous left path. Significantly, in the *Pèlerinage*, Occupation functions as a metonymy for the monastic life, the object of the narrator's "pilgrimage." Just as the contemplative performed manual work in the name of moral—rather than economic—profit within the monastery, so women were summoned to embrace a life of manual labor (housework) within the "cloister" of the domestic sphere. It is thus not surprising that moralists should promote a reclusive existence along with manual labor, as though to invite women to embrace a quasi-monastic existence. As much as possible, writes Bouchet, a young woman should strive to be a recluse in her house:

> La quatriesme condition d'une pucelle est que elle doit estre solitaire, et se tenir le plus que elle pourra recluse en la maison à ce qu'elle puisse eviter mauvaises compaignies.[11]

> [The fourth condition for a girl is that she should be solitary and live as much as possible as a recluse in her house in order to avoid improper company.]

While Bouchet is here speaking about an unmarried woman, seclusion was generally understood to increase with marriage. Vives observes that married women should appear even less often in public since "they have what unmarried women seem to be looking for"—namely, a husband.[12] Bouchet's choice of the word "solitary" only reinforces the religious undertones of the passage. Petrarch, for instance, used "the solitary life" as a synonym for the contemplative life in *De vita solitaria*.

As for Sundays and holidays, Vives and Bouchet again concur. Women's leisure should be devoted to religious instruction, worship, and charitable work. On holidays, writes Bouchet, women must "frequenter l'église le service divin et les sermons, lire ou faire lire en quelque livre spirituel et moral, non ès livres lascivieux et provocans à sottes amours. . . ."[13] Vives similarly dictates that women read on Sundays, holidays, and other days "when they have finished their daily household chores."[14] Yet the kind of reading he recommends does not resemble the increasingly popular "hobby" of reading and composing literature, as practiced by the gentlemen of the Fourth Estate. Reading should have a manifest religious impetus for women. He carefully limits any reading to a short list composed of saints' lives, Boethius, the lives of church fathers, and compendia of moral precepts.[15]

How women should occupy their time is condensed into a simple rule of thumb that concludes Vives's discussion of idleness: women should divide their time between "sainctes cogitations" and "operations manuelles": *ora et labora*—long the backbone of the monastic existence.[16] In the guise of a moral code for the Renaissance woman, Vives offers a condensed and scaled-down version of the contemplative life: like domestic *religieuses*, women should lead an existence of manual labor and holy thoughts while residing in semi-reclusion.[17]

In an age witnessing the growing secularization of leisure, moralists projected the vanishing ideal of the contemplative life onto women's quotidian existence within the secular sphere. Men were increasingly using *otium* to pursue the eminently earthly goals of prestige, power, and professional advancement. But women were instructed to elevate their leisure to loftier heights, to use leisure as an occasion to know and celebrate God, without, of course, attempting any of the subtleties reserved for theologians. Ruth Kelso observes that during the Renaissance, ideals for women remained Christian in contrast to the more secular orientation of masculine ideals.[18] Moralists' attitudes toward women's work and leisure seem to confirm this point: in the convent or the home, bourgeois women were instructed to lead a life of obedience, humility, manual labor, chastity, piety, and semi-reclusion.

Eros and Idleness

Moralists drew from religious ideals in defining the code of social behavior for women; but they also turned to a strictly secular source. Ovidian love psychology was the perfect complement to the lessons taught by moralists; it added an aura of inevitability to the moralists' agenda while furnishing a scenario for how idle women end up as fallen women.

In the *Remedia Amoris*, Ovid writes that if you avoid idleness, Cupid's arrows cannot harm you.[19] This rather poetic motif was given the weight of a medical fact during the Renaissance. Physicians and moralists glossed Cupid's preference for idlers by noting that idleness could trigger erotic melancholy. They attributed to idleness what we today would call *aphrodisiac* properties, perceived during the Renaissance to imperil both physical health and moral virtue.

In *L'Antidote d'amour*, Jean Aubery delineates the "particular dispositions" that make one susceptible to passion and thus to love-sickness. Chief among these are idleness, youth, luxury, and springtime.[20] When all of these factors are present, passion is inevitable. Why are artisans and laborers exempt from erotic melancholy, even during springtime and even if they are young? Because, the author concludes, they know neither luxury nor idleness.[21] Citing ample authorities, the physician prescribes the avoidance of idleness as the best prevention available: "qu'il bannisse du tout l'oysiveté, comme l'unique & principale nourrice de ses folles cupiditez. . . ."[22]

Reappropriated by medical discourse, Ovid's rule for causing (and curing) love also permeated conduct books and literary texts. Paraphrasing the *Remedia* (vv. 135–40), Vives writes:

> Pour ce il [Ovid] escript pour remede d'amours estre preciput, que la sajette de cupidité ne nous surprenne oyseux, car se tu oste oysiveté, l'art de cupidité demeure perie & extaincte.[23]

> [Ovid thus writes that the primary remedy for love is not allowing Cupid's arrow to surprise us idle, for if you eliminate idleness, then Cupid's amorous art remains dead and extinguished.]

Montaigne refers in passing to this medical condition, observing that in the young (and thus susceptible), idleness induces passion.[24]

If idleness causes passion, then labor is its antidote or "remedy" to quote the title of Ovid's poem. In fact, it is one of the few contributing factors over which one has any control since there is little one can do against other triggers such as youth and springtime. When in the *Tiers Livre* Panurge consults Rondibilis on his marital dilemma, the physician immediately prescribes "labeur assidu" as one of the five remedies for pathological desire. The ensuing discussion opens with physiological explanation: assiduous labor curbs libidinal desire, for it acts directly on the blood flow, begins the physician. But this technical presentation soon becomes indistinguishable from a recitation of moral axioms: "idleness is the mother of lust." This movement suggests an affinity between the physical, bodily world and the moral world. The passage concludes with an absurdly literal gloss on Ovid's topos in a gesture of Rabelaisian verve: Cupid, it would appear, strikes idlers more often simply because their preference for stasis over movement makes them easy prey compared to more elusive moving targets.[25]

Nothing, in short, is more foreign to eroticism than hard labor. Renaissance medical theory here concurs with twentieth-century sexology: the Kinsey report revealed that in the nonworking underworld, sexual activity was five times higher than in the disciplined and productive workforce.[26]

The medico-moral gloss of the Ovidian topos had profound consequences for women. A simple causal chain made idleness the cause of a woman's dishonor: *oisiveté* causes passion, which seeks "carnal union," which, in turn, leads to a woman's dishonor (her loss of chastity). Given this cause-effect relationship, the moral imperative that women "avoid idleness" becomes manifest. Hence the conduct books' insistence on perpetual busyness: chastity itself depended upon it.

If women's "moral guides" exhorted them to avoid idleness, their would-be lovers had a vested interest in promoting it. It is thus hardly surprising that one of the period's greatest seducers should elaborate a poetic discourse around his mistress's idleness. A rapid survey of Ronsard's love lyric reveals that his mistresses are prone to idleness, indolence, even laziness. In fantasies, he represents the object of his desire on the very threshold between wakefulness and sleep, as in sonnet XX in the first book of *Les Amours*. Appropriating the myth of Danaé, he imagines himself descending in golden rain onto his mistress's breast just as sleep is creeping into her eyes: "Lors qu'en ses yeulx le somme va glissant."[27]

"Mignongne, levés-vous, vous estes paresseuse,"[28] he writes to one young woman playfully accused of sleeping in too late. Sonnet XXIII of the *Continuation des Amours* concludes with the poet adopting a stance of mock severity, threatening to "punish" this lovely young *oisive* for her sloth:

> Ian, je vous punirai du peché de paresse,
> Je vois baiser cent fois vostre œil, vostre tetin,
> Afin de vous aprendre à vous lever matin.²⁹

> [I surely will punish you for the sin of sloth,
> I am going to kiss your eye and your breast one hundred times,
> In order to teach you to get up early.]

The cultural intertext for this scene was the Feast of the Innocents ("La fête des Innocents"). On December 28 it was customary for "lazy" women to be given a spanking if they were caught oversleeping. To administer such a spanking was termed "to innocent" (*innocenter*). But, as Ronsard suggests, the sin of sloth offered a convenient pretext for men to visit women still in bed and take advantage of the full erotic potential under the pretext of administering a ritual spanking.³⁰ The eroticism latent in idleness provided a backdrop for the scenario, playfully confirming the axiom that an idle woman was by definition lascivious. The ritual also offered an occasion to dramatically violate the interdiction against idleness, followed by a *carnavalesque* punishment, thereby making a temporary farce out of the laws prohibiting women from practicing idleness.

LES ANGOYSSES DOULOUREUSES: A CASE STUDY OF EROTIC MELANCHOLY

The *eros/oisiveté* equation provides Hélisenne de Crenne with a moral justification for publishing her novel. The original title specifies that the narrative "exhorte toutes personnes à ne suyvre folle Amour." Casting herself as Cupid's victim, she implores women to avoid idleness:

> O tres cheres dames, quand je considere qu'en voyant comme j'ay esté surprinse, vous pourrez eviter les dangereulx laqs d'amours, en y resistant du commencement, sans continuer en amoureuses pensées. Je vous prie de vouloir eviter ociosité, et vous occupez à quelques honnestes exercices. (*AD* I, 97)

> [O dear ladies, when I consider that in seeing how I was caught, you will be able to avoid the dangerous snares of love, by resisting love from the outset, without persisting in amorous thoughts. I beg you to try to

avoid idleness, and to occupy yourselves with some honorable activity.]³¹

Is it because Hélisenne did not busy herself with "honnestes exercices" that she was imprisoned in the "snares of love"? This is the premise underlying her status as a negative example. Presenting her story as an edifying warning to women provides a sanction for the rather daring first person narrative of a woman's illicit passion. It also represents a significant departure from both Boccaccio's *Fiammetta* and Jacopo Caviceo's *Peregrino*, Crenne's primary literary sources. In these texts, idleness may be invoked (Boccaccio refers in passing to a religious holiday),³² but it shapes neither the unfolding drama nor the depiction of Genevre or Fiammetta. In contrast, Crenne makes idleness into a coherent subtext with direct bearing on her heroine's plight.

While the narrative action hinges on the story of Hélisenne's tragedy, medical discourse permeates many of the descriptions of her mental and physical suffering. A number of passages in the first part read like a veritable medical case study of the cause and symptoms of erotic melancholy.

Soon after the fatal exchange of gazes between Hélisenne and her beloved, Guenelic, she diagnoses her condition as *melencolie* (*AD* I, 106). The authors of medical treatises observe that those who suffer from this condition "continually represent the image of their beloved."³³ Hélisenne thus notes: "La semblance, effigie ou similitude du jeune jouvenceau, estoit paincte et descripte en ma pensée" (*AD* I, 105) [The image, effigy or semblance of the young man was painted and limned in my mind] (11). Specialists of lovesickness further contend that lovers' sighs derive directly from this condition: because the mind is so preoccupied contemplating the image of the beloved, they explain, it forgets to breathe regularly, resulting in irregular bursts of breath in which nature catches up for this forgetfulness.³⁴ When her husband points to her lover, visible through the window, Hélisenne is indeed forced to draw back in order to conceal a profusion of sighs brought on by the sight of her lover: "fuz contraincte me retirer pour l'affluence des souspirs, dont j'estoye agitée . . ." (*AD* I, 107) [I was forced to withdraw because of the rush of sighs that agitated me] (13).

The first description of Hélisenne's condition (*AD* I, 107) includes a cascade of the symptoms of erotic melancholy found in medical treatises. She manifests nearly all of the signs that a trained physician would use to diagnose erotic melancholy:

L'Antidote d'amour	*Les Angoysses douloureuses*
(symptoms of erotic melancholy: p. 30r)	(Hélisenne's symptoms: p. 107)
"l'amaigrissement du corps"	"je perdis l'appetit de manger"
"la couleur pâle"	"devins palle"
"les souspirs"	"affluence des souspirs"
"veilles"	"de dormir m'estoit impossible"
"le refroidissement des parties externes"	"[devins] froide"
"l'embrassement des internes"	"puis apres une chaleur vehemente, licencia de moy la palle couleur, et devins chaulde, et vermeille"
"les pensees"	"[l]ong seroit à racompter et difficile, les pensemens que j'avoye"
"le silence"	"quand je voulois prononcer quelque propos, par manieres de plainctes et exclamations, l'extreme destresse de ma douleur interrompoit ma voix"
"la solitude"	"fuz contraincte me retirer"

Only three symptoms mentioned in *L'Antidote d'amour* are absent ("les pleurs," "les songes," and "l'extase"), all of which occur elsewhere in the narration. In this scene and, indeed, throughout the first part of *Les Angoysses*, Crenne meticulously catalogs the symptoms of a serious case of lovesickness.[35] Medical discourse clearly made for a compelling model, even within the context of a poetic and tragic language like the one used by Crenne in *Les Angoysses douloureuses I*.

The force of medical discourse in shaping constructions of women's idleness also suggests the difficulty of contesting an ideology cloaked in scientific fact. Any challenge to the axiom that "women must not be idle" would have directly countered medical discourse (Ovidian love psychology), moral imperatives (idleness jeopardizes chastity), and the code of women's honor (virtuous women are by definition industrious). A synthesis of such authoritative discourses may help us understand why women writers rarely openly challenge their exclusion from *otium*, why, without exception, they state their determination to avoid idleness while their male counterparts may adopt a more ambiguous stance. Should we, then, conclude that the honorific idleness used to such good effect by male writers such as Michel de Montaigne was simply inconceivable for women writers? Given the recognized importance of idleness for literary practice, this question assumes even higher stakes.[36] A common complaint of humanists, reiterated in their correspondence, is insufficient leisure. How much more difficult it must have been for women to practice *otium*, given that idleness was deemed perilous for the "feminine condition."[37]

Hélisenne's Idle Pursuits

There remained one widely recognized and practiced mode of honorific idleness available to women: the beautiful attire and careful grooming personified by Oiseuse. Although the role of Lady Idleness in redefining the aristocracy as "a leisure class" has been discussed above, it may be useful to briefly recall her salient traits. In *Le Roman de la Rose*, Oiseuse proclaims pleasure and aesthetic perfection to be her sole concerns: her *toilette* testifies to a life of leisure, offering tangible evidence of a delicate withdrawal from all forms of useful employment. Her mirror and gloves become the emblems of this new ideal. Both accessories signify an aristocratic rejection of "servile" functionality, for the mirror suggests (self-)contemplation while gloves insure that the hands serve primarily an ornamental function. To what extent does this model apply to Hélisenne's idleness in *Les Angoysses douloureuses*?

Hélisenne fell in love during a period of indolence, as was noted above. In the narration of her story, she carefully provides a description of the day before the *innamoramento* scene. "Ce jour se passa en toutes recreations, et voluptueulx plaisirs," she notes (*AD* I, 102) [The day was spent in all sorts of amusements and delightful pleasures] (19). She later uses the same two terms to describe the atmosphere: "passasmes le temps en recreation et voluptueulx plaisirs" (*AD* I, 124). In the *Epistres invectives*, this combination is revealed to be a pernicious one: "il est facile à congnoistre que ociosité accompaignée de voluptez, font . . . naistre les vices . . ." (*EI* V, 158) [it is easy to realize that idleness accompanied by voluptuousness is responsible for creating . . . vices].[38] Hélisenne seems to invite the reader to apply this formula to the *Angoysses doulour-*

euses as well: indeed, was it not the heroine's idleness, accompanied by voluptuous pleasures, that engendered vice? Why else would Crenne carefully draw the reader's attention to the way Hélisenne spent her time doing exactly what conduct books state women should *not* do?

This leisurely atmosphere continues in the early stages of her passion—a time when occupation is crucial according to medical treatises. Pretending to be distressed by Hélisenne's "soubdaine melencolie," her husband only promises her more idleness:

> ... je vous prometz avoir tel soing, que n'aurez cause de vous irriter, et ne vous soulciez de riens que de faire bonne chere, et prendre recreation. (*AD* I, 107)

> [I promise you I shall take such care that you shall never have cause for concern; don't worry about anything other than eating well and enjoying yourself.][39]

This gesture was equivalent to throwing oil onto an already raging fire. Work was the only "remedy" for love. Had Hélisenne followed the lessons of moralists and physicians, she would instead have taken refuge in hard work, busying herself about the house, for instance. Or perhaps she would have embraced good works, doing charity to take her mind off the stirrings of the flesh. For during the early stages of love, it is imperative to avoid idleness, as Hélisenne explains in her dedicatory epistle.[40]

Beyond providing the catalyst for Hélisenne's passion, idleness informs her characterization. The narrator further notes her complete withdrawal from all household affairs, even before she fell in love. Although it was on account of business that Hélisenne and her husband moved to the town where the drama was to take place, Hélisenne professed to take no interest in this "important matter"—a lawsuit concerning their property:

> Doncques parvenue au logis, incontinent me vins appuyer sur une fenestre, et regardois, en tenant propos joyeulx à mon mary, sans me soulcier de la chose qui nous avoit contrainct de venir, ce qui estoit de grande importance. (*AD* I, 102)

> [Thus once we had arrived at our lodgings, I immediately went to lean on the windowsill and look out, chatting lightheartedly with my hus-

band without worrying about the matter which had caused us to come there, and which was of great importance.]⁴¹

Adopting an indolent posture, she leans nonchalantly against a windowsill. She further engages in idle chatter *(tenant propos joyeulx)*. Here again, this description was inspired by none of Crenne's literary sources and appears to serve no purpose beyond establishing Hélisenne's frivolity.

In another passage, she indulges in that most canonic form of idle speech: gossip. Laughing with her attendants, she ridicules an ugly woman, who is described in detail.⁴² In a narrative recounting a woman's mental and physical anguish in a tragic *crescendo* of violence and suffering, this episode stands out. The depiction of the lovestruck heroine laughing with her attendants at an old woman's ugliness seems markedly out of place. If Crenne nevertheless included it, despite its incongruity, was it not because it further established the frivolity of her character? Conduct books criticize women for precisely this sort of idle gossip.⁴³

Hélisenne thus manifests all the telltale signs of chronic idleness: she adopts indolent postures, engages in idle chatter, gossips, and has no concern for household affairs. Work appears to be foreign to her very being, for she is never described performing any task even remotely related to spinning or managing the household which, the conduct books reiterate, should be a woman's condition. Although the narrator does not portray her wearing lovely white gloves, one of Oiseuse's emblems, she certainly could have done so, given that she apparently never engages in wholesome manual labor.

As it was for Lady Idleness, personal grooming appears to be Hélisenne's sole endeavor. "J'estois fort curieuse en habillemens, c'estoit la chose ou je prenoye singulier plaisir," she declares (*AD* I, 124). Here again, Crenne has inverted the ideal put forth by conduct books, which commonly dictate simplicity of dress.⁴⁴ On several occasions, Hélisenne's preoccupation with finery and the ritual of getting dressed comes into play. She notes that it was while she was dressing that she first glimpsed Guenelic: ". . . en m'habillant vins ouvrir la fenestre, et en regardant à l'aultre part de la rue, je veis ung jeune homme, aussi regardant à sa fenestre . . ." (*AD* I, 102) [getting dressed, (I) went to open the window. Looking across the street, I saw a young man also looking out his window] (10). Later, she is depicted donning "riches et triumphantz habillementz" (*AD* I, 159). Another passage describes the care she took adorning herself with "belles brodures, et riches pierres precieuses" (*AD* I, 123). Like Oiseuse, she associates herself with the mirror: "je me retiray ung petit, affin de prendre conseil à mon miroir, de mon accoustrement, grace, et contenance" (*AD* I, 111) [I withdrew a bit so as to consult my mirror concerning my dress, appearance, and countenance] (15). She describes herself strutting and preening in front of a mirror "like a peacock in its beautiful feathers" (*AD* I, 123). In this last instance, after finishing her intricate *toilette* and leaving the house, she adopts a *leisurely* gait. As she strolls down the street, everyone gazes upon her, confirming the function of leisure as a spectacle for public consumption:

> . . . sortasmes de la chambre, en la compaignée de mes damoyselles, je cheminoie lentement, tenant gravité honneste, tout le monde jectoit son regard sur moy . . . (*AD* I, 123)

> [And so we went out of the room in the company of my attendants I walked along slowly, maintaining a respectable gravity. Everyone looked at me . . .][45]

The lingering gait and dignity that characterize Hélisenne's carriage recalls Castiglione's portrait of the *donna di palazzo*, a reminder that the body's movement was as permeated by social codification as was the clothing that covered it.[46] Even the smallest gestural unit could fall under the empire of social value.

To appreciate Crenne's portrayal of her character as an early modern *oiseuse*, one has only to compare Hélisenne to Floride, the heroine of another sentimental romance, *Les Avantures de Floride* (1592). Béroalde de Verville prefaces the narrative with a brief treatise on conduct in the form of a dedicatory epistle. He here assimilates women's idleness to "the cause of all their woes."[47] As though to illustrate this moral truth in the novel itself, he carefully describes his chaste heroine's industriousness, which she apparently shares with most virtuous women:

> Ceste belle Demoiselle vivant comme la plus part des Dames honnestes, ne demeuroit paresseusement sommeillante en l'oisiveté.

> [This beautiful young lady, living like most virtuous women, did not spend her time lazily dozing in idleness.][48]

Among the many talents that signal her arrival "au but de la perfection" (1v) are music, erudite conversation, and an enchanting skill at embroidery:

> si elle traçoit un bel ouvrage, elle addressoit si dignement son aiguille, repassant sur les ombres selon l'ordonnance de la pourtraicture, que l'on craignoit de s'y arrester trop long temps, de peur d'entrer en telle admiration que l'entendement s'en alterast. . . .
>
> [if she embroidered some beautiful work, she used her needle so deftly, going over the shaded-in parts according to the design of the pattern, that one was afraid to linger too long, for fear that admiration would unsettle one's mind. . . .][49]

Never idle and skilled at embroidery, Floride emerges as a paragon of the Renaissance's "new woman." Hélisenne in contrast seems to indulge only in the most frivolous pursuits: idle chatter, indolence, personal adornment, and self-display.

Beyond Exemplarity

Crenne's depiction of Hélisenne as an early modern *oisive* fulfills her promise to provide a negative example. Her antiheroine does precisely and systematically what conduct books state women should not do. Is Hélisenne not the very personification of "feminine vanity"? Disappointment no doubt awaits readers today approaching *Les Angoysses douloureuses I* in search of open contestation of the ominous predictions made by moralists and promoted by Renaissance proverbs such as this one:

> Fille oisive,
> a mal pensive
> Fille trop en rue,
> tost perdue.

[An idle girl / has evil thoughts / A girl too often in the streets / is soon lost (loses her chastity).][50]

Yet depicting a paragon of chastity, industry, and modesty (Béroalde's Floride, for instance) would hardly have done greater service to "la cause des femmes." Both alternatives only reinforce the dominant ideology.

Crenne's literary project to fashion a woman's (fictional) biography placed her squarely before the tradition of literature as a source of *exempla*. To be sure, this provided a convenient narrative frame, almost an inevitable one for prose narrative in the 1530s.[51] Yet it also tended to give women writers the rather unsatisfying choice of writing the life of either a good or bad example, neither alternative presenting much of a challenge to the *doxa*. For the rhetoric of exemplarity seemed destined to reinforce the code of female behavior promoted by moralists with a vested interest in preserving the status quo. In short, this false debate was inscribed within the tradition of biographical prose narrative of Hélisenne's time, given the quasi-inevitability of the *exemplar*, whose "virtue" or "vice" obeyed preestablished criteria. It also suggests the difficulty of writing outside existing gender biases and outside the ideological framework reflected in conduct books.

If this problem derived from the narrative form of *Les Angoysses douloureuses*, Crenne turned to the epistolary genre for a solution. In her collection of letters first published in 1539 (one year after the *Angoysses douloureuses* appeared), she presents political and social critique. She also comments indirectly on the novel, using the epistolary form as a narrative and ideological mode outside of the conventions of the romanesque. She can thus return to many of the same problems at stake in the three parts of her novel, including dissimulation (*EF* VIII, *EF* IX), passion (*EF* V, *EF* VIII, *EF* IX, *EF* X), friendship (*EF* XII), and slander (*EF* III) along with the institution of matrimony and a husband's abuse of power (*EI* I, *EI* III). She never really refers explicitly to her novel in the *Epistres*; however, many parallels are so close that the reader inevitably makes connections.[52]

The theoretical discussions in the *Epistres* thus offer an occasion to circle back and reflect on elements of her novel, but from the vantage point of the epistle, a genre Crenne clearly found to be better suited to analysis. This solution to narrative constraints recalls the *Heptaméron*, where individual novellas are followed by a nuanced discussion among the group of *devisants*. Marguerite de Navarre was clearly not content to allow her often exemplary tales to "speak for themselves" either, for she charged her storytellers with the task of bringing ideological positions into the open and then submitting them to careful scrutiny and debate. Crenne's crisscrossing of novel and epistle fulfills much the same function: it allows her storyteller (Hélisenne) to provide nuanced discussion of problems also at stake in the *Angoysses douloureuses*.

The *Epistres* can thus offer explicit political commentary often frustratingly absent from *Les Angoysses douloureuses*. They comment on the ideological framework underlying what is depicted in the novel as Hélisenne's weaknesses or shortcomings. Her treatment of dissimulation serves as a case in point. Hélisenne engages in apparently endless subterfuge in the *Angoysses douloureuses*. But in the *Epistres*, women's deceit is shown to be a sometimes necessary stratagem in the patriarchal social order.[53] She addresses a letter to Clarice, exhorting her to persist in dissimulating her love since she is completely subject to the will of her guardians:

> Je te exhorte de nyer en apparence, ce que plus affectueusement desireras, pour evader que tu succumbe en l'indignation de ceulx, lesquelz par juste raison de toy à leur arbitraige peuvent faire.... (*EF* VIII, 95)

> [I beg you to pretend to deny what you most desire so as to avoid arousing indignation in those who have control over you.][54]

This passage refers specifically to the legal context that made justice *(juste raison)* subject to the arbitration *(arbitraige)* of those in power to the exclusion of women like Clarice. As "eternal minors," women were indeed condemned to obedience before the authority of their legal guardian (father or husband), as Evelyne Berriot-Salvadore has shown.[55] If "justice" was thus stacked against them, what recourse did women have besides ruse? This reasoning invites the reader to reach a political interpretation of Hélisenne's continual dissimulation of her true intentions from her husband in *Les Angoysses douloureuses I*. After a certain point, she simply could not resist her passion. Unable to either cease loving Guenelic or openly contest her husband's will, Hélisenne turned to deceit as the only alternative.

Idle Women and the Male Leisure Class

The *Epistres familières et invectives* also return to the question of idleness. They offer lucid metacommentary on the feminine "frivolity" and "idleness" displayed by Hélisenne and denounced by conduct books. The third of her *Epistres invectives* offers a persuasive reevaluation of the true nature of the feminine idleness in her social world, laying bare the logic at stake in a number of key episodes of her novel. Although castigated by moralists, women's idleness was in fact a key pawn in the male social order, as Hélisenne argues.

She first observes that a carefully manicured woman dressed in sumptuous clothing—Oiseuse and her avatars—is involved in an enterprise of prestige. However, all symbolic profits from her "conspicuous leisure" are channeled back into a strictly male economy of honor. In reply to her husband who has attacked "la curiosité féminine"—the care women take in adorning themselves—she writes:

> & quant ad ce que tu dis de la curiosité femenine, en sumptueulx & riches accoustremens, Sainct Hierosme a redigé par escript, que les femmes & filles sont desireuses de precieulx vestemens, & scavoit plusieurs dames pudicques le faire, non pour complaire aux folz, ne par orgueil: mais par honnesteté ayant regard à l'estat & noblesse de leurs mariz, ou de leur pere. (*EI* III, 144–45)

> [As for what you say about women's willingness to experiment in rich and sumptuous clothes, Jerome has written that women and girls desire expensive clothes; and he knew several chaste women who did so, not in order to satisfy foolish men nor out of pride, but out of honest regard for the social rank and nobility of their husbands and fathers.][56]

Any symbolic capital generated by a woman's performance of idleness goes not to her (she remains "modest"—*pudique*), but rather to her husband or father, whose own social standing is confirmed or enhanced: "ayant regard à l'estat & noblesse de leurs mariz ou de leur pere."[57] She unmasks the bad faith involved when men, like her husband, denounce feminine frivolity: in fact, men had considerable interest in promoting the manifest idleness of their wives and daughters. For, to paraphrase Hélisenne's reasoning, an idle wife or daughter was a potential resource in a man's patrimony: a strategic display of the leisure and ornamentation of female subordinates could be used to good effect in an ongoing competition with male rivals.

Thorstein Veblen analyzes the exploitation of women's idleness by the male leisure class. In fact, Veblen's model for understanding this phenomenon is remarkably close to the argument Hélisenne makes in her third invective epistle. He notes that in a patriarchal social order, women's leisure is not their own. Rather, a spectacle of idleness is extracted from them by their husbands or fathers. Men, that is, make women their delegates in leisure. Women are not idle for their own sake but are instead used as instruments of "vicarious leisure" for men.[58] A man's conspicuous abstention from utilitarian activity can increase his own honor; how much greater the effect, then, if he also charges members of his household with being idle on his behalf. Delegating idleness to subordinates such as a servant or a wife has long been a strategy employed by leisured elites.

Veblen's primary point of reference was nineteenth-century bourgeois society, with its servants in livery and the ever-symbolic white gloves. But royal courts during the Renaissance followed a comparable logic of conspicuous leisure. A suite of idle courtiers fulfilled a crucial function: they reflected their monarch's majesty, proclaiming the royal prerogative to enlist other people to engage in nonutilitarian activity (playing games, gallantry, conversation . . . all of the activities popular at court). Renaissance aristocratic and even bourgeois households imitated the processes of opulent display employed at court, although on a more modest scale. Hélisenne is thus careful to appear in public sumptuously dressed. She is also accompanied by her attendants, who have no manifest task to perform besides contributing to the spectacle of idleness. For Hélisenne to do otherwise would be to undermine her husband's honor. Given the structure of the social order, men had a vested interest in flaunting the "triviality" of their female subordinates.

This context elucidates a rather curious episode in *Les Angoysses douloureuses* when Guenelic steps on Hélisenne's cloak. This seemingly insignificant event enrages Hélisenne's husband and becomes a central moment in the drama. Before examining the symbolic logic at play, it may be useful to recall the entire sequence, since Crenne elaborates a very precise chain of events.

The scene is first set as one of a number of "festes solenneles" that occur in the first part of *Les Angoysses douloureuses*. These holidays provide the town's bourgeoisie with an occasion for conspicuous idleness as the temple and surrounding streets become the theater for self-display and rivalry. Indeed, religious devotion seems to serve mostly as a pretext for this secular function of leisure as pursuit of status.

The day before one such holiday, Hélisenne's husband orders her to dress in her finest clothing for the occasion:

> Il est demain le jour d'une feste solennele, parquoy je veulx et vous commande que vous accoustrez triumphamment, affin que vous assistez au temple avec moy, car doresnavant ne vous sera permis de sortir de la maison, sinon en ma compaignie . . . (*AD* I, 122)

> [Tomorrow is the day of a solemn observance, and therefore I wish and command that you put on your most triumphal garments in order to go to the temple with me; from now on you will be allowed to go out of the house only in my company. . . .]⁵⁰

But when they are within the temple, Guenelic is "inopportune." In passing near Hélisenne, he steps on her white satin cloak: ". . . ne differa ses importunitez, car il venoit passer si pres de moy, qu'il marchoit sur ma cotte de satin blanc" (*AD* I, 124) [he did not cease his importunities, for he passed so near me that he stepped on my white satin cloak.] (22). In a fit of fury, her husband returns home, followed by Hélisenne. His anger derives from the "grande presumption" Guenelic exhibited in treading on her satin cloak (*AD* I, 124). After this episode, her husband orders Hélisenne to dress simply when they return to the temple the next day.

Interpreting this incident in light of its ideological subtext, we can better grasp how Guenelic's gesture is a "grande presumption." The husband initially delegates leisure to his wife by ordering her to appear in public bearing all the traces of her leisurely existence, confirming or perhaps enhancing his standing. When he orders her to appear in public in her finest clothing, he in effect stages her performance of *oisiveté* and prepares to reap the profits. Renaissance legal treatises testify to the highly codified language of prestige inherent in how one dressed. They delineate the sumptuary rights (or even obligations) of the gentry and aristocracy, translating specific materials or types of clothing into a corresponding social rank. Hélisenne's cloak is described as white (a color traditionally favored by leisured elites as testimony to an existence "unsoiled" by work; as we recall, Oiseuse's gloves are white). It is also made of satin—a material reserved for the upper echelons of society. Contemplating his wife's dressing ritual, he manifests considerable pleasure:

> quand je fuz accoustrée, je commencay à me pourmener, en me mirant en mes sumptueulx habillemens, comme le paon en ses belles plumes

> ... cependant mon mary se habilloit, lequel prenoit singulier plaisir en me voyant ... (*AD* I, 123)

> [When I was ready, I began to walk about, admiring myself in my sumptuous garments, like the peacock with his beautiful feathers. . . . Meanwhile, my husband had been getting dressed; when he saw me, he was very pleased. . . .][60]

We can assume that he would be equally pleased to note the admirers circling around his wife as she walks majestically through the streets.

The performance is clearly working in her husband's favor when Guenelic intervenes. When the latter steps on Hélisenne's cloak, her husband perceives the gesture as a public challenge from his rival. By stepping on her finery, the lover is in a sense publicly "treading" on the husband's proprietary claim to Hélisenne and her display of opulence and leisure. Guenelic's gesture amounts to a bourgeois equivalent of tagging, for he leaves a signature of kind (a footprint) on the property of another man.

In a patriarchal system of monogamy, a wife's lover poses a serious threat. He jeopardizes the husband's monopoly on his wife's capacity to generate symbolic capital as well as on her reproductive capacities. Guenelic's gesture has precisely this effect. Indeed, after this episode, Hélisenne's husband threatens to initiate a separation—to relinquish the material resources he gained through marriage—if she disobeys him again:

> et sy vous n'observez ce mien commendement, j'ay ferme propos et deliberation de me separer de vous: vous avez du bien de par vous, terres et seigneuries plus que je n'en ay, lequel je ne vous veulx retenir. Car je ne vouldroye aulcunement proffiter du bien d'une femme lascive. (*AD* I, 125)

> [If you do not observe this commandment of mine, I have the firm intention and design to separate myself from you. You have your own property, more lands and fiefdoms than I have, to which I shall not lay claim, for I should not want to profit from the wealth of a lascivious woman.][61]

So powerful is the symbolic realm that her husband would sooner sacrifice great wealth (Hélisenne has more property than he does) than continue to suffer the loss of honor incurred by Hélisenne's behavior. He is willing to renounce the material resources to which he is entitled as her legal husband if he cannot profit from her symbolic resources as well.

Realizing that advertising his wife's leisure is not increasing his own honor, Hélisenne's husband then forbids her to perform any further public spectacles: ". . . au lendemain . . . me vouluz lever et accoustrer d'habillementz riches et sumptueulx: ce que mon mary ne voulut permettre . . ." (*AD* I, 125) [the next day [. . .] I wanted to get up and dress myself in rich and sumptuous clothes, which my husband refused to permit] (22). The dense narrative sequence suggests that Hélisenne's husband is ultimately the proprietor of her *oisiveté*, for he alone can impose or prohibit it, always in function of what he perceives to be his own interest.

Women's Conquest of *Otium Litteratum*

Hélisenne de Crenne appears perfectly lucid when it comes to the function of women's ornamental idleness in the male social order. Louise Labé is also cognizant of the alienation of women's idleness. Both writers situate the problem of idleness in a properly political context, unlike the authors of conduct books who speak only in "moral" and "scientific" terms.

In her famous *Epître Dédicatoire*, Louise Labé criticized both terms in the leisure/work dichotomy reserved for women. At a time when moralists defined spinning as the essence of women's work, she exhorted women to "lift their minds above their distaffs and spindles."[62] Yet she also criticized the dominant ideology of women's leisure. In this new era, she writes, women can aspire to loftier ambitions for their leisure than self-adornment. The time has come for women to participate in culture, in the "sciences et disciplines" that have long been a male monopoly:

> Estant le tems venu, Madamoiselle, que les severes loix des hommes n'empeschent plus les femmes de s'apliquer aus sciences et disciplines: il me semble que celles qui ont la commodité, doivent employer cette honneste liberté que notre sexe ha autre fois tant desiree, à icelles aprendre: et montrer aus hommes le tort qu'ils nous faisoient en nous privant du bien et de l'honneur qui nous en pouvoit venir: Et si quelcune parvient en tel degré, que de pouvoir mettre ses concepcions par escrit, le faire songneusement et non dédaigner la gloire, et s'en parer plustot que de chaines, anneaus, et somptueus habits: lesquels ne pou-

vons vrayement estimer notres, que par usage. Mais l'honneur que la science nous procurera, sera entierement notre: et ne nous pourra estre oté, ne par finesse de larron, ne force d'ennemis, ne longueur du tems.[63]

[Now that the time has come, Mademoiselle, that the severe laws of men no longer prevent women from applying themselves to science and learning, it seems to me that those who are able, should make use of this honorable freedom that our sex has so desired by studying, and show men how wrong they were to deprive of us of the good and honor that could result from such study. And if a woman reaches the point of being able to record her conceptions, she should do so carefully without disdaining glory and adorn herself with this glory rather than with chains, rings, and sumptuous clothing; for these things can only be deemed ours according to custom. But the honor that learning will grant us will be entirely ours, and will be taken away neither by a thief's ruse, nor an enemy's force, nor the passing of time.]

Labé denounces the traditional modality of women's idleness because the honor it generates does not really belong to women: the "chains, rings, and sumptuous clothing" procure only the illusion of personal honor while in reality reinforcing male hegemony. Instead of serving as the delegates of male rivals, women should enter into the game on their own behalf. They should, that is, claim proprietary privileges on the symbolic capital they generate through conspicuous leisure. And the best means to this end is not Oiseuse's elaborate *toilette*. Rather, they should channel their leisure into activities that produce honor for themselves, thereby "adorning" themselves with their own glory instead of with the beautiful garments that procure honor for men: "l'honneur que la science nous procurera, sera entierement notre." Men have long deprived women of learned leisure and the honor it generates, Labé writes, but now women can aspire to the *otium* espoused by their male counterparts. Only in this way can women break the monopoly men hold on culture, including *otium litteratum*. The time has come for women to partake of idleness in their own name, to liberate themselves from their subservience to a male leisure class.

For women to reap the glory they deserve from their learned leisure, they must make public their *otium litteratum*. Louise Labé exhorts women to publish the fruits of their idleness, like she herself did. She concludes the *Epître* by inviting her addressee, Clemence de Bourges, to publish *(mettre en lumiere)* a book "mieus limé" and "de meilleure grace" (43) than her own. But this was a path fraught with obstacles and risks given reigning doctrine on uxorial conduct. Any "public act," including literary publication, was considered to be a transgression of feminine chastity. In the early modern period, for a woman to be seen or heard in public, even via the medium of print, was to expose herself to slanderers, always eager to assimilate a published woman to a "public woman," as a number of critics have observed.[64]

If the sole basis for a woman's honor lay in her chastity, and if a reputation of chastity itself could be jeopardized by "appearing in public," Hélisenne de Crenne's literary project was a risky one indeed. Her erudition alone was a gesture of audacity, not to mention her decision to publish the story of a woman's illicit passion written in the first person. Louise Labé, who also wrote passionately of erotic love in the first person, was labeled a "harlot" by some of her contemporaries.[65] Her fate testifies to the risk at stake for a woman to "expose" her writing in public. How then does Hélisenne relate public idleness to published writing, and what narrative mode does she adopt for her own *otium litteratum*?

Pour Éviter Ociosité

In the first of the *Epistres invectives*, addressed to her husband, Hélisenne appears to cite the axiom "women must avoid idleness," writing:

> . . . la precipiteuse charge de ton cueur, à telle ymagination t'a conduict, que tu as estimé cela (que pour eviter ociosité j'ay escript) eust esté par moy composé, pour faire perpetuelle commemoration d'une amour impudicque. Et d'advantaige tu crois que telle lascivité se soit en ma personne experimentée. (*EI* I, 125–26)

> [Your heart's hasty judgment has led you to imagine that my *Angoysses* (which I had composed, in fact, only to pass the time) were intended to immortalize an illicit love. You believe, moreover, that I really experienced the lasciviousness about which I wrote.][66]

Taking her discursive mode from forensic rhetoric, she here refutes her husband's charge that her prose *(cela)*[67] commemorates an amorous passion she herself experienced. The dispute hinges on the status of this writing. In his "accusation," her husband argued that her first person narrative was a confession, long held to be "the queen of proofs" in a trial.[68] Hélisenne contests this charge, arguing that what her husband defined as a confession was merely a literary exercise, a hobby she practiced during her leisure hours: "pour eviter ociosité j'ay escript."[69]

A number of critics have singled out this passage as a central argument in Crenne's defense of women's writing. Constance Jordan points out that while Hélisenne's literary stance is frequently confessional, in this crucial passage she claims that as a writer she is entitled to create fiction, including a fictional persona named "Hélisenne." Given the moralists' insistence that women should not partake of feigning and fictionalizing, this claim had important political implications: at a time when women were supposed to be transparent to their husbands, Crenne defended their right to fictionality.[70] Jerry Nash similarly sees in this passage a rejection of an "autobiographical pact": Hélisenne's fictional "I" *(ma dame Hélisenne)* does not equal the historic person who composed *Les Angoysses douloureuses* (Marguerite Briet writing under the name of Hélisenne de Crenne).[71] Kathryn Ann Jensen also interprets this passage as a defense of fictionality as opposed to autobiography. She argues that Crenne here attacks a commonplace that has long beleaguered women: namely, the assumption that when women write, they simply record their lives, as though women's writing were somehow destined to be autobiographical in the first degree.[72] In short, Hélisenne here claims the prerogative to create a fictional universe with no simple, mimetic relationship to her own life, warning her husband (and her reader) that her art does *not* imitate her life.

These critics make a point of unquestionable merit, allowing us to appreciate the full political impact of Hélisenne de Crenne's assertion that she wrote what we, today, would call "literature," not a diary. Yet this passage conceals a more complex rhetorical strategy than is at first apparent, for it closely reproduces a scene from *Les Angoysses douloureuses*. Reading her manifesto in the first invective epistle alongside its twin in *Les Angoysses douloureuses* will thus allow us to nuance the interpretation of the critics mentioned above.

A particularly dramatic moment in Hélisenne's story occurs when her husband kicks open her bedroom door to find her rereading the letters she and Guenelic exchanged. So sudden is his entry and so surprised is Hélisenne that she does not think to hide the letters ("je n'euz advis ne discretion de cacher les lettres," *AD* I, 134). Seizing the letters, which Hélisenne has spread out on her bed, the husband reads them and then strikes her in the face, a blow that sends her crashing to the ground. "Come here and look at this letter of yours," he then commands, "and tell me, without the clever lies you now know how to use, who is the person to whom you intend to send such writing?"[73] Hélisenne's reply is to assert that she wrote the letter as a hobby, a literary exercise "pour eviter ociosité"—the very same argument that she uses in the invective letter when her husband accuses her of writing a confession. This episode and the passage in the first invective letter are thus set up in mirror reflection of one another. In each case Hélisenne's husband has read her writing and taken it as evidence of her guilt; he gives each piece of writing the status of a confession. And to each accusation, Hélisenne replies with precisely the same phrase, stating that her writing is sheer fiction, an exercise "pour éviter ociosité."

However, in the scene from *Les Angoysses douloureuses*, she supplies interior monologue that reveals her self-defense to be a ruse:

> Quand il eust ce dict, commencay à mediter et penser, et disoye à moymesmes: Helas, je ne me scauroye excuser, car ma lettre de ma main escripte rend cler tesmoignage de ma vie, puis je disoye au contraire, si m'est il necessaire de le nyer: car à face hardie, une prouve ne nuyt. (*AD* I, 136)

> [Then I began to meditate and reflect, and I said to myself: "Alas! I can hardly excuse myself, for a letter in my own handwriting testifies very clearly to what I have been doing." Then I said to myself: "On the other hand, I have to deny it, for a proof can do nothing against a bold face."][74]

While noting mentally (and to the reader who is privy to her thoughts) that her writing gives a "clear testimony of her life," she tells her husband that it is sheer invention. Is the reader not entitled to suspect that the second instance, when she addresses these same words to her husband in her invective letter, is an "artificiel mensonge" as well? In other words, when her husband claims that her writing is a "confession" in her *Epistres invectives*, and when she replies that she wrote "only to avoid idleness," should we not interpret this as a ruse as well? The perfect parallel between these two scenes invites interpreting the epistle in light of the interior monologue from *Les Angoysses douloureuses*: "car ma lettre de ma main escripte rend cler tesmoignage de ma vie . . . si m'est il necessaire de le nyer." All signs point to an implicit wink to the reader, summoned to see in Hélisenne's reply a defensive artifice, a false denial. This parallel has the effect of establishing a secret complicity between Hélisenne and her reader, a connivance that makes the reader privy to a confession from which her husband is, himself, excluded.

Pursuing the implications of this interpretation reveals a paradox. In *Les Angoysses douloureuses*, she seems to state: "I am lying (dissimulating the truth) when I tell my husband that I am lying (composing fiction)"—or parallel formulation, "I say that I lie (in my writing) even though I speak the truth (in my writing)." She thereby posits the confessional value of her novel using what is, in fact, a classic example of a paradoxical *énonciation*, what is often known as "the liar's paradox." For to say that one is lying is a logical contradiction (if I speak the truth when I say that I lie then I am not lying).[75]

What effect does Hélisenne's use of the liar's paradox have on the status of her writing? In the first place, it effectively makes the confessional value of *Les Angoysses douloureuses* undecidable. Crenne projects her narrative into a realm where it is logically impossible to discern truth (confession) and fiction (literature). If "by lying" I somehow tell the truth, then truth becomes only a paradoxical form of fiction. The seemingly simple commonplace "I wrote to avoid idleness" enmeshes *Les Angoysses douloureuses* in a rhetorical hall of mirrors in which it becomes impossible to distinguish "the truth of the matter" from its fictional counterpart. Fiction or confession? Potential censors and slanderers are disarmed by a paradox. The reader is first tantalized with the possibility that Hélisenne de Crenne's writing is in fact confession (after all, the only other time that she explicitly denied its confessional value, we know that she was lying); at the same time, this "confession" depends on an act of *énonciation* that effectively undermines its truth value. This strategy creates a zone of indeterminacy in which Crenne can draw from the resources of the confession while neutralizing the danger that any public "confession" of intimate secrets might entail. Male writers like Montaigne may provocatively state "je me confesse en publicq, religieusement et purement" (III, 5,

846b), but such a "signed" confession from a woman would incur a harsh penalty.[76]

Only with this most elaborate system of safeguards in place does Crenne explore a confessional discursive mode in *Les Angoysses douloureuses I*. The carefully structured puzzle serves a crucial function: it allows Crenne to make public the most private, the most secret, of narratives in published *otium litteratum*, yet all the while professing her determination to avoid idleness and reveal no intimate secrets. What remains to be seen is the nature of this confessional rhetoric, the narrative and cultural function it fulfills, and the literary resources Crenne mobilizes in fashioning it. To be sure, the confessional mode creates an "effet de réel."[77] But it also brings into play questions of subjectivity and anonymity, of private and public discourse, of the sacred and the profane, all of which are central to sentimental romance as practiced by Hélisenne de Crenne.

Confessional Fiction: True Lies?

Crenne elaborated a poetic language of confession unique to French prose narrative of her generation. Boccaccio's *Fiammetta* and Jacopo Caviceo's *Peregrino* both pretended to be intimate declarations. She clearly found in these texts part of the inspiration for her narrative mode and plot. But she also elaborated on and sometimes transformed their confessional elements, creating new narrative situations and exploring new problems while drawing from Renaissance confessional practices and terminology. The narrative mode and content in *Les Angoysses douloureuses I* echo confessional practices from the first half of the sixteenth century.

Although an ecclesiastical decree of 1215 made a yearly sacramental confession obligatory for all members of the Christian faith, this broad framework still allowed for considerable variation and redefinition.[78] By the Renaissance, sexuality and privacy had become central to confessional practices.[79] Manuals for confessors gave precise strategies to elicit confession of illicit sexual acts from reticent penitents, particularly from young women, supposedly more likely to feel shame in narrating intimate details. Secrecy in particular was thought to facilitate confession. With the invention of the confessional box in the mid-sixteenth century, the confessant was placed in a semi-private space, symbolically and materially isolated from the rest of the faithful, with a grille hiding the confessant's face from the priest.[80] But even before the confessional became a fixture in Catholic churches, confessors' manuals directed priests to avert their gaze, particularly when hearing the confession of a young woman. By averting his gaze, the confessor signaled a symbolic refusal to identify the confessant in the act of revealing shameful secrets.

This brief picture suggests that a number of the fictional elements of Hélisenne's novel find their corollary in sacramental confession, with its emphasis on sexuality and privacy. As the story of a woman's illicit passion, Hélisenne's adultery of intention if not of act, *Les Angoysses douloureuses* covers precisely the sort of material reserved for confession. The narrative mode only adds to this effect, given that confessions require, by definition, the first person. A semi-anonymous work, *Les Angoysses douloureuses* also suggests the disembodied voice of the confessant, for it promises to reveal a woman's deepest secrets while masking her identity. To be precise, however, Hélisenne de Crenne did not completely disguise her true identity. By assuming the name "Crenne," her husband's name, she left the shadow of her true identity (Marguerite Briet) discernible.[81] Like the grille in the confessional box that mostly (but not entirely) veils the identity of the confessant, this name allowed informed readers to guess her true identity, just barely visible through the "grille" of the assumed name "Crenne."[82]

In short, the confession would have constituted a natural discursive model, given Hélisenne de Crenne's literary project. At a time when women's speech and sexual freedom were strictly policed, "sacramental confession was one institution that required women to speak," as Mary McKinley observes.[83] In her first person narrative of a woman's illicit passion, a narrative mode that both "reveals" intimate secrets while mostly preserving authorial anonymity, Crenne adapts a confessional paradigm to romance. In both the confession and *Les Angoysses douloureuses*, privacy is *produced* within an intersubjective context that simultaneously consecrates its status as "private discourse"; privacy is paradoxically achieved only when hidden truths are revealed.

The parallel between Crenne's sentimental novel and sacramental confession is further established by Hélisenne's would-be confession, a scene set up as a *mise en abyme* of the novel itself.[84] In this episode, which takes place near the middle of *Les Angoysses douloureuses I*, Hélisenne visits an "auctentique religieux" residing in a "devot monastere" (*AD* I, 145). She explains that her husband brought her to the monastery so that she might "reveal her misfortune in confession": "me mena en ung devot monastere, affin que en confession et sans difficulté je voulusse exhiber mon infortune et descharger mon cueur à ung auctentique religieux" (*AD* I, 145). At first reticent, Hélisenne soon seizes the opportunity to confess all of her story, knowing that the seal of confession guarantees that she can reveal her secrets in all impunity: ". . . je luy peulx bien le tout reciter, Car par ce que je luy diray en confession, il ne l'oseroit jamais reveler" (*AD* I, 146). She and her confessor then retire to "ung petit lieu secret et devotieux" (*AD* I, 147). After she recites her story, the monk confirms that she has completely revealed her most intimate secrets: ". . . vous m'avez du tout exhibé le secret de vostre cueur, sans riens reserver . . ." (*AD* I, 152). Confessors were indeed encouraged to elicit a complete confession of what was most hidden, most secret.[85] Finally he professes his "compassion": "j'ay bien distinctement pensé, et consideré l'inestimable douleur de vostre afflict cueur, qui me provocque à grand compassion" (*AD* I, 152). Likewise, manuals advise confessors to exhibit compassion when listening to a confession. Appearing stern or manifesting disapproval or disgust at a confessant's declaration would only make the latter more reticent. In contrast, a sympathetic demeanor facilitates a complete and truthful confession.[86]

The compassion manifested by the monk at hearing Hélisenne's story further suggests a parallel between confessional discursivity and sentimental discourse in *Les Angoysses douloureuses*. Both novel and confession presuppose a specific intersubjectivity—an "I" addressing a "you." In her dedicatory epistle, Hélisenne professes to be driven by the need to avow, the need to declare her story to "toutes dames honnestes": "C'est à vous mes nobles dames, que je veulx mes extremes douleurs estre communicquées" (*AD* I, 96). Moreover, both Hélisenne's narration and her pseudo-confession have a performative quality: as perlocutionary acts, they both elicit a response of compassion from the listener and consolation from the speaker, as she explains to her readers. "Car j'estime que mon infortune vous provocquera à quelques larmes piteuses: qui me pourra donner quelque refrigeration medicamente" (*AD* I, 96). In short, the perlocutionary value of Hélisenne's "declaration" along with the intersubjectivity it presupposes suggest an underlying affinity with confessional speech.[87]

But if the confession is a speech act, it is of course intended to elicit more than compassion and consolation. Although this psychological dimension has always been present in confession, it is secondary to its theological finality: absolution. To confess and be absolved requires felicity conditions (to quote J. L. Austin's terminology) quite clearly missing from both *Les Angoysses douloureuses I* and the confessional scene that takes place at a monastery. Confessional discourse in *Les Angoysses douloureuses I* lacks two central ingredients necessary to any religious confession: the confessant's truthfulness and contrition. Crenne effectively made the truth value of her "declaration" undecidable, as was seen above. As for contrition, this notion is at the heart of the discursive transformation underway in the sentimental universe of *Les Angoysses douloureuses*. Eclipsed throughout most of *Les Angoysses douloureuses*, contrition suddenly reappears at the end of Hélisenne's story. This sudden return to a religious framework resembles a desperate, final-hour repentance. It also situates the true finality of Hélisenne's idle pursuits and Crenne's learned leisure within the realm of the sacred. Here, the heroine finally casts off the role of *oiseuse*, devoting the last hours of her leisured existence to a confessional prayer.

Sentimental Romance, or, Confession without Contrition

Before inviting Hélisenne to speak, the monk stresses that he can give her penance only if she has a contrite heart.[88] Hélisenne observes in her narration of this scene that she is completely without contrition: "je n'en ay contrition ne repentance, mais suis ferme et stable en l'amour de mon amy" (*AD* I, 146). Without contrition, there can be no effective confession according to Church doctrine. Contrition and truth are of course two key factors distinguishing storytelling from religious confession. And as Hélisenne's exchange with the monk continues, the scene drifts further and further away from confession and toward romance. Indeed, as the monk begins to lecture her, exhorting her to cease loving Guenelic and return to the path of virtue, Hélisenne becomes irritated, cursing the monk mentally: "O mauldict vieillard" (156). Not only does she have no intention to stop sinning, she even wishes that Guenelic were occupying the role of her "confessor." If only her lover had disguised himself in a monk's habit and surreptitiously taken her confessor's place, she thinks wistfully, they could at that very moment be talking about their love:

> "je te [the monk] soubhaicte estre submergé en Scilla, ou Caribdis, et que mon amy fust en ton lieu avecq ton habit, et par ce moyen sans aulcune dubitation, pourrions deviser de noz amours . . ." (*AD* I, 156)

> ["And so I wish you [the monk] were submerged in Scylla or Charybdis, and that my beloved were in your place wearing your habit! In that way, without arousing suspicion, we could talk about our love . . ."][89]

The would-be "confession" thus turns into a fantasy complete with a romance scenario of the first order.

Caviceo's *Peregrino* includes just such a scene, one of the hero's many ruses to arrange a meeting with his beloved. The narrator describes how a friend distracted a priest while he took the latter's place in a dimly lit corner of the church reserved for confession. His intention, he explains, was to hear his beloved's "confession":

> . . . entre le sacre autel & le mur avoit une espace de quatre couldees. En ce lieu estoit la chaire sacerdotale: & le reste occupoit la personne qui devant estoit agenouillee. Le tout considere, deliberay voluntairement me faire prisonnier en cest autel / pour entendre combien Genevre estoit de moy amoureuse . . .[90]

> [Between the holy altar and the wall there was a small space. The priest's seat was in the space: and the person kneeling before occupied the rest. After some thought, I freely chose to make myself the prisoner of this altar, in order to hear how much Genevre was in love with me.]

Crenne no doubt had this in mind when she composed the scene at the monastery in *Les Angoysses douloureuses I*. For Hélisenne similarly imagines her lover in the place of the confessor.

The shifting interlocutor further establishes the scene at the monastery's function as a *mise en abyme* for the novel itself. The end of the novel reveals a similar displacement of her original addressee by her lover, for she concludes with the wish that her lover will somehow intercept her book, thereby bearing witness to her secret declaration:

> Moy estant en telle deliberation, subitement je donnay commencement à l'œuvre presente, estimant que ce me sera tres heureux labeur: et si

ceste felicité m'est concedée que[']elle tumbe entre les mains de mon amy . . . (*AD* I, 218)

[Having made this decision, I immediately began the present work, thinking it would be a very happy labor for me. If I am granted the felicity of having it fall into my beloved's hands . . .]⁹¹

The discursive mode thus drifts away from its avowed intersubjectivity (Hélisenne addressing compassionate *Dames*, her initial interlocutors) toward wish fulfillment, which takes the form of a virtual intersubjectivity (Hélisenne seeking to establish contact with her lover). So too does the addressee of her ostensible confession shift from a compassionate monk to her lover, whom she wishes would intercept her narration by replacing the monk.

Both scenarios stray from intersubjectivity (an "I" addressing a "you") toward a fantasy mode (a subject imagining the object of its desire magically bearing witness to an amorous confession). This movement accompanies a shift from an explicit moral finality (warning women to avoid the pitfalls of passion; seeking spiritual guidance from a monk) toward romance (communicating the heart's deepest secrets to one's beloved). The discursive mode wavers before crossing the line dividing confessional discourse (speech reaching toward the sacred) from sentimental romance (a secular universe governed by the pursuit of desire). We might even define sentimental romance as practiced by Crenne as confession without real contrition and thus without absolution. For sentimental discourse consists of intimate declarations that elicit human compassion, but not divine pardon. If all of the felicity conditions had been present at Hélisenne's pseudo-confession, if the monk had been able to utter *ego te absolvo*, then the story would simply have come to an end in the midst of what was after all only the first part of *Les Angoysses douloureuses*. As though Crenne sought to correct the dubious implications of a narrative mode blending confession and romance, the third book comes to a close with a confession stripped of romance. Like Augustine, Hélisenne addresses her confession directly to God: "O eternel et souverain dieu, qui voids noz cueurs et congnois noz pechez," she begins (*AD* III, 468). A kind of deus ex machina, this confessional prayer brings sentimental romance (*AD* I) and chivalric errantry (*AD* II) to an end. In recounting his own progression from error to grace, Augustine uses the story of Dido and Aeneas to signify the period before his conversion. This passage from Book I, 13 would be a natural intertext for Crenne, who not only fashioned her own confessional discourse, but also borrowed one of Dido's names (Elissa) for her literary persona (Hélisenne).[92] "I was obliged to memorize the wanderings of a hero named Aeneas," writes Augustine, "while in the meantime I failed to remember my own erratic ways. I learned to lament the death of Dido . . . while . . . I was dying separated from you, my God and my Life, and I shed no tears for my own plight. . . ." The end of the third book of Hélisenne's own imitation of epic and romance suggests that she too recognized her previous ways to be "erratic" and, by extension, her literary pursuits to be secular "wanderings."

Hélisenne here professes contrition "je manifeste mon grand peché, je accuse ma vituperation et turpitude, et deteste mes vices" (*AD* III, 470) [I acknowledge my great sin (. . .) I condemn my vituperation and turpitude] (186). She even paraphrases the Church's doctrine on confession: "Toutes les foys que le pecheur se retournera à Dieu par vraye penitence, tous pechez qu'il pourroit avoir commis ne luy seront imputez, ny ne l'empescheront d'avoir la vie eternelle . . ." (*AD* III, 468) [Whenever the sinner shall return to God in true penitence, all the sins he may have committed shall not be imputed to him, nor shall they prevent him from having eternal life] (185). She thus both defines the felicity conditions for confession to be successful and confirms that they are all present in her own confession. Hélisenne's story comes to a close with her reintegration into the community of the faithful via penance.

We might, then, conclude that France's first sentimental novel takes place precisely in the gap between consciousness of sin and genuine contrition, between storytelling and confession. The discursive mode Crenne elaborates, what we now term "sentimental discourse," is in effect a kind of secular confession. It displaces the religious finality (policing the faithful and absolving sin) while preserving its psychological function (consolation) and discursive mode (revealing intimate particulars).[93] Sentimental discourse rejects the confessor's moral rigor in favor of a pliant listener or reader; it does not seek to reintegrate the wayward creature, preferring instead to establish a kind of extramoral community of shared experience. For above all else, Hélisenne demands the complicity of her reader, called upon to participate in her story via *compassion* (literally, suffering with her).

Yet Crenne clearly found confessional psychology without theology to be a troubling state of affairs. Hence the conclusion to the third book, which reintroduces a theological framework by staging Hélisenne's final confession, complete with a mea culpa and request for absolution. With this confession, she retroactively brings her sentimental romance into an eschatological framework that redeems it. And in the process, she attempts a fragile reconciliation of idle romance with the sacred, as though the vagaries of romance still drew their meaning from a divine masterplot.[94] After lengthy digressions and romance scenarios of the first order, including lovers' trysts, the exchange of letters, and chivalric quest and errantry leading up to a dramatic rescue and escape on horseback, Crenne redefines her literary idleness as a sacred pursuit, culminating in the creature's confessional prayer, a request for pardon addressed directly to the Creator. Chapter 4 examines how subsequent romance production and consumption will in effect sever the tenuous bond linking idle romance to leisure's basis in the sacred.

4
Leisure as Commodity: The *Amadis* Serial

> Vendre les choses sainctes comme simoniacles
> —André Thevet, *Cosmographie du Levant*

THE *AMADIS* BOOKS ARE MOST REMEMBERED TODAY THANKS TO THEIR most famous critic (and imitator): Cervantes. Near the beginning of *Don Quixote*, the curate performs an auto-da-fé designed to purge Quixote's library of all but a few of its owner's romances. Curiously, though, the zealous curate preserves the first volume of *Amadis*. Garci Rodriguez de Montalvo's continuation—*The Labors of the Very Brave Knight Esplandian*—is in contrast thrown into the flames.[1] With this selective censorship, the curate targets not the idea of chivalric adventure but rather Montalvo's sequel to his original masterpiece. Under attack is less *Amadis* than the *Amadis* vogue, or more precisely, the *Amadis* serial.

This essay chronicles a central literary-historical event of the 1540s—conscious serialization. More than in the Spanish text on which it was based, it was in the French *Amadis* adapted by Herberay des Essarts that the serial crystallized.[2] The *Amadis* serial changed romance production in its immediate wake. It also elicited a sharp response from the intelligentsia of the time, for beyond its manifest content, *Amadis*'s very form threatened humanist ideals, hence the rearguard offensive mounted by humanists from Jacques Amyot to Miguel de Cervantes. The emergence of serialization in the 1540s was a decisive chapter in the ongoing secularization of time: underlying the literary serial was a new understanding of leisure as a commodity that could be bought and sold like any other temporal merchandise.

Idle Romance

In the course of their quest for the *mot de la Dive Bouteille*, Pantagruel and his band encounter numerous adventures of the most extravagant sort, which make up the narrative substance of the *Quart Livre*. But roughly three-quarters of the way through their voyage, the wind dies down, bringing the whole fleet to a halt. Rabelais then depicts the spectacle of idleness that takes place during this brief period of narrative stasis. As an allegory of idle pursuits, including reading romance, this scene proves an appropriate starting point.

During the windless calm, each character attempts to beguile the passing hours. Panurge blows bubbles; Frère Jean goes to the kitchen for a snack; and Ponocrates daydreams, tickles himself, and scratches his head (a gesture that connoted idleness during the Renaissance, much like twiddling one's thumbs does today).[3] As for the hero himself, Pantagruel reads a romance and dozes: "Pantagruel, tenent un Heliodore Grec en main, sus un transpontin au bout des Escoutilles sommeilloit"[4] [Pantagruel was dozing on a mattress beside the hatchway, with a Greek Heliodorus in his hand] (385). Rabelais's choice to put a romance in Pantagruel's idle hands is no gratuitous detail: for, more than any other genre, romance embodied *oisiveté*, from the earliest luxurious folio editions to the humble chapbooks sold by colporteurs at the end of the Renaissance.[5]

Reading romance, snacking, blowing bubbles, tickling oneself: by placing these activities on the same plane, Rabelais suggests an underlying conceptual affinity. In the first place, each of these pastimes seems poised between activity and inactivity. As the hero reads Heliodorus's romance, he dozes, appearing neither fully awake (active) nor asleep (inactive). His dreamlike state further suggests the dubious status of romance, often compared to dreams, and having little in common with the pursuit of knowledge generally associated with the written word.[6] The assorted idle pursuits further share their solitary nature. Indeed, this is perhaps the only episode in all of Rabelais's novels in which the four principal characters appear as insular beings—engaging in no dialogue, sharing no adventures or wine, exuding no exuberance. Finally, each activity seems to confer a rather ephemeral pleasure: snacking, for instance, remains relatively unsatisfying when compared to the pleasures of a true meal. Romance may be pleasurable, Rabelais suggests, but it offers only a hollow form of gratification. On a par with Panurge's idle bubbles, it is sheer surface with no real content.[7]

Romance entered the literary practices of the time in the guise of recreational literature, defined precisely as a "bubble"—a pleasant narrative surface with no "deeper" meaning. A brief discussion of recreation in the first book of Herberay des Essarts's *Amadis de Gaule* will allow us to better situate subsequent transformations. For the paradigm inaugurated by *Amadis* grew out of the existing tradition of recreation before definitively breaking with it.

Recreational Romance: Play to Work

Herberay des Essarts offered the first book of *Amadis* to Charles d'Angoulême, the son of François I, as a form of recreation—a modest *passetemps*. It was an accepted fact that aristocrats needed pastimes to occupy their leisure hours. The Renaissance inherited its conceptual terms from late medieval theorists of recreation, who took great pains to establish ethical parameters for aristocratic idleness.

"Il est deux manieres de oyseuses," observes Christine de Pizan in an attempt to resolve the conceptual uncertainty of idleness. She characterizes the first kind of idleness as a form of decadence, a lazy sensuality, which "renders life full of folly and useless for all good works, and makes it prone to voluptuousness and to yielding to the inclinations of sensuality" [fait la vie fole et impotent a toutes bonnes œuvres, et la rent encline a volupté et a acomplir les inclinacions de sensualité]. Christine immediately dismisses this dissolute idleness after briefly indicating the Ovidian topos from which it was derived. Her purpose, as she explains, is to expound upon "the other idleness"—recreation: "L'autre oiseuse est celle dont j'entens qui est sans vice." Recreational idleness is not only "without vice," it is also simply necessary. Noblemen sometimes have to rest in idleness, putting temporarily aside their great and worthy endeavors: "le prince, et semblablement tout homme chargié de gra[n]s et nottables occupacions, doit aucune fois cesser de œuvre et reposer en oysiveté."[8]

It is this second idleness, morally neutral and physically necessary, that romancers like Herberay claim as their justification, making it their vocation to entertain idle aristocrats.[9] Elaborating on the delights awaiting the reader, Herberay presents his first book of *Amadis* in the following terms:

> . . . si trouvera on en elle [Herberay's "traduction"] tant de rencontres chevaleureuses et plaisantes, avec infiniz propos d'amours si delecta-

bles à ceulx qui ayment ou sont dignes d'aymer, que toute personne de bon jugement se doit persuader (voyre quasi contraindre) à lire son histoire pour le passetemps et plaisir qu'il pourra recevoir en la bien voyant.[10]

[One will thus find in it (Herberay's adaptation) so many chivalric and pleasing encounters, with infinite talk about love so delightful to those who are in love or who are worthy of love that all people of good judgment must persuade themselves (indeed, almost constrain themselves) to read this story for the pastime and pleasure that they may receive by granting it their goodwill.]

Advertising the pleasures of *Amadis* to the point of redundancy, the construction proceeds from themes (lovers' words, chivalric encounters) to their pleasurable effect on the reader, from a literary content to the reader's experience.[11]

But in the midst of the language of pleasure (*delectables, passetemps, plaisir*), Herberay introduces the notion of obligation: "All people of good judgment *must* persuade themselves (almost *constrain* themselves) to read the story for the pastime and pleasure they will receive . . ." Constraint, obligation, these are concepts generally reserved for moral duty, but not pleasure. Doesn't the very idea of constraint imply countering, or at least limiting, pleasure? But here, in a paradox not unlike Thélème's only *rule*, "Do what you wish," the reader is required to play, obliged to experience pleasure. More than a clever advertisement ("Reader, it is your *duty* to delight in this story!"), this formulation sums up the idea of recreation underlying Herberay's defense of *Amadis*: it is precisely because it is play that *Amadis* is worthwhile and even necessary.

Parodying this convention in romance prologues, Rabelais's first novel begins with a similar injunction to play:

Et à la mienne volunté que chascun laissast sa propre besoigne, ne se souciast de son mestier et mist ses affaires propres en oubly, pour y vacquer [aux *Chroniques*] entierement sans que son esperit feust de ailleurs distraict ny empesché . . .[12]

[As far as I am concerned, I would have every man put aside his proper business, take no care for his trade, and forget his own affairs, in order to devote himself entirely to this book (the *Chroniques*). I would have him allow no distraction or hindrance from elsewhere to trouble his mind. . . . (167)

Like Herberay, Rabelais formulates an invitation to partake of idleness in an imperative mode *(que chascun laissast sa propre besoigne)*. He further inverts work (necessity) and leisure (distraction, play): it is work that is here defined as a nonessential "distraction" from the pleasant *Chroniques (sans que son esperit ne feust de ailleurs distraict)*. Idleness, that is, should take precedence over a trade *(mestier)*, duties *(besoigne)*, or personal business *(ses affaires propres)*. As is often the case with Rabelaisian prose, it is difficult to determine the degree of facetiousness. Yet the ambiguity in this instance also comes from the paradoxical thrust of Rabelais's underlying question: is it not by virtue of their superficiality that the *Chroniques* fulfill an essential calling? Blanchot describes this paradox as the first and surest justification of the *romanesque*.[13] Rabelais's "wish" could indeed be paraphrased as the desire to restore human time to play, no less of an imperative for being a free occupation.[14]

These paradoxical terms elucidate Herberay's insistence that the reader see in *Amadis* both a pastime and a requirement. On a more general level, a fundamental superficiality was thought to define all recreational literature—texts valued precisely for their lack of a profound moral content. Glending Olson observes that late medieval theories of recreation situated the locus of pleasure *(delectatio)* on the narrative surface. Embedded deep within the fiction, any useful didactic dimensions *(prodesse)* thus remained beyond the scope—and stamina—of readers of recreational fiction.[15] In other words, *Amadis*, like all recreational literature, was designed to be read literally, not allegorically. Accordingly, Herberay contrasted *Amadis* to "choses plus haultes et ardues."[16] He promised his reader a dilatory narrative surface unencumbered by an *altior sensus*. Exempt from the laborious *gradus* of allegory, *Amadis* was intended to be read horizontally, leisurely.[17]

In contrast, reading for a moral or philosophical content required effort. The reader had to work hard in order to reach a "higher" or "deeper" meaning. In fact, the reader's labor was thought to be a necessary part of hermeneutics, which, in turn, was understood to be training for exegesis. Here, too, effort remained crucial. In *De doctrina christiana*, Augustine explained that God purposely made the Scriptures obscure in order to help us "to conquer pride by work and to combat disdain in our minds" (II, vi). Far from being a contingency of exegesis, the reader's effort constituted an integral part of God's redemptive design: it promoted humility, the proper attitude for the exegete.[18]

Yet however antithetical they may be, effort (hermeneutics) and idleness (recreation) belonged to the same ethical paradigm. Both concepts found their place in a larger hierarchy of values and economy of time. At the summit of this hierarchy were arduous books—books requiring effort; worthy, but tiring, books. Still, idle books had their place and function. Herberay invited Charles to use *Amadis* as recreation *after* reading laborious books, in order to "recréer son gentil esprit."[19] In other words, *Amadis* was a form of leisure; but it was also intended as a propaedeutic for the labor of reading Greek and Latin, of digesting a philosophical content, of interpreting.[20] *Amadis* was thus part of a dialectic of work and leisure: lighthearted romance provided therapeutic rest and play, preparing the reader to return to the laborious pursuit of true knowledge. Hard work made leisure necessary, and leisure made one better able to work.[21]

Rabelais depicted one example of how chivalric romance might be effectively integrated into a dialectic of laborious study and recreational reading. Even Gargantua's education, with its strict time management, left room for a recreational use of chivalric romance. The young prince divided his mornings between study and athletics. But after such strenuous mental and physical exertion, he sat down for the midday meal and enjoyed refreshment and *apéritif* in the form of wine and chivalric romance:

> Cependant monsieur l'appétit venait: et par bonne oportunité s'asseyaient à table. Au commencement du repas était lue quelque histoire plaisante des anciennes prouesses, jusques à ce qu'il eût pris son vin.[22]

> [In the meantime my lord Appetite came in, and when the happy moment arrived they sat down at table. At the beginning of the meal there was a reading of some pleasant tale of the great deeds of old, which lasted till Gargantua had taken his wine.] (88)

Listening to romance read aloud constituted a necessary part of Gargantua's daily agenda of hyperbolic usefulness. Because it was effortless and gratuitous compared to his early morning activities, this brief respite actually helped Gargantua return to more demanding endeavors. Paradoxically, it was its frivolous nature that made chivalric romance able to serve higher moral or philosophical truths.

A pleasant respite in the pursuit of true knowledge: this was the humble place reserved for romance in the humanist curriculum. Yet its most salient formal quality belied using *Amadis* as a means to a higher end. Readers were told to use romance on a punctual basis as a refreshing break from more serious pursuits. Yet the narrative form itself defied teleology. *Amadis* had some twenty volumes, not to mention other romances branching off, including Herberay's *Dom Flores*.[23] Everything about romance conspired more to prolong the reader's pleasurable experience than to circumscribe it. Unwilling to "get to the point," *Amadis* embodied an early modern version of what Ross Chambers has termed "loiterature," texts that linger in an interminable "middle" rather than "hastening to the end" (to borrow the Horatian formula). Romance tended to submerge readers in a sea of prose instead of projecting them back into a difficult moral and intellectual journey. Under the force of an additional factor, serialization, *Amadis*'s already fragile ties with the ethical paradigm of recreation were in effect severed.

PANTAGRUEL: BEST-SELLERS AND THEIR SEQUELS

It was during the Renaissance that the book assumed the status of merchandise.[24] This new commercial context shaped the book's material form as modifications in format allowed literary entrepreneurs to reach a larger reading public. The producers of the French *Amadis*, for instance, told women readers that its new smaller *livre de poche* format was designed especially for their dainty hands.[25] Within this context, the serial represented a logical development. If material innovations served to attract new readers, narrative strategies were designed to retain them, drawing them from one book to the next.[26] One of the earliest writers to exploit this sort of narrative strategy was Rabelais, who attempted to capitalize on an earlier commercial success, the *Chroniques gargantuines*. He posited his *Pantagruel* (1532) as a would-be sequel to this immensely popular chapbook published at most only two months earlier.[27]

Masquerading as Alcofribas Nasier, Rabelais opens the prologue to his first book by flattering his readers ("Tresillustres et Treschevaleureux champions, gentilz hommes, et aultres . . ."), who are immediately characterized as the disciples of the *Chroniques gargantuines*. The success of the *Chroniques* appears to have been enormous, and Rabelais presents his *Pantagruel* as a mock sequel—a would-be son for the best-selling father. "Voulant doncques, je vostre humble esclave accroistre vos passetemps dadvantage, vous offre de present un aultre livre de mesme billon" (60) [Wishing therefore still further to increase your entertainment, I, your humble slave, offer you now another book of the same stamp] (168). He then undertakes a comic defense of the usefulness of the *Chroniques*, a matter of no small importance since *Pantagruel* is ostensibly of the same stamp *(de mesme billon)*.[28]

Alcofribas proceeds to enumerate the many uses that the *Chroniques* have served in a mock attempt to prove that they fulfill everyday needs: they have provided consolation *(réconfort)* for unsuccessful hunters; others have used them to cure toothaches by placing them between two warm cloths and applying them directly to the sore tooth; victims of pox and gout have included them in their treatments and felt great relief *(consolation)* from their suffering (58–59). The first and last of the uses the *Chroniques* have served, according to Alcofribas, are perfectly conventional. Consolation was in fact one of the therapeutic functions routinely attributed to recreational literature, as pleasure was believed to promote physical and mental well-being.[29] However, sandwiched between these two more canonic justifications is an absurdly literal version of the consolation topos: the *Chroniques* do more than console the victims of misfortune; they are also a cure for toothaches. In this case, it is not by providing pleasure, laughter, or delight of any kind that this wonderfully recreational text can restore health, but rather by direct application to the afflicted tooth. Anticipating a skeptical reaction, Alcofribas defends this claim by invoking the commercial success of the said *Chroniques*:

> Et le monde a bien congneu par experience infallible le grand emolument et utilité qui venoit de ladicte chronicque Gargantuine: *car* il en a esté plus vendu par les imprimeurs en deux moys, qu'il ne sera acheté de Bibles en neuf ans. (60; emphasis added)

> [The world has thoroughly acknowledged by infallible experience the great returns and benefits proceeding from this *Gargantuine Chronicle*. For more copies of it have been sold by the printers in two months than there will be of the Bible in nine years.] (168)

Using a comically false logical deduction, he mounts the following argument: clearly the *Chroniques gargantuines* have all of the uses I listed (including serving as a healing salve—*emolument*) *because* there have been more copies sold in two months than there will be of the Bible in nine years. That is, the *Chroniques* enjoy commercial success, therefore they possess fundamental utility. Underlying this deduction lies the all-important premise that commercial success reflects an object's true utility. In this way, Alcofribas plays at defending what Baudrillard describes as the founding illusion of consumption:[30] its ostensible vocation to satisfy human needs. Alcofribas's unspoken premise is precisely that people purchase what they need—and therefore, to conclude the reasoning, commercial production fulfills human needs. This justification excludes the possibility that 1) "needs" are the effect (not cause) of production and 2) desire, not need, drives the buyer. If it is ultimately the needs of production combined with the buyer's desire that are most at stake, then commercial production does not provide fulfillment or satisfaction. Alcofribas deliberately confuses moral utility (objects that satisfy "real needs"—curing toothaches, for example) and economic utility (all products that people can desire, be it only for the span of a passing whim).[31]

Clearly, though, Alcofribas's mock reasoning is not really intended to produce belief. Rabelais constructs a misleading enthymeme, counting on the reader to recognize its lightly veiled sophism. In both the *Topics* and the *Rhetoric*, Aristotle carefully differentiates dialectic from rhetoric: while the former uses syllogisms to arrive at certainty, the rhetorical enthymeme may be used only to determine probability because its premises are unreliable, being supplied by the audience.[32] The best-seller, then, becomes an extreme form of the enthymeme given the all-important role played by the public. The specious demonstration mounted in the prologue to *Pantagruel* amused its readers with a textbook example of a sophistic enthymeme. Yet it also hinted at a world in which an unreliable public established the dubious premises underlying society's truths—a comic deflation of what was, after all, a humanist's nightmare.

But Alcofribas also suggests how a consumer paradigm departs from the logic of the enthymeme insofar as its public is an anonymous, generalized voice. This marks a significant divergence from the rhetorical context, which always appeals to a specific audience (such as a jury in the case of forensic rhetoric). Moreover, in a commercial context, the public "speaks" only through the commercial act, which is no longer circumscribed by rhetorical parameters based on probability—and thus rationality. These deviations make the consumer model all the more subject to uncontrollable movements. Finally, in deliberately confusing economic utility with moral utility, Alcofribas defends the commercially successful *Chroniques* using precisely this logic. That is, he uses an economic logic to defend an economic logic, as though to suggest that commercial success were sufficient unto itself, rendering other paradigms obsolete. Reflecting wryly on the commercial phenomenon, Rabelais seems to foresee in it the perfectly self-contained system it was to become, a system having little use for any exterior sanction, be it rhetorical prowess or logic itself. Indeed, by the time Alcofribas took it upon himself to champion the cause of the *Chroniques*, his elaborate defense was superfluous. It arrived *after* the success of the *Chroniques*, which, one might add, ultimately had very little in common with their would-be sequel, *Pantagruel*.

At the time of his first book, Rabelais adopted an ambiguous position regarding sequels. He playfully maneuvered to capitalize on an immediate predecessor; yet he also hinted at the potential dangers of resorting to this strategy. The humanist pointed to the dubiousness of a practice that he was simultaneously exploiting to his own advantage. Humanists, including Rabelais, would later adopt a more rigorous position against serialization, defining their practice in opposition to works produced for consumption. Beginning in the mid-1540s, they were faced with new developments of the bestseller with the successful launching of the *Amadis* serial. Before turning to its reception, the following pages examine the conscious serialization of *Amadis*, focusing on the textual thresholds where this transformation is most manifest: at the beginning and end of the first eight books of Herberay's adaptation of *Amadis de Gaule*.[33] My aim is to determine how narrative modes accommodate the newly discovered vocation to insert each new installment into a growing series. What rules governed this new medium? How did the serial favor a new paradigm of reading, based on psychology rather than ethics, subject to the movement of desire rather than the quest for salvation?

From *Amadis* to *Amadis*: The Serialization of Romance

A rapid survey reveals an initial absence of any metadiscourse on the narrative form in the first three books of *Amadis*. Nothing in the first books encouraged the reader to look forward to a sequel, even though Herberay clearly planned to adapt at least the first four books from the very beginning. Several months before the publication of the first book, he had already obtained a six-year privilege for the first four books of *Amadis* and given it to his printers, Jean Longis and Vincent Sertenas.[34] After the enthusiastic reception of the first book, Herberay immediately agreed to provide the second, third, and fourth "as soon as possible."[35] Still, the narrative revealed no self-consciousness about its open-endedness, as though the narrator remained oblivious to the increasing number of "continuations."

Only beginning with the fourth book do narrative modes begin to encourage readers to keep reading from one book to the next, using each new book to program a desire for a sequel. The fourth book comments self-reflexively on its own place in what was, by then, clearly a *series* of *Amadis* books. An anonymous "amy du Seigneur des Essars" identifies the narrative mode as based on the deferment and satisfaction of the hero's—and the reader's—desire:

> En ce quart livre outre les precedens
> Un point y a pour plaire & contenter,
> Car tant de maux un seul bien retardans
> Cessent en fin de nuire & tourmenter . . .[36]

[And besides the preceding ones, this fourth book / Has a point to please and content / For delaying one sole good thing, so many bad ones / Finally cease to harm and torment . . .]

At the end of this fourth book, the hero's tribulations will finally come to an end, to his own good fortune and to the reader's satisfaction. Moreover, the function of the preceding books has apparently been to *delay* this satisfaction (. . . *tant de maux un seul bien retardans*). Like Amadis himself, the reader will finally experience gratification:

> Les troys premiers c'est l'enfer d'Amadis
> Plains de douleur d'infortune & de souffrance
> Ce quart luy donne amoureux paradis,
> L'heureuse fin de plaine jouyssance.[37]

[The first three (books) are Amadis's hell / Full of pain, misfortune, and suffering / This fourth (book) gives him an amorous paradise / a happy end of full gratification.]

The narrative appears to reach a resolution, culminating in the public marriage of Amadis and Oriane along with the hero's retirement from the vagaries of knight-errantry.[38] After deferring the end through four books of adventure, the long-awaited "happy end" finally arrives, leaving (for the first time) no narrative threads left hanging to prevent the reader from a complete sense of satisfaction.

But despite this closure, the *Amadis* cycle was far indeed from reaching its end. Even before the publication of the fourth book, Herberay had agreed to provide Longis, Janot, and Sertenas with the fifth and sixth books in one year's time.[39] In anticipation of a sequel, the narrator thus intervenes at the end of the fourth book to counter the sense of an ending with a sense of expectation.[40] The last words state: "We will leave Amadis and Oriane on l'Isle Ferme, ending this fourth book, *waiting for the fifth to be published*."[41] Montalvo made no such appeal to the reader at the end of his fourth book; nor is there any mention of a forthcoming book at this point. The fourth book in the Spanish *Amadís* concludes not with the reader waiting for a sequel, but rather with Amadis and his companions waiting for news of King Lisuart.[42] Herberay's transformation of the conclusion reveals a new set of rules. Montalvo's reader bears witness to a general open-endedness that defines much early modern literature. Herberay's reader is in contrast asked to participate in the process of serialization by actively awaiting the sequel. The continuation of the series is now dependent upon the reader's complicity. In other words, the reader's desire becomes the condition of the narrative that promises to both satisfy and renew this desire, just as the narrative itself is repeatedly concluded and renewed.

This brief intervention at the end of book four announcing a sequel ("waiting for the fifth to be published") thereby sets desire into motion once again. But desire for what? Is the reader not completely satisfied now that nothing prevents Amadis and Oriane from living happily ever after? Nevertheless, the reader *awaits* the next installment, *whatever it may hold*. The resolution of narrative tension has clearly ceased to function as a pretext, however weak, for the reader's desire; instead, the end of the fourth book programs desire for desire itself. Jacques Gohory, one of Herberay's successors in the *Amadis* cycle, would capture this idea with a personal device, signing his books with the enigmatic *ENVIE D'ENVIE ENVIE*, meaning "I desire desire out of desire"; or "I desire the desire of desire." The motto is appropriately circular in suggesting that desire is both the cause and the effect in a self-referential, self-perpetuating paradox.

Successive books continue to practice and reflect on the serialization of *Amadis de Gaule*. Concluding formulae turn self-reflexive, tantalizing readers with a preview of the next book. The fifth book (1544), for instance, concludes by suggestively evoking the "adventures estranges" and "maintz haultz faitz d'armes" contained in the next installment. The reader is figured eagerly awaiting the adventures that will be "recitez amplement aux livres subsequens, desquelz *vous pourrez jouyr* quelque jour, si Dieu & le temps permettent."[43] In effect, the fifth book's prefatory verse had also incited the reader's desire for a sequel. The following *douzain* is worth quoting in its entirety:

> Quand d'Amadis j'ay veu le Premier livre,
> Il me fait estre amoureux du Second,
> Et ceste amour ne me veult laisser vivre
> Sans voir le Tiers, tant me semble facond.
> Et puis ce Tiers, qui au Quart me semond,
> Me fait plus fort desirer le Cinquiesme.
> Mais n'y voyant encor point de Sixiesme,
> Je me souhaite estre au commencement,
> Pour le plaisir, & grand contentement,
> Que c'est de voir ce livre gracieux:
> Ainsi traduit aux hommes proprement,
> Comme s'il eust esté fait pour les dieux.[44]

[When I saw Amadis's first book, / It made me fall in love with the second: / And this love does not want to let me live, / Without seeing the third, so fruitful does it seem: / And then this third, which summons me to the fourth, / Makes me desire the fifth even more strongly. / But because I do not yet see the sixth, / I wish I were at the beginning, / For the pleasure, and great contentment, / That comes from seeing this graceful book: / Thus translated for men, / As though it had been made for the gods.]

The poem simulates the words of an enamored reader who proceeds from the first book to the fifth, each book engendering a crescendo of desire for the next. The meticulous enumeration of each of the successive books—*le premier, le second, le troisième* ...—reduces the structure of *Amadis* to a chain of installments with no center and no driving force beyond the reader's own desire. The imaginary reader of the fifth book hopes there will be a sixth, but in case there is not, wishes to simply begin again: *"Je me souhaite estre au commencement."* Endless romance, insatiable desire, the two terms have a potentially limitless capacity to play off one another. Future books in the *Amadis* series continue to offer self-reflexive meditations on the charm of serialization, its capacity to maintain the reader in a state of longing.[45]

If, to borrow McLuhan's famous phrase, "the medium is the message," then the significance of the *Amadis* serial did not derive from its manifest content (chivalric and amorous adventure). Rather, its new "message" corresponded to the pattern of moving from one installment to the next, of finishing in order to begin again: it conveyed the ideology of an eternally renewable world in embryonic form.

This modification had two consequences. In the first place, it instituted an eminently secular mode of reading since romance no longer pretended to contribute to a providential plan for humanity culminating in salvation. Romance affirmed its autonomy with respect to lofty truths and its capacity to manufacture desires (and frustrations) independently of any divine plan. At the same time and in keeping with this new secular orientation, the passage from an ethical paradigm to "entertainment" corresponded to a transition from the realm of finite necessity to a realm of infinite desire. As long as desire was its driving force, there could be no end to romance; for unlike need, desire is able to attach itself to an unlimited string of objects in succession, responding instantly to the creation of new objects never before imagined by the person experiencing desire. With capitalism still in its infancy, *Amadis* seems to foretell that consumption would be better adapted to generating desire than to satisfying needs.[46]

The French Serial: Before and After

In some ways, when the producers of the French *Amadis* collaborated in making France's first literary serial, they did so within an established literary tradition of prose romance cycles. Since the thirteenth century, popular romance narratives had been given "continuations" (as in the *Perceval Continuations*) or even absorbed into vast cycles (as in the *Lancelot* prose romance). In each of these examples, a rather short verse romance by Chrétien de Troyes became the basis for a multivolume literary labyrinth prolonged over many years. Thus, when Herberay followed the first book with a second, and the second with a third, this gesture made sense within the logic of romance continuations and cycles.

Yet Herberay's literary venture departed from late medieval antecedents by virtue of its time frame and new self-consciousness. The first eight books of the French *Amadis* serial came out at roughly one-year intervals between 1540 and 1548, at a scale and velocity unimaginable for a medieval cycle. By releasing a new volume so quickly, those responsible for the French *Amadis* were able to exploit the momentum that the printing process made possible. Moreover, Herberay's *Amadis* was not only self-reflexive about its own serialization, but it turned this self-consciousness into an advertising ploy. Herberay and others who supplied liminary verse engaged in a playful dialogue with the reader as buyer of present *and future* volumes. This dialogue shaped the very form of the text.

A second precedent to the creation of the French serial was its most obvious inspiration: Garci Rodriguez de Montalvo's *Amadís de Gaula*. Unlike its adaptation into French, the first four books of the Spanish *Amadis* were published together in one volume with the title *Los Quatro Libros del Virtuoso Amadís de Gaula: Complidos*.[47] However, Montalvo included in this volume some pre-publication advertising for his forthcoming fifth book. One thus finds the promise of a new book—chronicling the adventures of Esplandian—strategically placed in the prologue to Book I.[48] Like his French imitators some thirty years later, Montalvo created a climate of expectation, thereby paving the way for *Sergas de Esplandian* published separately two years later.[49] By using his prologue to prepare the way for a sequel, Montalvo took one tentative step toward serialization. After the fifth book, however, other authors took over, carrying the Spanish *Amadis* through book XII (1546).[50] As a result, the embryonic serial that the fifth book seemed to announce was never realized since subsequent books lacked the close collaboration that was to shape the French *Amadis*. Out of Montalvo's nascent recipe, the producers of the French *Amadis* would develop and orchestrate a coherent and sustained design.

The *Amadis* serial thus went beyond both its Spanish model and the medieval legacy of cycles. It marked a new era, and French romance production in its immediate wake reflected new publishing practices and reading habits. In the years following the French

Amadis, three new would-be serials were announced. In 1554, Jean Maugin's *Le Premier livre du nouveau Tristan* appeared. The "first" book of the *Nouveau Tristan* left off with the dejected hero suffering from the false premise that Yseult had a new lover. Maugin concluded, however, with the promise that the second book would see the hero's tribulations come to an end: "qui s'adoucira & appaisera au second livre, comme esperons le vous faire voir bien tost."[51] When in 1549, *Gerard d'Euphrate* appeared, it was similarly announced as the "first" book: *Le Premier Livre de l'Histoire & Ancienne Cronique de Gerard d'Euphrate*. Its anonymous author claimed to have been inspired by Herberay "who made the old knights of Great Britain live and flower again."[52] The preface concluded with the author's promise that if the reader found this first book enjoyable, more would follow: "[a]vec cette condition, toutesfois, que si son enfance vous est agreable, apres sa jeunesse, vous verrez l'aage viril: sinon (frustré de mon esperance & labeur) le feray r'entrer d'ou il est sorty" [With this condition, however, that if you find his childhood delightful, you will see him reach manhood after his youth; otherwise, (with my hope and labor frustrated), I will send him back to the place from which he came]. The six-year privilege accorded to the "translator" announced a total of *six* books.[53] Finally, Barthélemy Aneau presented his *Alector* (1560) as only the first book in a series, concluding with enthusiastic publicity for the many adventures awaiting the reader in an ostensibly forthcoming "second part."[54] None of these "first" books ever had their promised sequels, despite their authors' apparent eagerness to launch a new romance serial. Nevertheless, they suggest that the idea of the serial quickly penetrated the world of romance production. Writers and publishers proved most eager to apply the *Amadis* formula to new narratives. Within one year after Herberay's pivotal fourth book, the serial was established as a new medium in French literature. A wave of attacks on serial romance coming from humanist quarters followed soon thereafter.

Humanist Resistance to Serial Romance

When Herberay's adaptation from Montalvo's *Amadis de Gaula* first appeared in 1540, it was granted a highly enthusiastic reception. Marian Rothstein's recent study documents the many ways Herberay's *Amadis* spoke to its Renaissance readers: the pleasure of *Amadis* derived not only from its appeal to nationalist sentiment and the public's taste for chivalric romance, but also from its encyclopedic dimensions, its analogic form, and its perceived linguistic elegance. All of these factors combined to make *Amadis* an instant best-seller, the first in early modern France.[55]

But the enthusiasm with which Herberay's *Amadis* was first greeted proved to be short-lived. Uselessness, excessive length, perniciousness—these were among the grievances humanists began to voice. To be sure, from its very birth in twelfth-century France, chivalric romance had had its critics,[56] and the Renaissance's *Amadis* was in this respect no exception. Well before Herberay's adaptation appeared in France, the Spanish humanist Juan Luis Vives had complained about the pernicious effect of Montalvo's *Amadís* on women readers. He described romance as an active agent of moral degeneracy, comparing it to diabolical matches that ignite vice in young women: "car c'est peste d'applicquer buschettes seiches pour corrompre les corps de la personne, ja ardens & fomentez de delectations & de vices";[57] [for it is a curse to apply these dry twigs to corrupt a person's body already burning and fomenting with pleasures and vices]. He also denounced romances on the grounds of inutility, calling them "livres desquelz on ne peult rapporter aucun proffit, composez par gens oyseux ou inutiles"[58] [books from which one can derive no use composed by idle or useless people].

New to the debate, however, was a growing impatience with *Amadis*'s formal qualities, particularly its length. Morally "useless," romance was also formally pointless, its critics began to object. They increasingly likened romance to babble—volumes without end. The fact that critics denounced *Amadis* on the basis of its sheer length suggests that they were reacting not to *Amadis* itself, but rather to its capacity to prolong its success with a stream of sequels. By 1560, *Amadis* was drawing criticism from humanists reacting specifically to its serial form.[59]

Tabourot forged a new verb to signify the useless length of the *Amadis* serial. To "Amadis-de-gaulize," he observed, was to fill an entire page with what could be written in two lines. For Tabourot, a gratuitous prolongation of discourse characterized the new *ars poetica* of *Amadis de Gaule*.[60] This indictment of *Amadis*'s length becomes all the more significant if one recalls that normally amplitude (a defining trait of epic) was highly valued during the Renaissance.

Jacques Amyot mounted a more sustained attack on otiose romance in the prologue to his translation of the *Histoire Æthiopique* (1547). Enumerating the flaws of existing romances, he denounced their lack of erudition, their irrelevance to understanding antiquity or anything else for that matter, and the narrative structure itself:

> ... la plus grande partie des livres de ceste sorte, qui ont anciennement esté escrits en nostre langue, outre ce qu'il n'y a nulle erudition, nulle cognoissance de l'antiquité ne chose aucune (à brief parler) dont on peust tirer quelque utilité encore sont ils le plus souvent si mal cousu & si éloignez de toute vraye semblable apparence qu'il semble que ce soient plustot songes de quelque malade resvant en fievre chaude . . .[61]

> [not only do most of the books of this sort, that were written in our language in the past, have no erudition, no knowledge of antiquity, nor anything (to speak succinctly) from which one can draw any usefulness, but they are also usually so badly sewn together and so far from any appearance of verisimilitude that it seems that they are instead the dreams of a sick man dreaming during a high fever . . .]

Amyot's criticism of the content of chivalric romance comes as no surprise. More unexpected are the pains he took to criticize its *dispositio*, describing romance as "mal cousu." Drawing on a Horatian intertext, Amyot suggested that romances resembled febrile nightmares in their lack of verisimilitude and their failure to constitute a harmonious whole.[62] How indeed could romance have constituted a harmonious "whole" given its formal endlessness, its capacity to forever begin anew?

In 1555, Etienne Jodelle referred to then common humanist complaints that romances were endless and useless. They contained "mile adventures" and were "choses inutiles," its critics were objecting. He himself claimed to have called romance a "perte de temps," as opposed to humanist books described as "doctes et laborieux."[63] François de la Noue similarly accused romance of being both useless and pernicious.[64]

Useless *and* pernicious: to be sure, this induction is hardly a surprising one. For something to be useless and thus somehow immoral was a widely shared assumption during the Renaissance. Yet, strictly speaking there is an implicit contradiction in terms. From a logical point of view, how can romance be both useless and deleterious? How can it have both no effect *and* a decidedly pernicious effect? This amalgamation rests on a specific attitude toward time.

Underlying humanist attacks on romance was the assumption that time, and particularly leisure time, was not an individual's private possession. One could not spend—or waste—time as one wished. In humanist attacks on "useless" romance, remnants of an older notion of the sacredness of time persisted. In this perspective, to waste time was not an indifferent gesture, a mere abstention from action; it was a Promethean gesture, an act of mutiny or rather simony, for to waste time was to consume what rightfully belonged to God. Romance was useless and *therefore* pernicious.

The sacred value ascribed to time was at the heart of a question disputed by Franciscans during the fourteenth century: could a merchant charge interest? The conclusion was that interest was not legitimate because reaping a profit from the passage of time amounted to selling time, which belonged not to the merchant, but rather to the Creator. By the Renaissance, however, the sacredness of time had undergone significant erosion. The long-standing interdiction of interest was officially abolished during the sixteenth century, a conciliatory gesture toward commerce and its disciples.[65] With this interdiction lifted, it became legally permissible to buy and sell time. It is within this new secular attitude toward time that one should situate the birth of the salary, another Renaissance invention. What was the effect of the salary if not to institutionalize a commercial exchange between a buyer of work time (employer) and a seller of work time (worker)? As an entertainment commodity, the literary serial translated the very same logic to the realm of leisure. Both the salary and the serial reduced time to the status of a commodity to be bought or sold, wasted or well used. For along with popular chivalry, it was leisure itself that was marketed through romance. No longer based on a physical need for rest (recreation), on the participation of humanity in divine existence (the religious holiday or contemplation), or even on the Dionysian pleasure accompanying festive life, leisure had become a commercial product. Those who produced entertaining romance were, in a sense, merchants of leisure, appealing to an ever-complicit public. Humanist condemnation was aimed equally at both ends of the commercial exchange: both producers and readers were guilty of degrading leisure, of depriving it of its transcendence.

Humanist attacks on romance can thus be understood within the broader context of secularization sweeping over all aspects of life. In the face of these changes, humanists mounted an often fierce resistance. One humanist critic of squandering leisure called "wasting time" no less than a form of sacrilege.[66] But like many of his contemporaries, he wavered between ascribing to time a sacred quality and giving it a civic virtue, as in Erasmus's omnipresent adage *nemo sibi nascitur*. Ultimately, however, whether time belonged to the Creator or to the collectivity, it transcended the individual subject, who was not free to dissipate it with impunity. Humanists resisted the desacralization of time and leisure, a generalized movement that risked reducing both concepts to the status of merchandise. The logic of the serial made the threat of this transformation all the more manifest. By attempting to catch the reader in a loop, from *Amadis* to *Amadis*, both time and *otium* were brought into a decidedly new era.

With no available concept for what today is known as "the serial," humanists had recourse to elaborate circumlocutions. They focused alternately on romance's length, pernicious inutility, and repetition. The language of myth, however, presented a register singularly well suited to capturing the mechanisms of serialization.

Sisyphus, Tantalus, Danaides

Shortly after *Amadis* had taken a decisive turn toward serialization, one finds Sisyphus used to characterize both writers and readers of literary cycles and serials. The most famous instance is found in the prologue to the *Tiers Livre* (1546), where Rabelais compares himself as a writer to Diogenes and then Sisyphus. Composing the *Tiers Livre* was somehow like Sisyphus's condemnation to roll a rock to the top of a mountain, watch it slide back down, only to roll it back up again in an eternal cycle of futility. In the eleventh *Amadis* (privilege 1554), Diogenes-Sisyphus appears again. Indeed, Jacques Gohory may very well have borrowed this figure from Rabelais. This time the image is invoked in order to represent how learned people perceive the readers of chivalric and sentimental romance.[67]

In both cases the figure of Sisyphus captures the crisis of finality threatening multivolume prose narratives of the mid-sixteenth century. In effect, his condemnation to eternally roll his stone, without ever reaching his goal, amounts to a form of serialization. Sentenced to play out a cycle of sterile repetition, he resembles *Amadis*'s imaginary reader who reaches the end of one book only to begin the next, or even (as liminary verse in the eighth book suggests) to start all over again: *vouloir aura de . . . recommencer*. If Rabelais and Gohory both chose this figure as a dubious emblem of their narrative ventures, was it not because both humanists were writing within the broader context of a series?

Rabelais playfully proclaimed his first book to be a sequel to the popular *Chroniques*. But a decidedly defensive tone permeates the prologue of his third book, as though in the mid-1540s continuations were no longer to be taken so lightheartedly. Not only did Rabelais find himself composing in the wake of *Amadis de Gaule*, but he was also beginning his third book, the number three being the symbolic threshold separating a perhaps random repetition (two terms) from a possible series (three or more). As both a continuation of the first two books and a prelude to the *Quart Livre* (which prolonged the unfinished quest), the *Tiers Livre* seemed to enact romance's eternal return. Like endless romance, Rabelais's *tonneau-livre* may have appeared "inexpuisible"—indeed, the ten-year privilege accorded him the right to publish an unspecified number of continuations: "ceulx qu'il delibere de nouvel mettre en lumière" (9). Finding his own position compromised, the humanist self-consciously tried to differentiate his writing from the literary serial. The *Tiers Livre*, Rabelais insisted, neither produced nor exploited never-ending desire.[68] Promising that his book would not leave the reader desiring or "thirsty," he adamantly opposed his own "satisfying" cornucopian book to the *bussart des Danaïdes* (29), an allusion to the mythological figures sentenced to a particularly frustrating punishment consisting in endlessly pouring water into a bottomless barrel. To appreciate this veiled allusion to the *Amadis* paradigm, one has only to recall liminary discourse in the fifth book of *Amadis*, published only two years before Rabelais's *Tiers Livre*. In his poem addressed to readers, Mathurin Behu promised that each successive book of *Amadis* would only increase the reader's desire for the next. Like the Danaides' barrel, *Amadis* appeared to be bottomless rather than fulfilling, a *bussart des Danaïdes*, to borrow Rabelais's metaphor.[69]

Sisyphus, the Danaides, one might add Tantalus, all three myths figure tragically insatiable desire. Indeed, their tragic dimensions distinguish them from the readers of the *Amadis* serial, whose desire was nevertheless apparently equally insatiable. No angry gods intervened to impose a harsh punishment on *Amadis*'s readers: for they were perversely made complicit by the nature of desire—a constraint within the subject and so requiring no all-powerful gods to enforce the punishment, to torture or tantalize their victim.[70] If the reader of the *Amadis* serial was a kind of Sisyphus, we must imagine this reader happy, provided happiness be defined as the flight of desire rather than as contentment.

Roughly fifty years after the birth of the romance serial, Cervantes's curate complained that even the popular classes were consuming leisure through romance. At the moment of its birth in the twelfth century, romance was founded on the exclusion of "ignobles." Implicitly recalling the aristocratic origins of the genre, the curate lamented its current popularity, which he interpreted as a symptom of a decaying society, a society suffering from generalized idleness. In "well organized republics," he observed, "romance is reserved only for the leisure class, an elite not required, forced, or even able to work": "algunos que ni tienen, ne deben, pueden, trabajar."[71] In a similar vein, Charles Sorel would later contend that *Amadis de Gaule* was luring young men away from pursuing a "useful profession." *Amadis*, it would appear, was causing young men to indulge in aristocratic dreams of knight-errantry rather than applying themselves to a useful trade.[72] The allure of idleness proved to be one of its most enduring enticements. Well into the seventeenth century, romance continued to invite willing readers to partake of *oisiveté*.

While the literary worlds depicted in Renaissance romance belonged to a vanishing feudalism and its values, romance offered its readers a distinctly modern form of leisure. This new mode of *otium litteratum* was neither pursued by the philosopher nor granted by the gods. Instead, leisure had become a product widely available on the marketplace and, by virtue of this very fact, a fundamentally unattainable object.

5
"*en pleine oysiveté*": Idleness in the *Essais*

> Vacate, et videte quoniam ego sum Deus
> —Psalm 45.11

IN MONTAIGNE'S MILIEU, IDLENESS BELONGED TO A LOGIC OF SELF-improvement, itself part of a larger enterprise of class definition. In this process of ennoblement studied in chapter 2, classical models framed the debate and gave an ethical impetus to the pursuit of idleness. Conspicuously absent from this picture was the dominant mode of meditative leisure in the Middle Ages: religious contemplation. In the *Essais*, subjectivity emerged as a new alternative to the world of commercial operations and mental disquiet. The idle self, master of its own leisure, was indeed a newcomer in the ongoing secularization of leisure.

Montaigne's rhetoric of *oisiveté* explicitly rejected the two dominant discourses on idleness in his time: the moralist rhetoric against idleness and his own class's cautious rhetoric *pro otio*. Far more troubling, however, was the displacement of the religious model of contemplation. Passed over in silence by the essayist, this absence paradoxically shaped the *Essais* more than his conspicuous targets, his rhetorical straw men. If the contemplative's practice of leisure was a way of knowing or celebrating God, idleness for Montaigne became a way of knowing himself.[1] In the place long held by God, Montaigne posited the self, *un sujet merveilleusement vain et ondulent*, as the basis of leisure.[2] As a result, much of Montaigne's rhetoric of idleness is a rhetoric of compensation, an ongoing search for a lost plenitude.[3] To make up for this loss, he turned to a surrogate plenitude found in Epicureanism and commerce, two cultural forces contributing to a desacralization of culture during the Renaissance.

My discussion focuses on the early essays, closest in theme and in time to Montaigne's so-called retirement in 1570 as well as on those passages devoted to his famous tower library. Beneath the conventional rhetoric of these early essays lies an intimate mythology of idleness composed of gods, cannibals, aristocrats, and merchants—heterogeneous components perhaps, but all part of a coherent logic. Montaigne's reinvention of leisure was modeled on an Epicurean ideal, inflected in turn by Renaissance assumptions regarding nobility and its *derogeance*. Beyond the rhetorical play, *oisiveté* in the *Essais* is a concept: a hyperbolic freedom from work and an idealized self-sufficiency, two sides of the same coin for Montaigne.

Refuting the Moralists

Long held to be the friend of leisure and the victim of a melancholic idleness,[4] Montaigne has recently been shown to take a more ambiguous stance. Critics and commentators have begun to uncover Montaigne's deep and enduring interest in *oisiveté*—with all the dubiousness this term connoted during the Renaissance.[5]

A rapid survey of the concept of idleness in the early essays reveals a highly rhetorical use of this concept, which may have been borrowed from any number of miscellanies. Borrowed from them perhaps, but only to better subvert their conventional wisdom. For Montaigne's praise for idleness is literally a paradox—an attempt at countering the *doxa* whose many spokesmen included Pierre Messie (Pero Mexia—probably Montaigne's original source for "De l'oisiveté"), Jean des Caurres, and Pierre de La Primaudaye, who all wrote against idleness—*mère et nourrice de tous les vices*.[6]

Idleness, the miscellanies teach us, should be blamed and avoided. For idleness as commonplace—and idleness was first and foremost a commonplace—was shaped by the long-standing tradition of exemplarity along with a complementary rhetoric of praise and blame *(epideictic rhetoric)*.[7] Montaigne's position in the early essays is a studied inversion of this conventional wisdom: idleness, the *Essais* teach us, is something to be praised and practiced. In "De la vanité," he declares "idleness" and "freedom" to be his "very favorite qualities" (741).[8] The inverse is true as well: for work, he maintains, is foreign to his very being. Montaigne likes to profess his indolence, stating, for example "how little I like to work" (737) [Qui connoistra combien je suis peu laborieux . . .] (III,

9, 965b). The object of his praise, idleness also becomes an ideal he actively cultivates: "Extremely idle, extremely independent, both by nature and *by art*" (486) [extremement oisif, extremement libre, et par nature et *par art*] (II, 17, 642c; emphasis added). In "De mesnager sa volonté," quoting Ovid, he will describe himself as born in—and for—idleness: *"fugax rerum, securaque in otia natus"* (III, 10, 1003b). Even as a child he could not be drawn out of his state of idleness to play, as he explains in "De l'institution des enfans": "I was withal so sluggish, lax, and drowsy that they could not tear me from my sloth, not even to make me play" (129) [j'estois parmy cela si poisant, mol et endormi, qu'on ne me pouvoit arracher de l'oisiveté, non pas pour me faire jouer] (I, 26, 174a); and again "[t]he danger was not that I should do ill, but that I should do nothing. No one predicted that I should become wicked, but only useless. They foresaw loafing, not knavery" (130) [(l)e danger n'estoit pas que je fisse mal, mais que je ne fisse rien. Nul ne prognostiquoit que je deusse devenir mauvais, mais inutile. On y prevoyoit de la faineantise, non pas de la malice] (I, 26, 175–76a). From the beginning of the *Essais* to their end, he returns again and again to one of his favorite themes: his own cultivated idleness and distaste for business of any sort.

The beginning of "De la solitude" illustrates the logic of work and idleness in the early essays. If Erasmus's adage *nemo sibi nascitur* formed the basis of work morality, Montaigne turns it against itself using the logic of paradox. He will thus begin "De la solitude" by announcing that it is in fact work that is for those who were "born for themselves":

Laissons à part cette longue comparaison de la vie solitaire à l'active; et quant à ce beau mot dequoy se couvre l'ambition et l'avarice: Que nous ne sommes pas nez pour nostre particulier, ains pour le publicq, rapportons nous en hardiment à ceux qui sont en la danse; et qu'ils se battent la conscience, si, au rebours, les estats, les charges, et cette tracasserie du monde ne se recherche [sic] plutost pour tirer du publicq son profit particulier. (I, 39, 237a)

[Let us leave aside the usual long comparison between the solitary and the active life; and as for that fine statement under which ambition and avarice take cover—that we are not born for our private selves, but for the public—let us boldly appeal to those who are in the midst of the dance. Let them cudgel their conscience and say whether, on the contrary, the titles, the offices, and the hustle and bustle of the world are not sought out to gain private profit from the public.] (174)

Here we learn that Erasmus's adage functions as a smoke screen. It is not used to promote civic ideals: on the contrary, it serves only private interests. More serious still, its would-be proponents use it as an instrument of mystification: it serves to hide personal ambition and greed under the veil of public service. The rigorous rhetorical construction of the opening of "De la solitude" reinforces its polemical thesis. The essayist structures his attack on the bad faith proponents of work morality, using a crisscrossing of public and private:

what they say: "nous ne sommes pas nez pour nostre *particulier*, ains pour le *publicq*"
        private → public

what they do: "tirer du *publicq* son profit *particulier*"
        public → private

Montaigne's idea is itself a kind of chiasmus: they claim to submit private concerns to the public interest, but in reality they use the public sphere to pursue a private agenda. In response to this situation, Montaigne humorously proposes to "retire" the age-old debate pitting the contemplative life against the active life ("laissons à part cette longue comparaison de la vie solitaire à l'active"), explicit irony given his active participation in the debate, even though it is *au rebours*, to quote another *topicqueur*.

Having rejected the moralists' rhetoric against idleness, Montaigne does not turn to the positive version of idleness that his century made available. He does not, in other words, embrace the learned leisure his peers cultivated.

Excluding the Robe

The Fourth Estate's project to redeem leisure by uniting idleness and letters had no happier outcome than the *Essais*. When Montaigne retired to the "breast of the learned virgins" it was in the name of *tranquillitas*, *libertas*, and *otium*. Initially he shared his peers' faith in the Senecan maxim *otium sine litteris mors est*. Indeed, the *Essais* would have been virtually inconceivable without his class's project of learned leisure. However, he later disavows learned leisure in several key passages, a posture that has led a number of critics to invoke his famous "nobiliary pretention."[9] Rather than laboring over books, Montaigne would like his reader to imagine him casually flipping through one book, then another, a dilettante of leisure, not an entrepreneur:

> . . . je feuillette à cette heure un livre, à cette heure un autre, sans ordre et sans dessein, à pieces descousues; tantost je resve, tantost j'enregistre et dicte, en me promenant, mes songes que voicy (III, 3 828b).[10]

> [. . . I leaf through now one book, now another, without order and without plan, by disconnected fragments. One moment I muse, another moment I set down or dictate, walking back and forth, these fancies of mine that you see here.] (629)

Divorcing his activity of reading from the book's own discursive logic (*à pieces descousues*), and divorcing the book itself from its place in a larger humanist *curriculum* (*je feuillette à cette heure un livre, à cette heure un autre, sans ordre et sans dessein*), Montaigne makes reading obey a biological rhythm, as though it were a continuation of his own organic processes. Inextricably linked in the *Essais*, reading and writing do not belong to an enterprise of learned leisure, insists Montaigne. The essayist thus counters his peers' culture of learned leisure with his own so-called idle nature ("extremely idle . . . by nature").

Beyond his desire to extract himself from the world of *negotium*, Montaigne wishes to exclude his *otium litteratum* from the circulation of cultural capital. He concludes his "Au Lecteur" by telling the reader that the *Essais* are not a good use of leisure: "ce n'est pas raison que tu *employes ton loisir* en un subject si frivole et si vain" (3; my emphasis) [you would be unreasonable to spend your leisure (literally "to *employ* your leisure") on so frivolous and vain a subject] (2; my emphasis). According to traditional assessments, this phrase is simply a variation on the modesty topos. In fact, though, this phrase hides a competitive maneuver on the part of the essayist who seeks to situate his own literary idleness beyond the reach of rivals. The choice of the verb *to employ* ("reader, do not employ your leisure on such a vain pursuit . . .") is a play on words, but also a subtle reminder that leisure and work are not incommensurable. *Otium* can be "employed"; it can be used to the same end as *negotium*. It is his awareness of the compatibility of idleness and business that makes the essayist anxious about losing exclusive rights to the cultural capital generated by his own literary idleness. For by publishing his *otium litteratum*, Montaigne knew he was putting it back into circulation. It could as a result be mobilized by other idle gentlemen eager to use the *Essais* to their own advantage.[11] That is, readers looking for a leisure investment could use the *Essais* to *employ* leisure well, applying the lessons learned from theorists such as Laval, author of "*Du Loysir* et Comme on le Peut *Employer* Honnestement" (my emphasis).[12] Always eager to invest any temporary respite from their busy professional lives in *otium litteratum*, these men knew that idleness was far from the gratuitous pursuit that Montaigne liked to pretend it was. A good use of leisure sometimes led to professional advancement and was in all cases a coveted ornament.[13] Indeed, despite Montaigne's resistance to this outcome, the *Essais* would remain required reading for aspiring *bourgeois gentilshommes*, becoming a virtual breviary for ambitious idlers, as Huet observes near the end of the seventeenth century:

> Son esprit libre, son style varié et ses expressions métaphoriques . . . ont principalement mérité cette grande vogue, dans laquelle il a été pendant plus d'un siècle, et où il est encore aujourd'hui: car c'est, pour le bien dire, le Bréviaire des honnêtes paresseux et des ignorants studieux qui veulent s'enfariner de quelque connaissance du monde et de quelque teinture de lettres.[14]

> [For the most part, his free spirit, his varied style and his metaphorical expressions earned him his current popularity, which he has enjoyed for more than a century, and which he still enjoys today: for, truly, it (the *Essais*) is the breviary for urbane loafers and ignorant pseudointellectuals who want to cloak themselves in some knowledge of the world and add some literary hues.]

Turning now to "De l'oisiveté" (I, 8), which Montaigne may have originally intended to serve as a prologue to the as yet untitled *Essais*,[15] the following pages examine a third absent from Montaigne's conception of idleness, a specter that he cannot reduce to derision by rhetorical prowess, that he cannot simply exclude, and that subtly haunts the *Essais*.

Displacing the Divine

In the second part of "De l'oisiveté," Montaigne gives a lyrical account of his retirement to his family estate.[16]

> Dernierement que je me retiray chez moy, deliberé autant que je pourroy, ne me mesler d'autre chose que de passer en repos, et à part, ce peu qui me reste de vie (I, 8, 33a)

> [Lately when I retired to my home, determined so far as possible to bother about nothing, except spending the little life I have left in rest and seclusion . . .] (21)

Villey confirms that "De l'oisiveté" was indeed composed shortly after Montaigne resigned from the Bordeaux Parlement in 1570. "De l'oisiveté" also echoes the inscription he had carved on the wall of his *cabinet* in 1571. This manifesto proclaimed his intention to dedicate what remained of his life to "liberty," "tranquillity," and "idleness." If his thirteen years as a magistrate had been dedicated to others, his leisure was to be for him alone: the "greatest favor" he could do for his mind was to leave it in full idleness *(en pleine oysiveté)*, free to converse with itself *(s'entretenir soy mesmes)*, to come to rest *(s'arrester)* and to settle down to itself *(rasseoir en soy)*.

Is this focus on the self a descent into solipsism or part of a redemptive process akin to an examination of conscience? The essay seems to invite both of these mutually exclusive conclusions. Montaigne seems to invoke a latent solipsism with an initial comparison of idle minds to women who conceive without the benefit of (male) semen—solipsism transferred to the realm of human reproduction. The latter give birth only to "shapeless masses and lumps of flesh"—*mola uteri*, in the physiological terms of the time.[17] Likewise, his idle mind gave birth to equally useless "chimeras and fantastic monsters" (20).[18] His reaction was to keep a careful record of them *(les mettre en rolle)* in order to leisurely contemplate their "ineptitude" and "strangeness." Notwithstanding this subtext, Montaigne suggests that his self-scrutiny might also serve as a kind of examination of conscience. He does invoke shame as the intended result, vaguely suggesting a connection to repentance: "esperant avec le temps luy en faire honte à luy mesmes" (33a); [hoping in time to make my mind ashamed of itself] (21). However, future essays clarify the true nature of this *mise en rolle*, as repentance and its avatars are dismissed.[19] "If I had to live over again, I would live as I have lived" (620), he writes near the end of "Of Repentance."[20] In "De la vanité," he reformulates the *mise en rolle* announced at the end of "De l'oisiveté," preserving the role of idleness, but effacing shame as the ostensible goal. "Qui ne voit que j'ay pris une route par laquelle, sans cesse et *sans travail*, j'iray autant qu'il y aura d'ancre et de papier au monde?" (III, 9, 945b; emphasis added) [Who does not see that I have taken a road along which I shall go, without stopping and *without effort*, as long as there is ink and paper in the world?] (721; emphasis added). *Oisiveté* and *franchise* are, he adds later in the same essay, his "qualitez plus favories" (969c). As Gisèle Mathieu-Castellani argues, the *folie*, uselessness, and idleness announced in "De l'oisiveté" become the de facto paradigm of value in the *Essais*.[21]

Entirely absent from his account of his retirement (and from his rhetoric of idleness in general) is any religious impetus. Elsewhere in the *Essais*, when he does refer to religious contemplation, he situates it on so lofty a height as to be completely out of reach—without, that is, the help of grace.[22] Near the end of "De la solitude," Montaigne praises those who lead a life devoted to solitary contemplation of God: "Ils se proposent Dieu, object infini et en bonté et en puissance," adding

> Et qui peut embraser son ame de l'ardeur de cette vive foy et esperance, reellement et constamment, il se bastit en la solitude une vie voluptueuse et delicate au delà de toute autre forme de vie. (I, 39, 245c)

> [And he who can really and constantly kindle his soul with the flame of that living faith and hope, builds himself in solitude a life that is voluptuous and delightful beyond any other kind of life.] (180–81)

While religious contemplation remains "the best share," Montaigne clearly did not choose to make this life his own—or, perhaps it is Montaigne who *was not chosen* for this life, for the phrase remains ambiguous ("Et qui peut . . ."). Instead, Montaigne's original intention, he explains, was simply to retire to his country estate in order to find sustained rest: "deliberé . . . de passer en repos, et à part, ce peu qui me reste de vie" (33a) [determined so far as possible to bother about nothing except spending the little life I have left in rest and seclusion] (21). Insofar as no manifest religious sentiment drives his desire for *repos*, Montaigne's wish for solitary rest marks a breaks with the long-standing doctrine of rest in God. This doctrine defined any intermittent rest enjoyed in this world as a prefiguration of the everlasting peace to be enjoyed after death—when the creature rested not in itself, but in the Creator.[23] Messie concludes his essay on idleness with this vision of rest. "Blessed are those who are received by the Lord after death," he writes, "for their spirits rest [se reposent] from their labors. . . ."[24]

Preserving leisure's ethical imperative but evacuating its sacred meaning, Montaigne posits a new figure of the contemplative—a creature that Josef Picpcr describes as theoretically impossible, if the basis of leisure is divine worship.[25] In Montaigne's case, the importance of the contemplative life for the preceding centuries gives added weight to this hypothesis. Underlying the monastic life, from the High Middle Ages on, was the injunction *"vacate, et videte quoniam ego sum Deus"* (Psalm 45:11). Augustine elaborated a clear doctrine: *De civitate dei* defined leisure as the activity of contemplating God in anticipation of the eternal rest of the next life.[26] Aquinas also made explicit the eschatological framework underlying the contemplative life on its most general level: he defined the purpose of work as leisure and the purpose of leisure as God, the divine telos of contemplation and of life itself.[27]

In the place of *contemplatio dei* Montaigne thus instituted *contemplatio sui*, turning contemplative vision back toward the self.

C'estoit un commandement paradoxe que nous faisoit anciennement ce Dieu à Delphes: *Regardez* dans vous, reconnoissez vous, tenez vous à vous . . . *Voy* tu pas que ce monde tient toutes ses *veues* contraintes au dedans et ses *yeux* ouverts à *se contempler soy-mesme*? (III, 9, 1001b; emphasis added)

[It was a paradoxical command that was given us of old by that god at Delphi: "*Look* into yourself, know yourself, keep to yourself; bring back your mind and your will. . . ." Do you not *see* that this world keeps its *sight* all concentrated inward and its eyes open to *contemplate* itself?] (766; emphasis added)

Subject—and object—of its own contemplation, the self imitates the world by turning its gaze inward. Replacing leisure as religious culture with a culture of the self amounts to putting the lowly self in the place long occupied by the divine. David Quint's study of the new historical consciousness that informed Renaissance conceptions of literary creation provides us with a broader context in which to situate this gesture. With its emphasis on originality over a divine origin, this consciousness contributed to an understanding of the text as the creation of a human author rather than the vehicle of a transcendent nonhistorical truth. It thus accounts for tentative attempts at self-authorization made by writers such as Montaigne.[28] Seen in this light, for the creature to affirm autonomy in leisure is but a continuation of the writer's autonomy in the act of creation.

One of Montaigne's imitators from the first years of the seventeenth century must have perceived with acuity the absence of any religious dimensions in the ideal of leisure in the *Essais*. His reaction was to systematically restore the religious basis of leisure. In imitating "De la solitude" in his own chapter with the same title, Louis Guyon quoted entire passages verbatim from Montaigne. However, he carefully added a new—explicitly religious—context of interpretation. He exhorts anyone wishing to practice idleness in solitude to make this practice an *imitatio Christi*:

> Voila le premier point, que doit tenir le solitaire, de ne recercher pas la vaine gloire, mais la vraye, à sçavoir la divine & celeste, à l'exemple de Christ.[29]

> [The first rule that the solitary person must respect is to not seek vain glory, but the true one, that is, divine and celestial glory, following Christ's example.]

This passage firmly establishes the context in which Guyon wished to resituate Montaigne's ethics of leisure. For with the very next sentence begins a long series of direct citations and paraphrases from Montaigne's essay (I, 39, 239a *passim*). He thus continues:

> Cela fait il faut chasser loin de nous l'avarice, l'irresolution, la timidité, la peur & les concupiscences, lesquelles ne nous abondonnent pas aisément, mais nous suivent coustumierement, jusques dans les cloistres, & dans les escoles de Philosophie. Ni les deserts, ni les rochers creux, ni la haire, ne nous en desmelent ou delivrent.[30]

> [We must drive away avarice, irresolution, timidness, fear, and lust, all of which do not abandon us easily, but often pursue us even into the cloisters and the schools of philosophy. Neither deserts, nor rocky caves, nor hair shirts free us of them.]

Guyon proceeds to transpose the most famous maxims from "De la solitude," including, to cite only a few: "gagnons ce point sur nous, de pouvoir vivre à nostre aise"; [let us win from ourselves the power to live really alone and to live that way at our ease];[31] "il se faut reserver une arrière boutique, toute nostre, toute franche, en laquelle nous establissons nostre vraye liberté, principale retraicte et solitude" [We must reserve a back shop all our own, entirely free, in which to establish our real liberty and our principal retreat and solitude];[32] "c'est assez vescu pour autruy, vivons pour nous au moins ce bout de vie" [We have lived enough for others, let us live at least this remaining bit of life for ourselves].[33]

This brief excursion into the "fortunes of Montaigne" serves to show how his ideal of leisure was firmly reintegrated into a religious economy by one of his imitators. For Montaigne's part, his own response was entirely different, although he was no less aware of the absence his new ideal of leisure created than was Guyon. To counterbalance the vertigo of self-authorized leisure, the essayist drew a repertoire of concepts and metaphors from the world of commerce and from Epicureanism, prominent secular discourses of his time.[34] In fashioning an imaginary of leisure on a human scale, Montaigne paradoxically turned to the world of business and to the meditative serenity personified by the Epicurean divinities. Why did the essayist privilege these two discourses in shaping his personal mythology of idleness? This choice appears all the more perplexing in light of their dubious status during the Renaissance, associated as they were with atheists and merchants, no doubt among the least popular social categories. If Montaigne turned to these two unlikely sources, it was because they offered compensation for the loss of the religious finality that had long shaped leisure. No longer seeking union with the Creator through contemplation, Montaigne's autonomous contemplative turned to a compensatory plenitude. This he found in Epicurean philosophy (Epicurus and his disciples sought to free the thinker from desire and thus from lack) and in commerce (a means of producing material wealth). Out of these two languages—a prosaic language of work and a poetic language of Epicurean beatitude—he reconfigured the dynamic between leisure and work, self and world.

The Gods Must Be Idle: Montaigne's Annotated Lucretius

The recent discovery of Montaigne's annotated copy of Lucretius provides the reader of the *Essais* with a privileged opening into how

Montaigne read *De rerum natura*—or rather how he read, reread, and annotated it. In his critical edition, Michael Andrew Screech transcribes Montaigne's notes, which fall into four general categories: pen-strokes against many of the lines of verse; marginal notations in French and sometimes Latin; notes in Latin on lexic, grammar, and scansion found on the flyleaves; and another series of Latin notations also on the flyleaves, but which concern Lucretius's argument itself. Screech suggests that Montaigne may have intended this last category to serve as a list of loci or even as an index.[35] These notes reveal that not only did Montaigne admire the poetic language (the *Essais* themselves had already proven this fact),[36] he also meticulously followed the argument. He sought to understand *De rerum natura* on its own terms rather than refute the materialist theories expounded in beautiful verse, as Lambinus tended to do in his notes.[37]

The first reference to the gods' idleness occurs at the beginning of *De rerum natura*: "omnis enim per se divom natura necessest / inmortali aevo summa cum pace fruatur / semota ab nostris rebus seiunctaque longe . . ." [the very nature of divinity must necessarily enjoy immortal life in the deepest peace, far removed and separated from our affairs. . . .][38] Montaigne included this page, the first of nine references on the flyleaves, under the general heading "Dij nihil curant res nostras & otio fruuntur sempiterno" [The gods have no concern for our affairs, and they enjoy everlasting idleness.][39] "Impia sententia," observed Lambinus in his note to this passage.[40] He perceived the gods' idleness to be a frontal attack on religion because it denoted their complete withdrawal from the affairs of mortals.[41] This element did not escape Montaigne, either. Some references to the idle gods also figure among the passages he labeled "contre la religion."[42] Yet what most interested Montaigne in the figure of the Epicurean gods was the meditative serenity they embodied.

The meticulousness with which he studied these passages—gathering them all together under one single heading, noting echoes between them, and making marginal annotations on several passages—testifies to Montaigne's interest in Epicurus's idle gods.[43] The following pages take these notes, which constitute a kind of archaeology of the *Essais*, as a point of departure in studying Montaigne's conception of idleness. By suggesting how Montaigne read one of his favorite poets, they offer new insights into one of his favorite themes: *oisiveté*.

Montaigne began reading Lucretius at the age of thirty-one, six years before he resigned from the Parlement of Bordeaux in 1570. It is thus hardly surprising that the ideal of leisure that he encountered in *De rerum natura* would shape the early essays, composed shortly after his own retirement, particularly those essays on the subject of leisure itself (I, 8; I, 39). The fact that Epicurus's gods served as a model is a reminder that Montaigne's idea of idleness should not be taken as a reflection of his daily life. After his "retirement" in 1570 he went on to serve two terms as mayor of Bordeaux (1581–85), perform important diplomatic service, and be very successful at managing his family estate. The hyperbolic idleness embodied by the Epicurean divinities in no direct way resembled Montaigne's own busy life. But it did profoundly shape the representation of idleness in the *Essais*. The *Essais* thus function as a mediating structure between an imaginary of *oisiveté*, partly inaccessible, and the reality of Montaigne's works and days. How, then, can his notes on the idle gods illuminate the notion of *oisiveté* in the *Essais*?

Montaigne noted Lucretius's description of the gods' idleness by writing "Dieus oisifs & en repos."[44] This note appears in the margin near the passage describing the deep peace the gods enjoy far from human business ("... *cum pace fruatur / semota ab nostris rebus seiunctaque longe*").[45] Another annotation Montaigne made simply states: "Dii otiosi prolixe," followed by page references.[46] One of the notes covering the flyleaves, this observation may be read as an abbreviated form of: "Lucretius writes copiously of the idle gods." However, without a verb to signify that it is Lucretius's *writing* that is "copious," the more literal reading is simply "the Gods are copiously idle."[47] In condensing these two notions (idleness and copiousness), Montaigne's brief annotation sums up the essence of Epicurean divinity, the very antithesis of the state of work and lack that troubles humanity. In other words, the gods can enjoy an existence of idleness and abundance because they are completely sufficient unto themselves, autarkic, unlike human beings who are plagued by needs, desires, fears.

The symbolic association of plenitude with leisure resurfaces in the *Essais* with, appropriately, the essay "Of Idleness." For it is in the name of *pleine oysiveté* (I, 8, 33a) that Montaigne first retired to his family estate. "Idle fields" are also lush and fertile, he tells us at the beginning of the essay (*terres . . . grasses et fertilles*) [32a]. In "De la solitude" he qualifies retirement as "lush" and "plentiful": *en cette pleine et grasse rectraicte* (I, 39, 244a). The concept of plenitude in idleness is central for both Seneca and Epicurus, whom Montaigne praises as the only true philosophers of leisure in "De la solitude."[48] For the latter, wisdom requires detachment from "empty" desires, including ambition, which is endless and thus destined to lead to frustration.[49] The wise man seeks to free himself from desire, which always implies a lack. "J'essaye à n'avoir expres besoing de nul," writes Montaigne in "De la vanité." (III, 9, 968b). "Se *contentus* est sapiens," wrote Seneca.[50] The wise man is "contented"—literally full: "plenus est."[51] This plenitude in turn conditions absolute serenity, as Montaigne suggests by associating plenitude and idleness: "passer en repos . . . en pleine oysiveté" (I, 8, 33a). Seen in this light, Montaigne's rhetoric of uselessness, so often associated with idleness in the *Essais*,[52] becomes a paradoxical form of plenitude.

Much later, we find plenitude, meditation, and the gods (this time, Aristotle's) once again associated together:

> Le *mediter* est un puissant estude et *plein*, à qui sçait se taster et employer vigoureusement . . . Les plus grandes [âmes] en font leur vacation . . . C'est la besongne des Dieus, dict Aristote, de laquelle nait et leur beatitude et la nostre. (III, 3, 819c; emphasis added)
>
> [*Meditation* is a powerful and *full* study for anyone who knows how to examine and exercise himself vigorously. . . . The greatest minds make it their profession. . . . It is the occupation of the gods, says Aristotle, from which springs their happiness and ours.] (621–22; emphasis added)

Aristotle's gods present an example of a perfect synthesis of meditation, plenitude, and happiness—an ideal the leisured philosopher strives to emulate. In the *Nicomachean Ethics*, Aristotle argues that happiness is found in *schole*, the sole pursuit of the gods themselves—indeed, reasons Aristotle, the idea of the gods engaging in business is absurd.[53] Aristotelian *schole* has the dual meaning of "study" and "idleness," and because it is not telic, directed out toward an object that must be lacking, meditative study can thus be autotelic or "full."[54] Aristotle's gods are thus shown to resemble Lucretius's gods: both figures present a hyperbolic form of autotelic idleness: turned inward, they are the sole object of their sole activity (happiness).[55] They offered a powerful metaphor for someone who, like Montaigne, used idleness to study himself, to be the subject *and* object of his activity. No other entity appears as far removed from work, business, the telic world of everyday existence. Only the cannibals approach this degree of idleness, perhaps equally mythical in the way they are represented in the *Essais*. As Montaigne imagines how he would describe them to Plato, he begins by noting "it is a nation where there is no commerce," adding, "they know only idle pursuits."[56] Sprung straight from the gods (*"viri a diis recentes"*) [I, 31, 207c], the cannibals are themselves godlike. And they too are both subject and object of their defining activity. For in their act of cannibalism, the subject ultimately becomes its own object:

> J'ay une chanson faicte par un prisonnier, où il y a ce traict: qu'ils viennent hardiment trétous et s'assemblent pour disner de luy: car ils mangeront quant et quant leurs peres et leurs ayeux, qui ont servy d'aliment et de nourriture à son corps. Ces muscles, dit-il, cette cher et ces veines, ce sont les vostres, pauvres fols que vous estes . . . (I, 31, 212a)

> [I have a song composed by a prisoner which contains this challenge, that they should all come boldly and gather to dine off him, for they will be eating at the same time their own fathers and grandfathers, who have served to feed and nourish his body. "These muscles," he says, "this flesh and these veins are your own, poor fools that you are. . . ."] (158)

Montaigne thus gives a wide spectrum of highly metaphoric meanings to plenitude. An autotelic category, leisure is what cannibals share with the gods and what philosophers seek. It offers an end to humanity's endless pursuit of desire, a form of cultivation (learned leisure defined as plenitude through letters, as in Pliny's advice cited in "De la solitude"),[57] and an aesthetic ideal (the *Cornucopian Text*, to quote the title of Terence Cave's study). Finally, all of these meanings stand in for the obvious one: idleness is conceivable only within a context of material plenitude—which is of course the unnamed bedrock on which Montaigne's ethics of idleness rests. Taken together, the tight associations of idleness and plenitude offered a symbolic solution to a cultural dilemma. The absence of the religious ideal of leisure left the autonomous contemplative with a residual sense of incompleteness. With leisure no longer offering privileged access to the sacred, he searched for an alternative plenitude, a kind of consolation for the new sense of the emptiness of his leisure. Idleness in the *Essais* is thus accompanied by a promise of plenitude from the very beginning, when in the essay "Of Idleness," Montaigne first articulated the desire to seek *pleine oysiveté*, to allow his idle mind to find rest in itself *(s'arreter et rasseoir en soy)* [33a], to "stop" and be "reseated in itself."

This last metaphor of the mind *seated* in itself recalls Lucretius's depiction of the gods found at the beginning of book 3. Montaigne included this portrait of the idle gods in his index on the flyleaves. The description begins:

> apparet divum numen sedesque quietae
> . . . .
> omnia suppeditat porro natura neque ulla
> res animi pacem delibat tempore in ullo.

[before me appear the gods in their majesty and their peaceful abodes. . . . There moreover nature supplies everything, and nothing at any time impairs their peace of mind.][58]

Complete unto themselves, the gods reside in an abode of perfect serenity. Rather than abode, however, the Latin word is *sedes*—seat. Indeed, only a seated posture would conform to their existence of idleness and self-sufficiency. In the *Essais*, Montaigne observes that although they have our (human) face and limbs, these limbs are of no use to them—"Epicurus faict les dieux luisans . . . revestus d'une humaine figure et de nos membres, lesquels membres leur sont de nul usage" (II, 12, 516c) [Epicurus makes the gods shining . . . invested in human form and limbs like ours, which limbs are of no use to them] (383). Far from being a gratuitous detail, Montaigne's choice of the verb *s'asseoir* (I, 8) to characterize quietude assumes strong philosophical resonances. As in *De rerum natura*, a seated posture is a metonymy for complete serenity. To be seated is to be without disquiet, without the desire and need that propel human beings into a state of perpetual motion.

Later, Montaigne appears to revise the ideal of self-seatedness, claiming to prefer to meditate as he walks, to think with his feet: "Mes pensées dorment, si je les assis. Mon esprit ne va, si les jambes ne l'agitent" (III, 3, 828c) [My thoughts fall asleep if I make them sit down. My mind will not budge unless my legs move it] (629). It is for this reason, he says, that he would like to have a *promenoir* constructed in his tower library, a gallery one hundred paces long and twelve wide: "je pourroy facilement coudre à chaque costé une gallerie de cent pas de long et douze de large, à plein pied . . . Tout lieu retiré requiert un proumenoir" (III, 3, 828c) [I could easily add on to each side a gallery a hundred paces long and twelve wide, on the same level. . . . Every place of retirement requires a place to walk] (629).[59] Significantly, it was his indolence that prevented him from undertaking such a major construction. As he explains, if he ultimately chose not to construct this gallery, it was more because of the *trouble* this would entail than the cost. "Et, si je ne craignoy non plus le soing que la despense, le soing qui me chasse de toute besongne, je pourroy facilement coudre à chaque costé une gallerie . . ." (828c) [And if I feared the trouble no more than the expense, the trouble that drives me from all business, I could easily add on to each side a gallery . . .] (629)]. Like the abode or *seat* of the gods, his tower thus remained essentially a seat: "C'est là mon siege" (828c).

There is perhaps no Renaissance space that embodies leisure more than Montaigne's tower. Modern imaginations tend to form a mental picture of Montaigne leading an isolated existence far from mundane preoccupations. The "ivory tower" library may well be one of the most enduring *mythologies* associated with Montaigne. Yet George Hoffmann has recently directed our attention back to the actual space Montaigne inhabited when he was in his third-story library, and in particular, to the vistas afforded by its three windows, reminding us that Montaigne preferred to look back on the courtyard and main building of the chateau instead of across the solitary landscape that lay in the opposite direction.[60] Montaigne was clearly not a protoromantic gazing off into the distance. What he claims to have liked best about the tower was not its isolation, but rather the view it commanded of his household:

> . . . ma librairie, d'où tout d'une main je commande à mon mesnage. Je . . . vois soubs moy mon jardin, ma basse court, ma court, et dans la pluspart des membres de ma maison (III, 3, 828b)

> [. . . my library, from which at one sweep I command a view of my household. I am over the entrance, and see below me my garden, my farmyard, my courtyard, and into most of the parts of my house.] (629)

Removed from the world of work below him, he was nevertheless able to *supervise* his servants and peasants engaged in the activities on which his livelihood depended. Supervision, or at least vision, for looking is perhaps the most indolent of all the actions the human body is able to perform.[61]

Removed from the laborious and painful world inhabited by human beings, the gods also enjoy a secret existence, for they are invisible to the eyes of mortals. Montaigne emphasizes this fact in the passage quoted above, observing that Epicurus "makes the gods shining, *transparent* . . . (516c)." Hoffmann notes that, from below, it was impossible to know for sure if Montaigne was watching from the tower. This contributed to maintaining a *passive* pressure on the peasants laboring below in the interior courtyard or in the fields.[62] In effect then, when he was seated in the tower, his activities were secret; he too was invisible, *transparent*.

Besides being a majestic "seat," a post of observation, and the secret locus of idleness, what most characterizes the abode of the gods is its location. For they reside in an ethereal interspace, as Montaigne observes: "Epicurus faict les dieux . . . logez comme entre deux forts, entre deux mondes" (II, 12, 516c) [Epicurus makes the gods . . . lodged between two worlds as between two forts] (383). Montaigne must have found this detail all the more striking given his tower's situation. In the tower, he entertained the meditations and reflections that make up the *Essais*: "tantost je resve, tantost j'enregistre et dicte . . ." (III, 3, 828c). At the same time, the tower library was suspended between two distinct worlds, the courtyard and the fields. Each one had its own population: servants labored in the *basse-court* while hired hands and tenant farmers worked the fields. The site reserved for the essayist's *otium*, the tower library, occupied what was to all intents and purposes a kind of interspace.

A final characteristic of the seat of the gods, related to its location in an interspace, is the total absence of weather. In the passage from the beginning of book 3 singled out by Montaigne and discussed above, Lucretius emphasizes this fact:

> apparet divum numen sedesque quietae
> quas neque concutiunt venti nec nubila nimbis
> aspergunt neque nix acri concreta pruina
> cana cadens violat semperque innubilus aether
> integit, et large diffuso lumine ridet.

[before me appear the gods in their majesty and their peaceful abodes, which no winds ever shake nor clouds besprinkle with rain, which no snow congealed by the bitter frost mars with its white fall, but the air ever cloudless encompasses them and laughs with its light spread wide abroad.][63]

With no wind, rain, snow, frost, or even clouds, the gods' interspace is without any seasonal variation—without weather. Simple in appearance, this fact is essential to the utter peace they enjoy because, as Montaigne observes in his notes on the flyleaves, (external) weather influences (internal) emotional state: "Calor iram mouet aura frigida pauorem aër tranquillitatem animi" [Heat moves to anger; cold wind to fear, air, to peace of mind].[64] Mortals can only take shelter from the weather and resist its effect on emotional state; only the gods live in an ethereal zone entirely without weather and thus without mental unrest. In the *Essais*, Montaigne will return to this idea to qualify his own leisurely existence. Like Lucretius, he mingles this weatherless state with *tranquillitas animi*:[65]

> où qu'elle [son âme] jette sa veuë, *le ciel est calme* autour d'elle: nul desir, nulle crainte ou doubte *qui luy trouble l'air*, aucune difficulté [c] passée, presente, future par dessus laquelle son imagination ne passe sans offence. (III, 13, 1112b/c; emphasis added)

> [. . . wherever she (Montaigne's soul) casts her eyes, *the sky is calm* around her: *no desire, no fear or doubt to disturb the air* for her, no difficulty, past, present, or future, over which her imagination may not pass without hurt.] (854; emphasis added)

Following *De rerum natura*, Montaigne fashions a metaphor of absolute serenity conditioned by meteorological calm.

In the tower library, Montaigne was thus able to practice his own form of *imitatio dei*, emulating an ideal existence of self-sufficiency, serenity, and idleness. Invisible, seated in an ethereal interspace, watching, but not doing, Montaigne, the contemplative without gods, became a godlike contemplative.

But he also drew a more general lesson from *De rerum natura*. Following its movement from physics to ethics, it was on a material foundation (the tower) that Montaigne elaborated an ethical ideal (idleness). The Epicurean divinities could exist only because of the nature of their liminary space; their existence—and the philosophical ideal it embodied—was inseparable from precise material conditions that Lucretius was so careful to describe. Montaigne, in other words, knew that the idle self he wished to cultivate was not an impenetrable fortress. Without a "physics" conducive to idleness, no amount of Stoic detachment from the vagaries of the real could offer the guarantee of a perfectly intact, private self, however desirable such intimacy and absolute self-mastery might have been.[66]

The intersection of Montaigne's notes on *De rerum natura* with his conception of the tower thus departs from the definite Stoic resonances in Montaigne's discourse on idleness in the early *Essais*. To be sure, the essayist borrowed extensively from the *Epistles to Lucilius* (in "De la solitude" alone, one counts at least thirty quotations or allusions). Montaigne also praises Seneca himself as a true philosopher of *otium*, and defends an interior space (the famous *arriereboutique*) miraculously preserved from the slavery of public life along with the demands it makes on us. In forging a new medium—the essay—it was to Seneca's letters that Montaigne turned.[67] Short and open-ended, the Senecan epistle provided a poetic model particularly suited to an incorrigible *oisif* like Montaigne:

> Ils ont tous deux [Plutarch and Seneca] cette notable commodité pour mon humeur, que la science que j'y cherche, y est traictée à pieces décousues, qui ne demandent pas l'obligation d'un long travail, dequoy je suis incapable, comme sont les Opuscules de Plutarque et les Epistres de Seneque, qui est la plus belle partie de ses escrits, et la plus profitable. (II, 10, 413a)
>
> [They both have this notable advantage for my humor, that the knowledge I seek is there treated in detached pieces that do not demand the obligation of long labor, of which I am incapable. Such are the *Moral Essays* of Plutarch and the *Epistles* of Seneca, which are the finest part of his writings, and the most profitable.] (300)

Written by the philosopher of learned leisure for the idle reader, Seneca's *Epistles* not only shaped the conception of leisure for Montaigne, but framed the debate for his generation and social milieu: indeed, at roughly the same time as Montaigne was composing the early *Essais*, his brother-in-law Geoffroy de La Chassaigne, *sieur* de Pressac, had undertaken the first French translation of the *Epistles*. In 1580, Montaigne and La Chassaigne presented their books to the king, each one offering a form of Senecan wisdom to this monarch and his court.[68] The rigorous *otium* defended by Seneca found a sympathetic public in Montaigne's *robe* peers—for he elevated idleness to a new dignity, making retirement into a superior—though paradoxical—form of "affairs." To quote La Chassaigne's translation, "Je me suis retiré . . . Je fay les affaires de la posterité, en escrivant ce qui luy pourra estre profitable" [I retired . . . I do business for posterity, writing what will be useful to it].[69] This idea, expressed here in the eighth *Epistle*, is given a full development in Seneca's treatise *De otio*, printed at the end of *De vita beata* for most of the sixteenth century.[70] In short, Seneca constituted a natural authority for anyone, like Montaigne, interested in practicing idleness.

Yet the Lucretian intertext suggests a very different picture. The Senecan form and content of the early essays on leisure is belied by Montaigne's imaginary of the tower. The Stoic sage has faith in the autonomy and integrity of the self mastering the self: yet everything about the tower library suggests a very porous self in need of protection. Because the self is permeable, because a human being armed with philosophy cannot withstand a hostile environment, Epicurus instructs his students to retire to a privileged society of friends in a garden removed from the misfortunes accompanying life in the public sphere. Seneca preaches mental detachment while Epicurus advocates mental *and* physical detachment from a harmful environment. For what happens in the realm of public life also happens in the realm of physics, where atoms in constant motion crash into one other: the self is as vulnerable as one small atom in a sea of turbulence.[71] No mere act of Stoic fortitude can change this physical reality. As much a mental construct elaborated by the essayist as an architectural structure, Montaigne's tower served a function comparable to the Epicurean garden: protection for a self ever vulnerable to its physical surroundings. It reflected the Epicurean axiom that a life in the image of the gods can exist only within a space worthy of divinities.

Degrading Work

Finally, Montaigne made another marginal annotation beside a passage where Lucretius again invokes the idle gods with a string of rhetorical questions:

> nam pro sancta deum tranquilla pectora pace,
> quae placidum degunt aevom vitamque serenam,

> quis regere immensi summam, quis habere profundi
> indu manu validas potis est moderanter habenas,
> quis pariter caelos omnis convertere et omnis
> ignibus aetheriis terras suffire feracis . . .

[For I appeal to the holy hearts of the gods, which in tranquil peace pass untroubled days and a life serene: who is strong enough to rule the sum of the immeasurable, who to hold in hand and control the mighty bridle of the unfathomable? who to turn about all the heavens at one time and warm the fruitful worlds with ethereal fires. . . .][72]

Lucretius asks his reader to put into question the idea of all-powerful, all-controlling divinities. It is improbable, he suggests, that any entity could be powerful enough to accomplish such a feat *(who is strong enough . . . ?)*. But Montaigne focuses not on the (im)possibility of such a direct, hands-on involvement, but rather on its (in)-appropriateness, noting "la vacation de manier le trein de nature sieroit mal a dieu" [the occupation of handling natural processes would be ill-suited to god].[73] Lucretius suggests that intervening in natural processes would be beyond the gods' capacities; for Montaigne, it would be beneath them. We know from the *Essais* that work clearly belongs to the "lowest" of all genres—the farce. As he observes in "De mesnager sa volonté": "La plus part de nos vacations sont farcesques" (III, 10, 1011b) [Most of our occupations are low comedy] (773).

An overarching social prejudice against work thus surfaces in Montaigne's brief annotation and is echoed in the *Essais*. The meditative beatitude embodied by the gods thus becomes part of the processes of social distinction at work in Montaigne's world. Highlighting Lucretius's metaphor of "holding *in hand [indu manu]* the mighty bridle of the unfathomable," Montaigne stresses that "*handling [manier]* natural processes" would be unsuitable for divinities. In his own world, manual labor and the so-called mechanical arts, both techniques of controlling natural processes, were deemed to be the responsibility of peasants. The Third Estate alone produced the resources consumed by all members of society and took charge of the mechanical arts. If these forms of labor amount to *derogeance*, if they would be inappropriate for nobles, then they would be ill-suited indeed *(sieroit mal)* to a divinity.[74] In short, Montaigne's annotation suggests that it was out of aristocratic disdain that the gods refused any direct involvement in either the affairs of mortals or the natural processes of this world—all the more given the strictly material, even mechanistic, universe described by Lucretius.

In his own case, Montaigne claims to have sought refuge from business in his tower library:

> J'essaie à m'en rendre la domination pure, et à soustraire ce seul coin à la communauté et conjugale, et filiale, et civile. Par tout ailleurs je n'ay qu'une auctorité verbale: en essence, confuse. (III, 3, 828c)

> [I try to make my authority over it (his tower library) absolute, and to withdraw this one corner from all society, conjugal, filial, and civil. Everywhere else I have only a verbal authority, essentially divided.] (629)

Everywhere else *(par tout ailleurs)*, his responsibilities required him to become involved in the business of running the family estate. Yet even when playing the role of lord of the household, he specifies that he did not "handle" business. Instead, he exercised only his voice, an extremely mediated form of involvement: *je n'ay qu'une auctorité verbale*. Withdrawn from any direct (manual) contact with material processes, Montaigne proffered only his voice, which had an apparently doubtful effect *(une auctorité . . . en essence, confuse)*.[75]

The last reference to the hands of the gods projects idleness back into the realm of social practices of Montaigne's world. It suggests an overlap between the intertextual unconscious in the *Essais* (including *De rerum natura*) and Montaigne's own social unconscious (inflected by the broader context in which work and leisure were highly charged notions). In his praise of idleness in the early *Essais*, Montaigne ironically drew part of his conceptual repertoire from the world of ordinary business, the very antithesis of the leisure ethos his class wished to represent.[76]

Idleness out of Commerce

Commercial discourse and Epicurean representations of divine beatitude constitute the raw materials for Montaigne's private ideal of *pleine oysiveté*. Montaigne calls upon these two metaphorical registers to serve much the same ends: they grant the autonomous contemplative what I have been describing as symbolic compensation. With their close association to plenitude, both metaphorical registers offer consolation for the loss of sacred uses of contemplation. Idle gods and merchants project an idealized image of perfect completeness and specularity back to Montaigne, whose essays circle back onto their idle subject. Yet they also reveal a world marked by an increasingly imperious economic paradigm. Montaigne's private imagery of idleness remains tributary to the world of *négoces*, supposedly the antithesis of the distinctive art of idleness cultivated in his milieu. Montaigne can seek freedom in leisure (to recall the liberation vocabulary he used to characterize his retirement). But his leisure remains a derivative of work, not an escape to an elusive elsewhere. In other words, the essayist can subtly bend commerce toward idleness, but this deflection also confirms the force of the new ideological context in which it is work that constitutes the primary term.

The conclusion to "De l'oisiveté" presents one of the most striking examples of Montaigne's use of a vocabulary of *négoces* to figure idleness. At the end of the essay, he announces his decision to record the monsters and chimeras generated by his idle mind. This problematic dialogue with oneself inherent in his practice of idleness evokes the "ame contournable en soy mesme . . ." (I, 39, 241a). Yet Montaigne figures this dialogue—and thus his new existence of leisure—with a metaphor of bourgeois accounting: *mise en rolle*. The contemplative as bookkeeper thus meticulously records each of the monstrous and chimeric births of his idle mind in a *livre de raison*, a common fixture in bourgeois households. Montaigne himself refers to the practice of keeping a journal of family events, a so-called *livre de raison*, in "D'un default de nos polices":

> En la police œconomique mon pere avoit cet ordre, que je sçay loüer, mais nullement ensuivre. C'est qu'outre le registre des negoces du mesnage où se logent les menus comptes, payements, marchés, qui ne requierent la main du notaire, lequel registre un receveur a en charge, il ordonnoit à celuy de ses gens qui lui servoit à escrire, un papier journal à inserer toutes les survenances de quelque remarque, et jour par jour les memoires de l'histoire de sa maison, tres-plaisante à veoir quand le temps commence à en effacer la souvenance, et très à propos pour nous oster souvent de peine: quand fut entamée telle besoigne? quand achevée? quels trains y ont passé? combien arresté? noz voyages, noz absences, mariages, morts, la reception des heureuses ou malencontreuses nouvelles; changement des serviteurs principaux;

telles matieres. Usage ancien, que je trouve bon à refraichir, chacun en sa chacunière. Et me trouve un sot d'y avoir failly. (I, 35, 223–24c)

[In his domestic administration my father had this system, which I can praise but not follow: besides the record of household affairs kept by his steward, in which were entered petty accounts, payments, and transactions not requiring the notary's hand, he ordered the servant whom he used as his secretary to keep a journal and insert in it all occurrences of any note, and the memorabilia of his family history day by day. A record very pleasant to look at when time begins to efface the memory of events, and very well suited to get us out of perplexity: When was such and such a thing begun? When completed? What retinues came? How long did they stay? Our trips, our absences; marriages; deaths; the receipt of happy or unhappy news; the change of principal servants; such matters. An ancient custom, which I think it would be good to revive, each man in each man's home. And I think I am a fool to have neglected it.] (166)

Despite his claim to have neglected this family tradition *(me trouve un sot d'y avoir failly),* in reality Montaigne did continue the tradition of making notations in his family copy of Beuther's *Ephemeris historica* (1551). In fact, Montaigne decided to resume the practice of recording events in his family's *livre de raison* shortly after he left the Parlement of Bordeaux.[77] Beginning in 1572 he duly noted trips, absences, deaths, and marriages as well as important visitors to Montaigne. However, revealing *lapsus*, most of his own notes concern births—the one category not mentioned in his long list of household events in "D'un default de nos polices." And just as he noted all *births* (some seventeen in all)[78] in his family Beuther, so he duly noted the monstrous births in the *Essais*, the *livre de raison* of his idle mind: "il [Montaigne's mind] *m'enfante tant de monstres et chimeres . . . que j'ay commancé de les mettre en rolle*" (33a) [it (Montaigne's mind) gives birth to so many chimeras and fantastic monsters . . . that I have begun to put them in writing.] (21).[79]

Se retirer, retraite, retrait, retraité: the notion of retreat or retirement functions as a leitmotif in Montaigne's discourse on leisure. Retiring to one's country estate was, after all, the consummate gesture of idleness. But this figurative meaning was secondary to a more literal sense derived from the world of business. In its substantive form, "rectraict" could denote return to a place one had left. But the primary and "conventional" meaning refers to a commercial term of acquisition: *retraict* designates an agreement whereby a seller buys back what has already been sold.⁸⁰ In essence, this transaction functions much like a loan, since the object in circulation leaves—and then returns to—its original owner. Montaigne activates this meaning with his metaphor of the loan, writing "Mon opinion est qu'il se faut prester à autruy et ne se donner qu'à soy-mesme . . . *fugax rerum, securaque in otia natus*" (III, 10, 1003b); [My opinion is that we must lend ourselves to others and give ourselves only to ourselves . . . 'Fleeing affairs, and born in idle ease'] (767). Born in and for idleness, Montaigne periodically "loaned" himself to the public, serving as magistrate, then later mayor and royal counselor.

Emblematic of the broader changes underway, the story of Martha and Mary is reconfigured in the *Essais*. With her position of quiet adoration at Christ's feet, Mary had long personified the medieval ideal of the contemplative life (Luke 10:42). Montaigne recasts the idea of the "best share" with a metaphor drawn from the world of commercial exchanges, observing "[i]l se faut reserver une arriereboutique toute nostre, toute franche" (I, 39, 241a) [(W)e must reserve a back shop all our own, entirely free, in which to establish our real liberty] (177). The famous metaphor of the *arriereboutique* is an idiom from the everyday world of commerce, for it was a common merchant practice to keep the "back of the store" for the best merchandise, as Jean Nicot observes.⁸¹ With self-conscious irony, Montaigne reshapes idleness using a metaphorical register from the world of *négoces*. Reserving the best share for himself, he partakes of idleness much like a merchant who would withdraw his best stock from circulation, keeping it instead for personal enjoyment.

Montaigne draws these last three metaphors of idleness from commercial vocabulary and practices. However, in each case he gives a new interior finality to commerce, as though to make it compatible with idleness. The idle subject engages in commerce, and this commerce necessarily takes place with others. Yet the process is somehow magically recuperated without sacrificing either idleness or autonomy—indeed, the tower imagery stands as a reminder of the utopian dimensions of Montaigne's ideal of idleness, for it suggests the profound vulnerability of the idle self to worldly turbulence. On a purely discursive level, the essayist can nevertheless envisage a fictional interplay of commerce and idleness that contributes to the subject's plenitude rather than disrupting it. Thus, through *retrait*, the idle self which has been "on loan" to others is redeemed. If the self is a kind of capital in circulation, Montaigne fantasizes about its place in a self-enclosed circle that always returns it back to the point of origin: it can be "loaned," but not sold. With the back shop metaphor, Montaigne figures the idle merchant as his own wealthy client, keeping his best stock all for himself, although with the perhaps half conscious assumption that this kind of "withholding" can ultimately increase prices, following a monopolistic logic. Finally, with the metaphor of the *Essais* as household account, Montaigne borrows the *livre de raison* only to make it better serve the mind's turn inward. Rather than noting the affairs of the household, Montaigne's idle self records its own idle children, becoming a masculine mother (for Socrates, the prototype of the contemplative).

Thus, out of commerce, Montaigne forms idleness. Or, to restate this movement using the underlying social paradigms: out of bourgeois commerce, Montaigne fashions aristocratic idleness—a conceptual redefinition that echoes the recent social cursus of Montaigne's family, from his enterprising great-grandfather to his own nobility and *condition oisive*.[82] His ideal of full idleness reveals its debt to the world of commercial operations just as his own idleness was indebted to his family's past in *négoces*. Montaigne's idleness was, in a very real sense, not so much the antithesis as the *extension* of commerce. At the same time, if Montaigne's *imaginaire* of idleness remained tributary to *négoces*, it was also because leisure was increasingly dependent upon an economic paradigm.

Having rejected his century's constituted discourses of idleness, Montaigne turned to an enterprise of "bricolage." In redefining idleness, he drew from varied, even contradictory, sources. The rhetoric of leisure in the *Essais* is marked by the metaphorical registers derived from the world of *négoces* and extrapolated from Montaigne's annotations to his Lucretius. Idle gods and merchants do make strange companions, but Montaigne's intertextual play respects none of the rigid lines society may impose in the realm of the real. If these two sources were privileged, it was because of their intimate connection to plenitude—wealth, bounty, fullness, completeness: the proverbial best share, but defined in secular terms. With their connection to plenitude, these two discourses offered a symbolic compensation for the loss of the completeness that had long been the promise of the contemplative life. This ideal, as it was embodied by Epicurus's idle gods and Montaigne's idle merchants, offered the essayist an alternative model with which to figure his own earthly pursuit of leisure that might be paraphrased as "have leisure and know thyself."

The *Essais* offer no direct challenge to religious contemplation; they are not, like Epicurean philosophy, an explicit and categorical attack *contre la religion*, to quote Montaigne's own annotations to *De rerum natura*. But they do pursue the objective sketched out in the inscription that dedicated the years left to him, the years of the *Essais*, to *tranquillitas*, *otium*, and *libertas*, quietly displacing leisure's basis in the sacred.

The problems Montaigne faced in attempting to realize an art of idleness were already those of the modern world, with its increasingly invasive economic paradigm and the loss of the transcendent dimensions of leisure. Montaigne's attempt to seek recourse in a leisured self divorced from the world of work made him the first modern contemplative. Subjectivity continues to offer symbolic compensation for the nearly unchallenged supremacy of the economic paradigm. It promises that we can always escape to a private self that remains miraculously preserved from a purely "exterior" reality of total work. Yet Montaigne remained conscious of the vanity of his own gesture, of the illusory nature of his "escape" from work to the self. He elaborated a personal mythology of leisure associated with an imaginary interspace: for leisure could no longer exist outside of utopian spaces. The relegation of idleness to the realm of compensatory practices marked the new reign of *homo œconomicus*.

Notes

INTRODUCTION

1. Ellery Schalk studies the Renaissance aristocracy as a functional class, a group that derived its identity from its social occupation in *From Valor to Pedigree: Ideas of Nobility in France in the Sixteenth and Seventeenth Centuries* (Princeton: Princeton University Press, 1986). On the robe, see for instance, Jonathan Dewald, *The Formation of a Provincial Nobility: The Magistrates of the Parliament of Rouen, 1499–1610* (Princeton: Princeton University Press, 1980). On the robe versus sword polemic, see James Supple, *Arms Versus Letters: The Military and Literary Ideals in the 'Essais' of Montaigne* (Oxford: Clarendon Press, 1984). On women's work, see Ann Rosalind Jones, *The Currency of Eros: Women's Love Lyric in Europe, 1540–1620* (Bloomington: Indiana University Press, 1990), esp. chapter 1; and Gisèle Mathieu-Castellani, *La Quenouille et la lyre* (Paris: José Corti, 1998).

2. "[P]our eviter ociosité j'ay escript," Hélisenne de Crenne, *Les Epîtres familières et invectives*, ed. Jerry Nash (Paris: Champion, 1996), 126; Herberay des Essarts explains how he read *Amadis de Gaula* "pour eviter la pernitieuse oysiveté" and then decided to translate the Spanish romance into French, "Prologue," *Le Premier Livre d'Amadis de Gaule*, ed. Hugues Vaganay and Yves Giraud (Paris: Nizet, 1986), vol. 1, xi; "Quant à moy tant en escrivant premierement ces jeunesses que en les revoyant depuis, je n'y cherchois autre chose qu'un honneste passetems et moyen de fuir oisiveté . . ." Louise Labé, *Œuvres complètes*, ed. François Rigolot (Paris: Flammarion, 1986), 43; "Sy ne veulx-je pourtant demeurer ocieux, / Ains comme je pourray je veulx laisser memoire / Que les Muses jadis m'ont aquis une gloire . . ." Pierre de Ronsard, "Elégie à Pierre l'Escot," in *Le Second livre des poèmes*, *Œuvres complètes*, ed. Paul Laumonier, (Paris: Droz, 1939), vol. 10, 300, vv. 4–6; in "De l'oisiveté" (I, 8), Montaigne relates how, during a period of extended idleness, he first began to compose the as yet unnamed *Essais*.

3. Examples of this way of framing the problem of leisure include Glyn Norton, *Montaigne and the Introspective Mind* (The Hague: Mouton, 1975); Michael Andrew Screech, *Montaigne and Melancholy: The Wisdom of the Essays* (London: Duckworth, 1983; reprint, Selinsgrove: Susquehanna University Press, 1984). André Tournon suggests interpreting Montaigne's ethic of idleness in light of the concept of "souci de soi," a concept that he links to the development of a "phenomenology of consciousness." See his "Vacances intérieures: L'*Essai* du loisir," in *Les Loisirs et l'héritage de la culture classique* (Actes du XIIIe Congrès de l'Association Guillaume Budé), ed. Jean-Marie André, Jacqueline Dangel, and Paul Demont (Brussels: Latomus, 1996), 559–66. Fausta Garavini examines the "monsters" born out of Montaigne's idle mind as a key to understanding the essayist's

unconscious. Garavini's study sheds new light on subjectivity in the *Essais*, understood in its Freudian sense as the locus of conflict, power, and desire. Her study, *Monstres et chimères: Montaigne, le texte et le fantasme*, trans. Isabel Picon (Paris: Champion, 1993) begins with a subtle reading of the essay "Of Idleness."

4. *The Theory of the Leisure Class* (1899; reprint, New York: Macmillan Company, 1917).

5. George Hoffmann, *Montaigne's Career* (Oxford: Clarendon Press, 1998); Philippe Desan, *Les Commerces de Montaigne: Le Discours économique des "Essais"* (Paris: Nizet, 1992).

6. Cathy Yandell, *Carpe Corpus: Time and Gender in Early Modern France* (Newark: University of Delaware Press, 2000), 128–74; see also Gary Ferguson, "Le Chapelet et la plume, ou, quand la religieuse se fait écrivain: le cas du prieuré de Poissy (1562–1621)," *Revue du Seizième Siècle* 19, no. 2 (2001): 83–99.

7. For a discussion of these questions in a medieval context, see Penelope D. Johnson, *Equal in Monastic Profession: Religious Women in Medieval France* (Chicago: University of Chicago Press, 1991).

8. Max Weber, *The Protestant Ethic and the Spirit of Capitalism* (1930; reprint, New York: Routledge, 1992); R. H. Tawney, *Religion and the Rise of Capitalism* (New York: Harcourt, Brace & Co., 1952).

9. See, for instance, Max Engammare, "Organisation du temps et discipline horaire chez Calvin et à Genève au XVIe siècle," *Bibliothèque de l'Ecole des Chartes* 157 (1999): 341–67.

10. See André Gorz, *Métamorphoses du travail: Quête du sens* (Paris: Galilée, 1988); Alain Lebaube, *Le Travail: Toujours moins ou autrement* (Paris: Le Monde Editions, 1997); Alain Lipietz, *La Société en sablier* (Paris: La Découverte, 1996); Jacques Robin, *Quand le travail quitte la société post-industrielle* (Paris: GRIT, 1993); Daniel Mothé, *L'Utopie du temps libre* (Paris: Esprit, 1997). The number of editions Lafargue's short treatise, *Le Droit à la paresse*, has known in the past ten years speaks of the prominent place leisure occupies in contemporary French political and cultural sensitivities. Most recently, Paul Lafargue's *Le Droit à la paresse* has been published in a collection devoted exclusively to essays in defense of idleness (Paris: Editions Allia, 2001).

11. Dominique Méda, *Le Travail, une valeur en voie de disparition* (Paris: Flammarion, 1998), 193–94.

12. See Ernst Robert Curtius, *European Literature and the Latin Middle Ages*, trans. Willard R. Trask (London: Routledge & Kegan Paul, 1953), 88.

13. *Les Diverses Leçons de Pierre Messie*, trans. Claude Gruget (Paris: Estienne Groulleau, 1554). See also Pierre de La Primaudaye, "De L'Oisiveté, et Paresse, & du Jeu," in *L'Academie françoise* (Paris: Guillaume Chaudière, 1581), 177–82; and Jean des Caurres, "De l'oisiveté, & maux procedans d'icelle," in *Œuvres morales et diversifiées* (Paris: Guillaume Chaudière, 1575).

14. For a gentleman, "le propre est de vivre de ses rentes, ou du moins de ne point vendre sa peine et son labeur . . ." Loyseau, *Traité des ordres et simples dignitez*, quoted in Etienne Dravasa, *"Vivre noblement": Recherches sur la dérogeance de noblesse du XIVe au XVIe siècles* (Bordeaux: chez l'auteur, 1965), 165.

15. This illustration of Lady Idleness was used in a large number of editions of *Le Roman de la Rose* printed during the Renaissance. See F. W. Bourdillon, *The Early Editions of "The Roman de la Rose"* (London: Chiswick Press, 1906).

16. The importance of the classical heritage on subsequent traditions has been brought to the fore by the recent collection of essays in *Les Loisirs et l'héritage de la culture classique*, ed. André, Dangel, and Demont. For an assessment of *otium* in the culture of ancient Rome, see Jean-Marie André, *L'Otium dans la vie morale et intellectuelle romaine* (Paris: Presses Universitaires de France, 1966). See also Michael O'Loughlin, *The Garlands of Repose: The Literary Celebration of Civic and Retired Leisure—The Traditions of Homer and Vergil, Horace and Montaigne* (Chicago: University of Chicago Press, 1978). A very broad summary of the history of leisure is provided by Byron Dare, George Welton, and William Coe, *Concepts of Leisure in Western Thought* (Dubuque: Kendall/Hunt, 1987).

17. "S'efforce qui voudra le laurier meriter, / Quant à moy, ie n'escris sinon pour eviter / Les trompeuses douceurs d'une langueur oisive." Pibrac, *Les Quatrains de Pibrac suivis de ses autres poésies*, ed. Jules Claretie (Paris: Alphonse Lemerre, 1874), 110.

18. "Lettre à Abel L'Angelier," in *Les Missives*, ed. Anne R. Larsen (Geneva: Droz, 1999), 108.

19. Arlette Jouanna, *L'Idée de race en France au XVIème siècle et au début du XVIIème siècle (1498–1614)* (Paris: Champion, 1976); also see Jouanna's *Le Devoir de révolte* (Paris: Fayard, 1989) and *La France du XVIe siècle, 1483–1598* (Paris: Presses Universitaires Françaises, 1996); George Huppert, *Les Bourgeois Gentilshommes* (Chicago: University of Chicago Press, 1977).

20. Evelyne Berriot-Salvadore, *Les Femmes dans la société française de la Renaissance* (Geneva: Droz, 1990).

21. Glending Olson, *Literature as Recreation in the Later Middle Ages* (Ithaca: Cornell University Press, 1982).

22. Jean Baudrillard, for instance, in *La Société de consommation: Ses mythes, ses structures* (Paris: SGPP, 1970).

23. I borrow Josef Pieper's notion of "total work," used to characterize the extent to which work has "invaded and taken over the whole realm of human action and of human existence as a whole." *Leisure: The Basis of Culture*, trans. Gerald Malsbary (South Bend: St. Augustine's Press, 1998), 6.

Chapter 1. Aristocratic Idleness

"Glossaire," *Œuvres* (Paris: Gallimard, 1995), 1789.

1. "[l]es gentilz hommes ne doyvent estre oyseux." "Troisième Epistre," in *Epistres morales & familieres du Traverseur* (Poitiers: Jacques Bouchet, 1545), 8–9. Unless otherwise indicated, all translations will be mine.

2. Des Caurres describes degenerate aristocrats as "faineans, inutiles, dissolus en delices." Book II, ch. 16 ("Des Enfans qui meurent devant aage Competant"), 102v-103r.

3. Nobles become "insolens, & par opulence & oisiveté delitieux, superflus, & effeminez," *Enseignements d'Isocrates et Xenophon [. . .] pour bien regner en paix et en guerre* (Paris: Michel de Vascosan, 1568), 59. In 1560 the Third Estate of Epernay demanded that "les gentilzhommes oyseuz et sans service au Roy payent tailles comme les roturiers." Quoted in Davis Bitton, *The French Nobility in Crisis, 1560–1640* (Stanford: Stanford University Press, 1969), 6.

4. Renaissance prologues reiterate exhortations that sword nobles (the intended public, at least initially) "work virtuously in their estate," to quote the preface to the 1533 *Lancelot* (Paris: Jean Petit [& Philippe le Noir], 1533); another prologue promises to help readers avoid idleness: "pour eviter oysiveté mère et nourrice des vices." *L'Histoire de Giglan* (Paris: Gilles et Jacques Huguetan freres, 1528); Jacques Gohory states succinctly that the *Amadis* books "conseillent le travail & exercice de guerre, abhorrent l'oysiveté." *Le Treizieme Livre traduit nouvellement d'Espagnol en Francois par JGP* (Paris: Estienne Groulleau, 1571).

5. Jean de Caumont (Paris: Jean Charron, 1586), 6r.

6. As Parlamente points out in the preface to the *Heptaméron*: "si nous n'avons quelque occupation plaisante et vertueuse, nous sommes en danger de devenir malades." Ed. Renja Salminen (Geneva: Droz, 1999), 8.

7. Catherine Velay-Vallantin summarizes the existing evidence for and against this theory, concluding that the tale of Bluebeard was formed out of a synthesis of Gilles de Rais's story and another tale of a jealous husband who murders his young wife. *L'Histoire des contes* (Paris: Fayard, 1992), 72–76.

8. He was found guilty of invoking demons, heresy, apostasy, sodomy, and violation of the Church's immunities by the ecclesiastical judges; the civil authorities found him guilty of the rape and murder of children. Eugène Bossard, *Gilles de Rais, Maréchal de France, dit Barbe-Bleue (1404–1440)* (Paris: Champion, 1885), 315; 224.

9. Bossard, *Gilles de Rais*, LVIII. I consulted Pierre Klossowski's translation into French for my own English translation. Georges Bataille, *Le Procès de Gilles de Rais* (1965; reprint, Paris: Pauvert, 1979), 252.

10. In his chapter entitled "De l'Oisiveté, & Paresse, & du Jeu," Pierre de La Primaudaye explains that becoming accustomed to idleness before judgment is formed by "la vraye intelligence" is extremely dangerous. Idleness may pervert judgment, making one unable to judge between virtue and vice. Living in idleness (*oisiveté*), one becomes bewitched (*ensorcellé*), falling prey to "faulses voluptez" that cause "plus grand nombre de douleurs & miseres," *L'Academie françoise* (Paris: Guillaume Chaudière, 1581; reprint, Geneva: Slatkine Reprints, 1972), 177v. According to Jean Des Caurres, "[les pères] doivent traiter leurs enfans en peine, & leur accouster les travaux." *Œuvres morales et diversifiées*, 50. For a discussion of the importance of *habitus* in moral philosophy, see Ullrich Langer, *Vertu du discours, discours de la vertu: Littérature et philosophie morale au XVIe siècle en France* (Geneva: Droz, 1999), esp. 28–29.

11. The belief that gluttony and lechery were "born from" idleness was widely shared. A fourteenth-century preacher's handbook apparently of Franciscan authorship emphasizes this cause-and-effect relationship. *Fasciculus Morum: A Fourteenth-Century Preacher's Handbook*, ed. and trans. Siegfried Wenzel (University Park: Pennsylvania State University Press, 1989), 398–99.

12. Bossard provides the inventory of Gilles de Rais's personal library in *Gilles de Rais*, 12.

13. Valerius Maximus, *Faits et paroles mémorables*, trans. C. A. F. Frémion (Paris: C. L. F. Panckoucke, 1835), vol. III, 232–34.

14. Bossard, *Gilles de Rais*, 60–97.

15. Ibid., 96–98.

16. The potlatch being, for Bataille, an extreme example of expenditure: "la

richesse apparaît comme acquisition en tant qu'un pouvoir est acquis par l'homme riche mais elle est entièrement dirigée vers la perte en ce sens que ce pouvoir est caractérisé comme pouvoir de perdre. C'est seulement par la perte que la gloire et l'honneur lui sont liés." "La Notion de dépense," in *La Part maudite* (Paris: Minuit, 1967), 34–35.

17. Bataille's theoretical inquiry is intentionally unclassifiable, borrowing as it does from anthropology, mysticism, and political economy. Bataille compared *La Part maudite* (which he considered to be his most important work) to a treatise of political economy while emphasizing his treatment of a broad range of phenomena generally excluded from the discipline. "I did not consider facts from the point of view of qualified economists," he stated. "My approach regarded human sacrifice, the construction of a church, or the gift of a jewel, as bearing no less interest than the sale of wheat." Quoted in Michèle Richman, *Reading Georges Bataille: Beyond the Gift* (Baltimore: Johns Hopkins University Press, 1982), 2.

18. "Gilles de Rais n'est pas seulement le monstrueux criminel, il est le prodigue insensé: la prodigalité est comme une ivresse. Jean de Craon [the grandfather who raised Gilles de Rais] avait pensé que, devenant un homme de premier plan, il saurait s'assagir: mais l'importance qu'il reçoit effectivement lui sert à s'enivrer davantage, elle le mène à céder sans mesure au besoin d'émerveiller par de magnifiques et féeriques dépenses." *Le Procès de Gilles de Rais*, 30.

19. Ibid., 49–50.

20. War, Bataille observes, had become the work *(le travail)* of the many, a *technè* unworthy of aristocrats. The feudal world, he concludes, could not be separated from immoderation *(la démesure)*. Ibid., 51–53.

21. Bataille's first gesture in "La Notion de dépense" is thus to demonstrate the "Insuffisance du principe de l'utilité classique." *La Part maudite*, 25–28.

22. See Bourdieu, *Esquisse d'une théorie de la pratique, précédé de trois études d'ethnologie kabyle* (Geneva: Droz, 1972), 171–83; *La Distinction* (Paris: Minuit, 1982); and *Raisons pratiques* (Paris: Seuil, 1994).

23. Kristen Neuschel discusses the significance of honor as part of a global pursuit of gain, provided this "gain" be understood to encompass both material and symbolic capital. "Nobles were 'rational' in their pursuit of gain. But we must work to understand what 'gain' meant to them and what means to pursue gain felt useful to them. Nobles' rationality in these matters bears little resemblance to current notions of economic rationality, and must be carefully delineated in its own terms." *Word of Honor: Interpreting Noble Culture in Sixteenth-Century France* (Ithaca: Cornell University Press, 1989), 18.

24. See Bourdieu's discussion of symbolic capital in *Esquisse d'une théorie de la pratique, précédé de trois études d'ethnologie kabyle*.

25. For a discussion of the vulnerability of Bataille's notion of the general economy, see Scott Cutler Shershow, "Of Sinking: Marxism and the 'General' Economy," *Critical Inquiry* 27, no. 3 (2001): 468–92. Shershow argues that "general" economics seems always circumscribed by a restricted economy and thus implicated with the ideas it claims to question.

26. Georges Duby, *Les Trois ordres ou l'imaginaire du féodalisme* (Paris: Gallimard, 1978), 42–43, 15.

27. Duby points to the appearance of a technical term *armiger* (squire) in the last quarter of the twelfth century. This term designated men who were born noble

but who were not knights. It thus signaled a distinction between noble status and the nobility's military specialization. Thus, in Chrétien's *Erec*, the word chivalry designated the military vocation while in *Perceval* the notion transcends the realm of concrete occupations in order to partake of an abstract, courtly ideal. Ibid., 354, 360.

28. In the earliest formulations, only prayer was deemed "leisure," and this leisure was necessary to all of society. Sustained by peasants and protected by noblemen, the clergy reciprocated with prayer, for only through their prayers could peasants and noblemen have their sins pardoned. With the feudal "revolution," however, a generalization of the privilege of leisure to all members of the nobility was necessary in order to justify (or rationalize) new modes of production. Ibid., 57–58, 61, 188–200. Duby believes that the agent in this transformation was the turbulent class of "jeunes," as he writes in a passage that recalls Bataille's vision of aristocratic excess. "Des gens de guerre vivant sur le pays, le saignant, forçant les paysans, libres ou non, à produire toujours davantage, pour procurer par leur travail les plaisirs de la vie à quoi les combattants professionnels n'ont pas renoncé, pour satisfaire le goût aristocratique du luxe et du gaspillage, qui ne peut plus s'assouvir dans les razzias extérieures. Et c'est là l'aspect économique," 188.

29. In 1190 the third function included *labor* and, principally, *negotium*. Ibid., 388–89.

30. "Chevaliers et clerc sans faille / Vivent de ce qu'ils [les paysans] travaillent." Etienne de Fougères, *Livre des manières* (ca. 1174–78). Quoted in Ibid., 342.

31. The identity of its author, *Guillaume de Lorris*, remains a mystery. K. A. Ott argued that he was a bourgeois, excluded from the society he purported to describe, but this hypothesis has been criticized, notably by Jean Batany in "Miniature, allégorie, idéologie: 'Oiseuse' et la mystique monacale récupérée par la 'classe de loisir,'" in *Etudes sur le Roman de la Rose de Guillaume de Lorris*, ed. Jean Dufournet (Geneva: Slatkine, 1984), 30–33.

32. Thérèse Bouché discusses the absence of prowess among the aristocratic virtues praised in the *Roman de la Rose* in "Les Personnages d'Oiseuse et Déduit dans le *Roman de la Rose* de Guillaume de Lorris," in *Les Loisirs et l'héritage de la culture classique*, ed. André, Dangel, and Demont, 491.

33. *Jardin*, according to the *Trésor de la Langue Française*, entered the French language only in the twelfth century to mean "terrain généralement clos, où l'on cultive des végétaux utiles ou d'agrément": from *gart*: or *clôture*.

34. "Lors m'en alai grant aleüre, / acernant la compasseüre / et la cloison dou mur querré / tant c'un huisset mout bien serré / trovai, petitet et estroit." Guillaume de Lorris, *Le Roman de la Rose*, ed. Felix Lecoy, vol. 1 (Paris: Champion, 1976), vv. 511–15. [Then I set off in great haste, skirting the enclosure and the wall that surrounded it on all sides until I found a very cramped, small, and narrow little door. Guillaume de Lorris, *The Romance of the Rose,* trans. Frances Horgan (Oxford: Oxford University Press, 1994), 10]. Quotes from the *Roman de la Rose* will be from Lecoy's edition and Horgan's translation. Verse and page numbers from the French and English texts respectively will be included after each citation.

35. Robertson and his students interpreted Oiseuse as a figure for *Luxuria*, a mortal danger for the Christian soul. (See D. W. Robertson Jr., *A Preface to Chaucer* [Princeton: Princeton University Press, 1962]; Charles Dahlberg, "Love and

the Roman de la Rose," *Speculum* 44 [1969]: 568–84; John V. Fleming, *The Roman de la Rose: A Study in Allegory and Iconography* [Princeton: Princeton University Press, 1969]). However, more recent scholarship rejects this (negative) assessment based on *Luxuria*, interpreting Oiseuse instead as an ambiguous figure if not an altogether positive one. She has thus been hailed as the emblem of an aristocratic existence (Armand Strubel, *Le Roman de la Rose* [Paris: Presses Universitaires de France, 1984]; as a figure for religious contemplation (Jacques Ribard, "Introduction à une étude polysémique du *Roman de la Rose* de Guillaume de Lorris," in *Etudes de langue et de littérature du Moyen Age offertes à Félix Lecoy* [Paris: Champion, 1973]); or as a combination thereof (Batany, "Miniature, allégorie, idéologie".) Thérèse Bouché provides a useful summary of these and other scholarly assessments of Oiseuse in "Les Personnages d'Oiseuse et Déduit," 492–94.

36. Thérèse Bouché suggests a parallel between the carefully groomed Oiseuse and the narrator himself, a parallel that seems to vindicate Oiseuse of narcissism. "Les Personnages d'Oiseuse et Déduit," 495. For a broad discussion of the aristocracy's aesthetic impulse, see Domna Stanton, *The Aristocrat as Art* (New York: Columbia University Press, 1980). Focusing on the *honnête homme* and the dandy, she studies how the aristocrat uses the self as a canvas. "Every signifier which the aristocrat can control—looks, clothing, gesture, manners, speech—will be recruited into the expression of his superiority," 5.

37. Veblen, *The Theory of the Leisure Class*, 35–67.

38. Very little is known about Guillaume de Deguilleville beyond the scant biographical details he includes in the *Pèlerinage de vie humaine*, the *Pèlerinage de l'âme*, and the *Pèlerinage de Jhesucrist*. For a summary of this evidence, see Edmond Faral, "Guillaume de Digulleville, moine de Chaalis," *Histoire littéraire de la France: Ouvrage commencé par des religieux bénédictins de la congrégation de Saint-Maur* 39 (1962): 1–11.

39. "En veillant avoie lëu / Considere et bien vëu / Le biau roumans de la Rose. / Bien croi que ce fu la chose / Qui plus m'esmut a ce songier / Que ci apres vous vueil nuncier." [While awake I had read, considered, and seen well the beautiful romance of the Rose. I believe that it was indeed the cause that most moved me to have this dream, which I want to recount to you below.] Guillaume de Deguilleville, *Pèlerinage de vie humaine*, ed. J. J. Stürzinger, Roxburghe Club, no. 124 (London: J. B. Nichols & Sons, 1893), vv. 7–14. This edition was printed from a fourteenth-century manuscript (BNF, *fonds franç.* no. 1818). All citations will be from this edition.

40. The *Pèlerinage de vie humaine* was one of the most popular allegories of the later Middle Ages, with fifty-three extant manuscripts of the first recension and eight of the second. Sylvia Huot, *The "Romance of the Rose" and its Medieval Readers: Interpretation, Reception, Manuscript Transmission* (Cambridge: Cambridge University Press, 1993), 226. Deguilleville composed the first recension (1330) for a lay public; the second appeared twenty-five years later with substantial changes and an explicit rejection of the *Roman de la Rose*, denounced as the work of Venus. Faral compares the two versions in "Guillaume de Digulleville, moine de Chaalis," 29–48. My discussion will focus on the first recension.

41. See Pierre-Yves Badel, who describes the *Pèlerinage de vie humaine* as an *Anti-Roman de la Rose*. *Le Roman de la Rose au XIVe siècle: Etude de la réception*

de l'œuvre (Geneva: Droz, 1980), 362–76; Huot, *The "Romance of the Rose" and its Medieval Readers*, 207–38; Steven Wright, "Deguileville's *Pèlerinage de vie humaine* as 'Contrepartie Edifiante' of the *Roman de la Rose*," *Philological Quarterly* 68, no. 4 (1989): 399–422; and Marion Lofthouse, "*Le Pèlerinage de Vie Humaine*, by Guillaume de Deguileville," *Bulletin of The John Rylands Library* 19 (1935): 170–215.

42. Boredom still had strong moral connotations. The preacher's handbook (roughly contemporaneous to the *Pèlerinage de vie humaine*) defines *acedia* partly as "boredom with respect to the good" *(accidea est tedium boni)*. *Fasciculus Morum*, 398–99.

43. It should be noted that the Church itself was not immune to secularizing trends. Just as secular culture absorbed elements from sacred institutions (Guillaume de Lorris's courtly "abbey" being an example), so too did religious institutions borrow from the secular sphere, sometimes even precipitating secularization. The papal court established in Avignon in 1309 thus closely resembles what we now know as the "modern court"—with its display of luxury and leisure. Here ecclesiastical princes from across Europe with no vocation other than that of serving the court's interest resided alongside beautiful women in an atmosphere of pomp and splendor. This court laid the seeds that were to flower in the court of François I, where women assumed a powerful role. According to Werner Sombart, whose analysis I have been paraphrasing, the "modern court society" was the result of a synthesis of gallantry, intrigue, and luxury. And the decisive factor in this formula was the role played by women at court, liberated from the strict confines of the domestic sphere and the domestic labor it implied. Hence the Pilgrim's observation in the *Pèlerinage* that Lady Idleness cared nothing for spinning and other labor. Werner Sombart, *Luxury and Capitalism* (1938; reprint, Ann Arbor: University of Michigan Press, 1967).

44. In ushering the pilgrim into a horrible place peopled by the Seven Deadly Sins personified, Idleness admits the pilgrim to the Garden of Delight, as in the *Roman de la Rose*, but seen from the soul's point of view rather than the body's. Wright, "Deguileville's *Pèlerinage*," 408.

45. Reinhard Kuhn, *The Demon of Noontide: Ennui in Western Literature* (Princeton: Princeton University Press, 1976), 53.

46. The *Pèlerinage* reflects the Church's ambiguous position regarding work in the later Middle Ages. In the period of commercial growth from the eleventh through the fourteenth centuries, the Church undertook a valorization of trades: each trade was given a patron saint, and commerce itself was less morally stigmatized. Yet despite a theoretical and spiritual justification of trades and even commerce, they continued to bear a social stigma, a view the Church shared with secular elites. On this ambiguity, see Jacques Le Goff, "Métiers licites et métiers illicites dans l'Occident médiéval," in *Pour un autre Moyen Age: Temps, travail et culture en Occident* (Paris: Gallimard, 1977), 91–107.

47. The popularity of the *Roman de la Rose* during the Renaissance will be discussed below. As for the *Pèlerinage de vie humaine*, like many other verse narratives, it was translated into prose in the fifteenth century: this version was the only one to be printed during the Renaissance. Three initial editions of the prose version were printed in 1485, 1486 (both in Lyons), and 1499 (Paris). Another printed and revised version came out in 1499 (Lyons); Antoine Vérard printed the

Pèlerinage de vie humaine followed by the *Pèlerinage de l'âme* in 1499. Two more editions appeared in the beginning of the sixteenth century, both based on a revised version of all three books undertaken by an anonymous monk. Faral, "Guillaume de Digulleville, moine de Chaalis," 130–31.

48. Josse Clichtove, *Le Traicté de la vraye noblesse* (Paris: Jean Longis, 1539).

49. "In sixteenth-century France . . . nobility was viewed quite differently then from what most scholars have assumed: it was thought of much more as a profession or function—something one did—rather than something one inherited." Schalk, *From Valor to Pedigree*, xiv.

50. Michel de Montaigne, *Les Essais*, ed. Pierre Villey and V.-L. Saulnier (Paris: Presses Universitaires de France, 1965), II, 7, 384a. *The Complete Essays of Montaigne*, trans. Donald Frame (Stanford: Stanford University Press, 1958), 277. Unless otherwise indicated, all translations from the *Essais* will be Frame's. Page numbers will be placed in parentheses following quotes.

51. Supple, *Arms Versus Letters*.

52. See James Wood, *The Nobility of the "Election" of Bayeux, 1463–1666* (Princeton: Princeton University Press, 1980), 11–12. Arlette Jouanna estimates that the percentage of noblemen actually performing military services oscillated between 6 and 30 percent. *La France du XVIe siècle*, 61–62. As Jonathan Dewald points out, "Even those most committed to ideals of military glory accepted that there were other valid forms of high status." *The European Nobility, 1400–1800* (Cambridge: Cambridge University Press, 1996), 35.

53. Less equivocal than Montaigne, Alcofrybas Nasier wistfully proclaims his own affinity for aristocratic idleness, which consists of: "faire grand chere, pas ne travailler, poinct ne [se] soucier, bien enrichir [ses] amis et tous gens de bien et de sçavoir." Rabelais, *Gargantua* (Lyons: François Juste, 1542), cited as a variant by Ruth Calder and Michael Andrew Screech, eds., (Geneva: Droz, 1970), 47.

54. Arlette Jouanna summarizes the importance of the aristocracy's status as a nonworking estate in the following terms: "Le noble, c'est d'abord un homme libre, ou plutôt libéré par le travail des autres, exempt des servitudes ordinaires de la condition humaine; un homme qui peut se redresser de toute sa stature, regarder plus haut que le sillon, l'établi ou le comptoir, et se consacrer de façon désintéréssée à la culture de son corps ou de son esprit, ou des deux à la fois. A la limite, un être inutile: si l'on prend la mesure de l'utilité par celle du travail rural ou artisanal, ou par celle du commerce." *L'Idée de race en France,* 232.

55. Ibid., 171.

56. Ibid., 187; Jouanna, *La France du XVIe siècle*, 61. See also Jouanna's *Le Devoir de révolte* (Paris: Fayard, 1989).

57. The risk in reducing nobility to a mere function was that it could then have been annulled if this function was not upheld. In other words, to be a nobleman one would have had to be a warrior. The lawyer Jean Lange used precisely this line of argument to attack the nobility at the Estates General in 1560: the nobility was a military function; therefore, those noblemen who did not perform military service should neither call themselves noble nor enjoy all the privileges thereof. Jouanna, *Le Devoir de révolte*, 44.

58. "Le principe de qualité détermine donc un classement qui se superpose à celui des professions et le transcende; on passe ainsi du *faire* à l'*être*. La noblesse, ici, n'est plus une fonction, mais une excellence humaine, ou une 'vertu.'" *La France du XVIe siècle*, 58–59.

59. Montaigne would have had occasion to observe such laws, perhaps even firsthand. While he was serving as mayor, a council was held in Bordeaux in 1583 to address the problem of public works for beggars. Its conclusion was predictable: the unemployed poor should be *"employés* à un travail utile." See Jean-Pierre Gutton, *La Société et les pauvres en Europe* (Paris: Presses Universitaires de France, 1974), 120.

60. *Les Vies des hommes illustres Grecs et Romains*, trans. Jacques Amyot (Paris: Michel de Vascosan, 1559), 38r. The anonymous speaker in this passage is identified as Herondas: "Hérondas se trouvant à Athènes alors qu'on venait d'y condamner quelqu'un pour cause d'oisiveté, et apprenant la chose, se fit montrer 'cet homme reconnu coupable d'avoir vécu en homme libre.'" *Œuvres morales*, vol. III, trans. François Fuhrmann (Paris: Les Belles Lettres, 1988), 185.

61. *Les Vies des hommes illustres Grecs & Romains*, trans. Amyot, 38r.

62. Ibid.

63. "Mais vous ne serez point accusé par moy de ceste loüable paresse que les Spartains disoient appartenir aux hommes nobles, bien que nous ayons d'autres loix meurdrieres de l'oisiveté, comme les Atheniens. . . .' Des Roches, *Les Missives*, 108.

64. Lecoy, "Introduction," Guillaume de Lorris, *Le Roman de la Rose*, xxxi. For a discussion of the 1529 adaptation, attributed to Marot, see Hope H. Glidden, "*Le Roman de la Rose* and Evangelical Poetics," in *Translation and the Transmission of Culture Between 1300 and 1600*, ed. Jeanette Beer and Kenneth Lloyd-Jones (Kalamazoo, Mich.: Western Michigan University Press, 1995): 143–74. Jean Molinet prepared a prose adaptation for Philippe de Clèves in 1500. In his moral glosses or *moralités* following each episode, he explains the importance of Lady Idleness in light of a mystical theological framework. Free of any moral ambiguity, she is revealed to be "contemplation" whose function consists of initiating the "virtuous young man" into *la parfaite religion.* The *Roman de la Rose Moralisé* thus celebrates not nobiliary idleness, but rather monastic *otium*. For a discussion of how Molinet transposes Guillaume de Lorris's *Ars amandi* (earthly love) to a theological context (divine love), see Michael Randall, *Building Resemblance: Analogical Imagery in the Early French Renaissance* (Baltimore: Johns Hopkins University Press, 1996), 13–39.

65. Noël du Faïl, 210. A 1518 inventory from the royal library included a list of books entitled: "Livres que le Roy porte communément." Among these: Petrarch, *Le Roman de la Rose, Le Livre des déduits, Le Chevalier délibéré*, a treatise on falconry, history books, and French translations of Greek and Roman historians. Gilbert Gadoffre, *La Révolution culturelle dans la France des Humanistes* (Geneva: Droz, 1997), 192.

66. On the affinity of the *jardin de déduit* to an abbey, see Batany, "Miniature, allégorie, idéologie," 22–23.

67. Citations from *Gargantua* will be followed by page numbers from Gérard Defaux's edition (Paris: Librairie Générale Française, 1994).

68. François Rigolot, *Les Langages de Rabelais* (1972; reprinted and revised; Geneva: Droz, 1996), 89.

69. The above quotations in English are all from *Gargantua and Pantagruel*, trans. J. M. Cohen (London: Penguin, 1955), 156.

70. Guillaume Budé, *Traitté de la venerie*, trans. Louis Le Roy, ed. Henri Chevreul (Paris: Auguste Aubry, 1861).

71. Of course, when François I praised its nonutilitarian dimensions, Budé could have objected that this superficial nonutilitarianism only made the hunt all the more useful: for a strong, fleet, and potentially elusive stag increases the physical demands made upon the hunters, and strength is a very useful virtue for warriors. That is, doesn't the aleatory telos (the stag) indirectly reinforce the aristocrat's true vocation (warfare)? Doesn't the hunt's "inefficiency" on a material plane make aristocrats more "efficient" when it comes to combat? Budé leaves this ambiguity floating. Whether or not the accursed share is redeemed, the hunt as *loisir* fulfills a primary distinctive function in Budé's treatise that is absent from Thélème.

72. Michel Beaujour, *Le Jeu de Rabelais* (Paris: L'Herne, 1969), 102.

73. "Le 'beau' y devient lassant: 'bel *alabastre*', '*beau* jardin', '*beau* labyrinthe': c'est d'un 'beau' médiocre, ordinaire, qu'il s'agit." Rigolot, *Les Langages de Rabelais*, 89. Rigolot departs from earlier appraisals of Thélème as a reflection of Renaissance aristocratic ideals. Raoul Morçay, for instance, writes: "Dresser un château splendide, plus beau que Bonnivet, Chambord ou Chantilly, avec toutes les commodités des plus parfaites demeures italiennes ou françaises, l'animer par une société choisie de gentils compagnons, d'esprits cultivés et de dames qui sont des fleurs de beauté, traduire, agrandi par une imagination débordante, le rêve de vie aristocratique qui hantait alors tant de cœurs . . ." *L'Abbaye de Thélème*, introduction (Geneva: Droz, 1949), xxxiv.

74. See Kathleen Wine's study of Honoré d'Urfé's pastoral novel. In an era of growing monarchic control and increasingly powerful rivals from the world of the "robe," *L'Astrée* elaborated a potent compensatory myth of aristocratic autonomy. In its privileging of autotelic pursuits (beauty, pleasure, elegant speech), pastoral *otium* offered a register of resistance to the ideological imperative that the nobleman be useful to the crown. The idle shepherds and shepherdesses in d'Urfé's romance proclaimed their indifference to the court and arms, the two forms of "occupation" reserved for aristocrats, just as Guillaume de Lorris eliminated aristocratic functions from the Garden of Delight. *Forgotten Virgo: Humanism and Absolutism in Honoré d'Urfé's "L'Astrée"* (Geneva: Droz, 2000), 25–26, 139–41.

75. Rabelais, *Gargantua and Pantagruel*, 159.

76. Ibid., 158.

77. Veblen, *The Theory of the Leisure Class*, 59–60.

Chapter 2. Work in Idleness in the Fourth Estate

1. "Cettuy-ci, tout pituiteux, chassieux et crasseux, que tu vois sortir apres minuit d'un estude, penses tu qu'il cherche parmy les livres comme il se rendra plus homme de bien, plus content et plus sage? Nulles nouvelles. Il y mourra, ou il apprendra à la posterité la mesure des vers de Plaute et la vraye orthographe d'un mot Latin." (I, 39, 241a)

2. Chevreul, introduction, Budé, *Traitté de la venerie*, xiii.

3. Only at two hours past midnight would Ronsard finally retire, regretfully, but not before awakening Baïf, who would take his candle—and take his place mounting a humanist guard against ignorance. See Frances Yates, *The French Academies of the Sixteenth Century* (London: The Warburg Institute, 1947), 14–

15. In his biography of Pierre Pithou, Loisel also praises Pithou's late-night industry: "il se retiroit en son estude, où il demeuroit jusques à deux ou trois heures du matin, ne se mettant au lict que lorsqu'il falloit, par manière de dire, resveiller les autres." Quoted in Louis de Rosanbo, "Pierre Pithou, biographie," *Revue du Seizième Siècle* 15 (1928): 281.

4. Pieper describes Erasmus's portrait (by Hans Holbein) in *Leisure: The Basis of Culture*, 16. The Toronto translation of his works into English has over eighty volumes. *The Collected Works of Erasmus* (Toronto: University of Toronto Press, 1974–).

5. The bee was one of the dozen or so personal emblems espoused by the members of the Palace Academy. See Yates, *The French Academies of the Sixteenth Century*, 34. On Ramus's motto, see George Huppert, *The Style of Paris: Renaissance Origins of the French Enlightenment* (Bloomington: Indiana University Press, 1999), 40.

6. A constant fixture of their intellectual life, Cicero accompanied members of Montaigne's milieu from their years in a *collège* through their professional lives. For a discussion of the role Cicero played in shaping not only debates in the Parlement, but the image the corps of lawyers and magistrats had of themselves, see Jean-Marc Châtelain, "Heros togatus: Culture cicéronienne et gloire de la robe dans la France d'Henri IV," *Le Journal des Savants* (July-December 1991): 263–87.

7. See Yandell's discussion of the humanist schedule, with its high premium on time, *Carpe Corpus*, 28–34.

8. See Méda, *Le Travail, une valeur en voie de disparition*; Lipietz, *La Société en sablier*; Robin, *Quand le travail quitte la société post-industrielle*; Mothé, *L'Utopie du temps libre*; Gorz, *Métamorphoses du travail*; Lebaube, *Le Travail: Toujours moins ou autrement*.

9. Montaigne uses this term as does Du Bellay in his "Ample Discours au Roy sur le fait des Quatre Estats du Royaume de France," in *Œuvres complètes*, vol. 4, ed. Léon Séché (Paris: Revue de la Renaissance, 1913).

10. On the intermingling of *robe* and *sword*, see Wood, *The Nobility of the "Election" of Bayeux* and Jonathan Dewald, *The Formation of a Provincial Nobility*. On the birth of the *robe* and early modern articulations of office and order, see Robert Descimon, "The Birth of the Nobility of the Robe," in *Changing Identities in Early Modern France*, ed. Michael Wolfe (Durham: Duke University Press, 1997) and Albert Cremier, "La Genèse de la notion de noblesse de robe," *Revue d'histoire moderne et contemporaine* 46, no. 1 (January–March 1999): 22–38.

11. Supple, *Arms Versus Letters*. See also Bitton, *The French Nobility in Crisis*.

12. For a useful summary of approaches historians have used to define the early modern aristocracy, focusing on such criteria as profession, reputation, and genealogy see Robert Descimon, "La Noblesse, 'essence' ou rapport social?," *Revue d'histoire moderne et contemporaine* 46, no. 1 (January–March 1999): 5–21.

13. I borrow this phrase from chapter 5 of Huppert's *Les Bourgeois Gentilshommes*. My study is indebted to Huppert's discussion of the ethos of the Fourth Estate although our conclusions regarding conceptions of leisure diverge.

14. In 1462 an edict that allowed nobles to deal in commerce concerned only with bulk goods was passed. However, during the course of the sixteenth century,

commerce was increasingly criticized, and in 1540 an edict was passed to ban nobles from engaging in commerce. There were, however, exceptions such as the merchant-gentlemen in Marseille who were given the right to engage in mercantile practices in 1566. Jouanna, *La France du XVIe siècle*, 64.

15. Quoted in Dravasa, *"Vivre noblement,"* 162. For a discussion of Tiraqueau's treatise *Tractatus de nobilitate* and a broad discussion of the principle of derogeance, see Bitton, *The French Nobility in Crisis*, 64–76.

16. André Tournon compares this obligatory dimension of leisure for the members of Montaigne's milieu to the military injunction: "at ease!" *(repos)* in "Vacances intérieures," 559.

17. II, 8, 389–90a.

18. "la vie noble faict finalement le noble," David Rivault, *Les Estats, esquels il est discouru du Prince, du Noble et du Tiers Estat, conformément à nostre temps* (1596), quoted in Jouanna, *La France du XVIe siècle*, 66.

19. Laval made a somewhat rapid ascent to nobility, giving him a shakier noble status than that of many of his peers. Born "Antoine Mathé," he began to sign his name "Ant. Math. de Laval Foresien," a clever abbreviation since "Math" was taken for "Mathieu"—a middle name instead of a surname. In 1605 he became simply "Antoine de Laval." Claude Longeon, *Les Ecrivains foréziens du XVIe siècle: Répertoire bio-bibliographique* (Saint-Etienne: Centre d'Etudes Foréziennes, 1970), 393. For a discussion of Laval's relationship to Montaigne, see George Hoffmann, "Croiser le fer avec le Géographe du Roi: L'Entrevue de Montaigne avec Antoine de Laval aux Etats généraux de Blois en 1588," *Montaigne Studies* 13, nos. 1–2 (2001): 207–22.

20. In "De la solitude," he criticizes Pliny and Cicero for having submitted leisure to the thirst for glory. "Cicero . . . dict vouloir employer sa solitude et sejour de affaires publiques à s'en acquerir par ses escris une vie immortelle" (I, 39, 244a).

21. Antoine (Mathé) de Laval, *Desseins des professions nobles et publiques* (Paris: A. L'Angelier, 1605), 303r.

22. On the changing meanings of boredom, see Patricia Meyer Spacks, *Boredom: The Literary History of a State of Mind* (Chicago: University of Chicago Press, 1995).

23. Hoffmann's discussion of a dinner party held by Pierre Forget de Fresnes, secretary of state in charge of Protestant affairs, conveys the smugness with which the Fourth Estate viewed its cultivation. If the guests at the party (including Montaigne's cousin Geoffroy, Antoine de Laval, and Jacques Davy du Perron) could not boast of their families' genealogies, they were secure in their knowledge that they possessed a degree of personal cultivation that most old nobles could not claim. *Montaigne's Career*, 137.

24. Near the beginning of the chapter, Laval first castigates stereotypical country gentlemen who fall apart if they are unable to engage in their usual pastimes (hunting, hawking, visits . . .), concluding: "tout cela peut manquer, ce qu'advenant voila un pauvre Gentilhomme fort empesché à ne rien faire." But he then extends the lesson to include *fonctionnaires*: "[a]utant en dis-je de toute autre personne qualifiee qui n'est pas tousjours employée à l'exercice de sa charge." *Desseins des professions nobles et publiques*, 302v.

25. Desiderius Erasmus, *Opera Omnia Desiderii Erasmi Roterodami*, vol. 2 (Amsterdam: Elsevier, 1969), 65–66.

26. See Arlette Jouanna, "Le Thème de l'utilité publique dans la polémique anti-nobiliaire en France dans la deuxième moitié du XVIe siècle," in *Théorie et pratique politiques à la Renaissance, XVIIe colloque international de Tours* (De Pétrarque à Descartes 34) (Paris: Vrin, 1977), 287–99.

27. Ronsard, for instance, accuses the courtier of never having worked "n'a jamais sué, ny travaillé . . ." (quoted in Pauline Smith, *The Anti-courtier Trend in Sixteenth-Century French Literature* [Geneva: Droz, 1966], 180).

28. *L'Imagination poétique* (Lyons: Macé Bonhomme, 1552), 131. This collection of emblems was first written in Latin in 1552 and entitled *Picta Poesis*. During that same year Aneau himself translated it into French under the title of *L'Imagination poétique*.

29. "Le miel est faict pour l'homme, & la cire odorante / Pour rendre à Dieu honneur, en clarté adorante."

30. "De l'oisiveté, & maux procedans d'icelle," in *Œuvres morales et diversifiées*, III, 17, 228r. The same universalizing criterion of public interest applied to nobles was also applied to "idle" monks and "idle" paupers. Using their position as civic administrators, *bourgeois gentilshommes* sought to implement their vision through public policy, the clearest example being public works programs. Poor Laws were enacted in order to eliminate idleness and begging among all able-bodied paupers who were forcefully enlisted in public works such as digging ditches. Further, these programs were intended to replace charity, long held to be both a form of poor relief and a means for the wealthy to assure their *private* salvation by giving alms.

31. "On accusoit un Galba du temps passé de ce qu'il vivoit oiseusement; il respondit que chacun devoit rendre raison de ses actions, non pas de son sejour. Il se trompoit: car la justice a cognoissance et animadvertion aussi sur ceux qui chaument" (III, 9, 946b).

32. Lettre VIII, "A Monsieur de la Croix," in *Lettres familières*, ed. D. Thickett (Geneva: Droz, 1974), 278.

33. (Paris: Robert le Mangnier, 1574).

34. Henri II made him president of the Parisian *Cour des Aides*, a prestigious position that he later had to vacate after his open conversion to Calvinism. One wonders if the works of his leisure did not contribute to his reentry into the active life. For he was later reinstated by Charles IX, the dedicatee of *Discours politiques* before dying soon after in the Saint Barthélemy massacre. See the entry for Pierre de La Place in the *Dictionnaire des Lettres Françaises*, vol. 1 *(Le Seizième Siècle)*, ed. Georges Grente (Paris: Fayard, 1951). A brief biography emphasizing his Calvinism is found in *Choix de Chroniques et Mémoires sur l'Histoire de France*, J. A. C. Buchon (Paris: A. Desrez, 1836), x–xii.

35. See Michel de L'Hospital's "Epître XIV" addressed to Barthélemy Faye. In a description of his activities on his Vignay estate, L'Hospital elaborates on the pleasures of leisure (which include merriment and poetry), while reminding his reader that he did not choose these activities; rather, his disgrace at court made it impossible for him to serve the public. *Poésies complètes du Chancelier Michel de L'Hospital*, trans. and ed. Louis Bandy de Nalèche (Paris: Hachette, 1857), 200.

36. La Place's list of valid reasons for retiring to *otium* is nearly identical to Cicero's. Compare to the preface to book III of *De Officiis*, esp. 1–4.

37. Regarding Montaigne's ostensible solitude, Hoffmann emphasizes the hus-

tle and bustle that surrounded him as he composed the *Essais*. Far from residing in an ivory tower, Montaigne supervised the work on his country estate from his tower-library: ". . . Montaigne's library office suggests less a purely interior space than a post of observation linking the inside to the outside." And even in his tower, he was not always engaged in solitary contemplation, but rather engaged the help of a secretary to whom he dictated part of the *Essais*. Hoffmann, *Montaigne's Career*, 15, 39–62.

38. Studying the Georgic poetry of the last third of the sixteenth century, Danièle Duport argues that the idle lord on his country estate worked vicariously through the labor performed by peasants. His supervision—or contemplation—of this labor resulted in an imaginary synthesis of work and leisure. "L'oisif en ses terres," paper delivered at "L'oisiveté au temps de la Renaissance," *Société Internationale de Recherches Interdisciplinaires sur la Renaissance*, Paris, 17 March 2000.

39. See his letters to his daughter, Madame de Belesbat, from 28 March 1571; 8 April 1571; 17 April 1571. A. H. Taillandier, *Nouvelles recherches historiques sur la vie et les ouvrages du Chancelier de L'Hospital* (Paris: Librairie de Firmin Didot Frères et Fils, 1861), 222–31.

40. "Il n'y a guiere moins de tourment au gouvernement d'une famille que d'un estat entier . . ." (I, 39, 238a). See Hoffmann, *Montaigne's Career*, 8–38.

41. ". . . l'estude des bonnes lettres est le seul & souverain remede pour attacher dans son ame a cloux de diamans une forme de bien vivre, pour dompter & adoucir sa nature sauvage & farouche . . ." *Le Gentilhomme* (Paris: Jean Petit, 1611), 14.

42. He proposes a three-way model of communication for interpreting *sprezzatura*: a "naive" public (implied or actual) is deceived by a performer-courtier who appears to be "naturally" or "magically" graceful rather than skillful; only a second public (composed of peers) sees through the illusion, appreciating the performer's art of appearing artless and of dissimulating effort. "*Grazia, Sprezzatura, and Affettazione* in Castiglione's *Book of the Courtier*," trans. Susan G. Beecher, *Glyph* 5 (Baltimore: Johns Hopkins University Press, 1979), 34–54.

43. "Le toit paternel n'est un lieu d'exil que pour celui qui laisse engloutir son oisiveté dans le vin et le sommeil, qui n'a de goût pour aucun travail et qui voudrait chaque soir être au matin et chaque matin être au soir." "Epître Première à Guy du Faur," in *Poésies complètes du Chancelier Michel de L'Hospital*, VI, 325.

44. "il faut . . . user en toutes choses d'un certain mespris & nonchalance . . ." *Le Parfait Courtisan* (Paris: Nicolas Bonfons, 1585), 65. Alain Pons discusses Chappuis's translation of this important concept in his edition of Castiglione's *Le Livre du Courtisan* (Paris: Flammarion, 1991), 54 n.

45. Joachim Du Bellay, *Deffence et Illustration de la langue francoyse*, ed. Henri Chamard (Paris: M. Didier, 1948) II, V, 135–36.

46. Aneau, *L'Imagination poétique*, 99.

47. Laval, *Desseins des professions nobles et publiques*, 304v.

48. Michel de L'Hospital requested that his collection of antique medals and coins not be dispersed after his death, as though by remaining intact, a collection commemorated its author. Taillandier, *Nouvelles recherches*, 340–42. Similarly, Pierre Pithou's last thoughts were to preserve his library's integrity. Rosanbo, "Pierre Pithou, biographie," 303.

49. Charles Thornton Forster and F. H. Blackburne Daniell, ed. and introduction, *The Life and Letters of Ogier Ghiselin de Busbecq*, vol. 1 (London: C. K. Paul, 1881), 2–3; 204–19.

50. See Hoffmann's discussion of Busbecq in "Rites Romains et autres dans l'essai 'Des cannibales,'" in *"D'une fantastique bigarrure": Le Texte composite à la Renaissance: Etudes offertes à André Tournon*, ed. Jean-Raymond Fanlo (Paris: Champion, 2000), 157–66.

51. Among the most distinguished visitors were Henri III and Sully. For a brief description of Laval's museum and library combined as well as a biography, see Claude Longeon, *Les Ecrivains foréziens du XVIe siècle*, 39. See also Hoffmann, *Montaigne's Career*, 137–41.

52. Gadoffre argues that early humanist scholarship obeyed the same logic of personal glory and primogeniture as the heroic exploit had for the *chevalerie*. *La Révolution culturelle dans la France des Humanistes*, 83 passim.

53. Pibrac, *Les Quatrains de Pibrac suivis de ses autres poésies*, 110.

54. "Et encore qu'au commencement il ne s'addonnast à ceste profession [poetry] que comme en se jouant, et la faisant servir à une autre passion . . ." Jacques Davy du Perron, *Oraison funèbre sur la mort de Monsieur de Ronsard*, ed. Michel Simonin (Geneva: Droz, 1985), 84.

55. ". . . quand il vid que ses vers estoient leuz avecques quelque louange, il commença de s'y affectionner à bon escient: Joint aussi que l'accident qui luy estoit avenu ["la debilité d'ouye"] l'empeschoit aucunement de pouvoir esperer à la Cour, ce qu'il y avoit esperé en matiere de faveur et d'avancement." Ibid., 84.

56. Laval, *Desseins des professions nobles et publiques*, 303r.

57. "Il n'est rien plus necessaire que les lettres, sans le benefice desquelles la vie humaine semblerait plustot estre mort que vie." Des Caurres, *Œuvres morales et diversifiées*, III, 87v. "Le moral Seneque allegue, que oisiveté, sans lettres ou estude, est la mort ou sepulture de l'homme: & que ceux-là seulement qui s'exercent en sapience, sont ceux qui scavent & ont la *vraye oisiveté*." Messie, *Les Diverses Leçons*, trans. Gruget, 90; emphasis added.

58. "An. Chr[isti 1571] æt. 38, pridie cal. mart., die suo natali, Mich. Montanus, servitii aulici et munerum publicorum jamdudum pertæsus, dum se integer in doctarum virginum recessit sinus, ubi quietus et omnium securus [quan]tillum in tandem superabit decursi multa jam plus parte spatii; si modo fata duint exigat istas sedes et dulces latebras, avitasque, libertati suæ, tranquillitatique, et otio consecravit." Montaigne, *Essais*, XXXIV.

59. *Les Œuvres de Maître Charles Loyseau* (1613) (Paris: Michel Bobin et Nicolas le Gras, 1678), 48.

60. On the triumph of the Fourth Estate's definition of literary culture as the sign of nobility over earlier conceptions of the warrior's *virtus*, see Jouanna, *Le Devoir de révolte*, 42–44.

61. There is a semantic ambiguity in the clause beginning with *comme*, which can be read as a comparative clause ("just as"), but also as a causal clause ("because").

62. Pasquier notes that living in the country connoted nobility: "ceux qui se veulent dire estre à bonnes enseignes Nobles, laissent les villes, pour choisir leurs demeures aux champs." Quoted by Hoffmann, *Montaigne's Career*, 17 n. The social dimensions assumed by Horace's *Epode II* ("Beatus ille qui procul

negotiis . . .") during the Renaissance also confirm the importance of land for living nobly. Nicolas Rapin's translation of the first stanza of Horace's *Epode II* in his *Plaisirs du gentilhomme champestre* (1575) is a case in point. Rapin gives a faithful translation of the first stanza; however, he adds a clause, qualifying the fields which ". . . ses peres / En propre luy ont delaissé" (vv. 14–15). This addition not only signals that the country gentleman did not purchase his property, it also specifies that land ownership goes back at least to the grandfather, for Rapin carefully puts "his fathers" in the plural form. With this simple addition, he establishes his *gentilhomme*'s noble status based on three generations of "living nobly" on the country estate. In *Œuvres*, ed. Jean Brunel and Emile Brethé (Geneva: Droz, 1982), 117.

63. See Huppert, *Les Bourgeois Gentilshommes*, 34–46; 84–102.

64. Pierre Eyquem de Montaigne made the transition to "living nobly," engaging in military campaigns and serving as mayor of Bordeaux, an office usually restricted to "genealogical" nobles. Michel de Montaigne was the first to drop the family name of Eyquem. See Roger Trinquet, *La Jeunesse de Montaigne* (Paris: Nizet, 1972) and Desan, *Les Commerces de Montaigne*, 47–82. In *De Officiis,* Cicero describes two kinds of men who retire to *otium*: philosophers and ernest thoughtful men. Among the latter are those who live in the country and manage their private estates. Marcus Tullius Cicero, *De Officiis,* (Cambridge: Harvard University Press, 1997), I, 20, 70.

65. In his commentary on Ronsard's sonnet XXI ("Qu'amour mon cœur, qu'Amour mon ame sonde . . ."), Muret glosses the runaway horse found in the two tercets as "appetit sensuel et desordonné, guidant l'ame aux voluptez charnelles" and explains that this allegory (of reason and sensuality) comes from Plato's *Phaedrus*. Marc-Antoine de Muret, *Commentaires au Premier Livre des "Amours" de Ronsard*, ed. Jacques Chomarat, Marie-Madeleine Fragonard, and Gisèle Mathieu-Castellani (Geneva: Droz, 1985), 12.

66. When Des Caurres adapts the same topos to his chapter on idleness, he emphasizes the "uselessness" of idle fields to the point of redundancy: ". . . la terre seule, qui est sans estre travaillee, & sans sentir la main industrieuse du laboureur, est celle, qui produit des ronces, des horties poignantes, & chardons *sans profit*, & les sillons des champs, que le coultre ne rompt, se voyent chargez le plus souvent de chardons espineux, & occupez *vainement* de plusieurs herbes *inutiles*." *Œuvres morales et diversifiées*, 227r–v; emphasis added. Messie, too, includes the image of idle fields in his lesson on work and idleness. "Si la terre n'est labourée & ouverte, elle ne peult produire que ronces, espines, chardons, & autres herbes *inutiles*." Messie, *Les Diverses Leçons*, 88r; emphasis added. One finds the same commonplace in La Primaudaye, who paraphrases Proverbs 24, in "De l'oisiveté, et Paresse, & du Jeu," 179v.

67. This device appears at the end of Jodelle's ode addressed to Etienne Pasquier and was included, among other liminary verse, in the 1554, 1555, and 1610 editions of Pasquier's *Le Monophile*, ed. F. H. Balmas (Milan: Cisalpino, 1957), 52–55.

68. Pasquier, "A Monsieur Airault, Lieutenant Criminel au Siege Presidial d'Angers," *Lettres familières*, 222. Cf. Nicolas Rapin's letter XVI to A. N. Perrot where he describes composing verse to fill a temporal void caused by the postponement of a trial: "Quando licet toties, dilatae examine causae / Ludere scribendis

otia carminibus . . ." [Puisqu'il m'est si souvent possible, chaque fois qu'on reporte l'examen de ma cause, de charmer mes loisirs en écrivant des vers . . .] (vv. 1–2), trans. Brunel, Œuvres, vol. 1., 231 and 752.

69. François Rabelais, Le Tiers Livre, ed. Jean Céard (Paris: Librairie Générale Française, 1995), 17–19.

70. Gargantua and Pantagruel, trans. Cohen, 282. Unless otherwise stated, all translations of Rabelais into English will be from this translation.

71. "puys, comme excité d'esprit Martial, ceignit son palle en escharpe, recoursa ses manches jusques es coubtes, se troussa en cuilleur de pommes, bailla à un sien compaignon vieulx sa bezasse, ses livres, et opistographes." Rabelais, Le Tiers Livre, 19. [Then, as if spurred by the martial spirit, he slung his cloak across his chest, rolled his sleeves up to his elbows, trussed himself up like an apple-gatherer, handed his wallet to an old comrade of his, together with his books and double-sided scrolls . . .] (282).

72. "Auquel respondit le philosophe, qu'à aultre office n'estant pour la republicque employé, il en ceste façon son tonneau tempestoit pour, entre ce peuple tant fervent et occupé, n'estre veu seul cessateur et ocieux." Ibid.

73. Compare to François Rigolot's reading of this passage, ". . . Diogène, dans sa frénésie gratuite, apparaît par la voie du discours, beaucoup plus *nécessaire* que ses concitoyens. La stérilité de ses gestes n'est qu'apparence; elle est mille fois compensée par la fécondité du langage." Les Langages de Rabelais, 102.

74. Pierre de la Place invokes this anecdote from the life of Solon as an example of circumstances that make idleness legitimate. Solon's attempt to prevent tyranny proved to be in vain, for none of his compatriots would listen to him. He was left shouting into the wind, so to speak, just as Diogenes was left faced with a Sisyphean task. But unlike the latter, Solon, in his wisdom, quickly realized that his efforts were useless and accepted to reside in idleness. Discours politiques, 108.

75. "ma deliberation est servir et es uns et es autres: tant s'en fault que je reste cessateur et inutile." Tiers Livre, 23. A number of critics have explored the allegory of the writer as Diogenes-Sisyphus including Floyd Gray, "Structure and Meaning in the Prologue to the Tiers Livre," L'Esprit Créateur 3 (1963): 57–62; Alfred Glauser, Rabelais créateur (Paris: Nizet, 1964); and Ullrich Langer, Divine and Poetic Freedom in the Renaissance (Princeton: Princeton University Press, 1990), 104–10. See also Edwin Duval's discussion of the Prologue in the Design of Rabelais's Tiers Livre de Pantagruel (Geneva: Droz, 1997). Duval argues that the absence of a formal telos takes nothing away from the very clear moral telos found in Pantagruel's evangelical lesson on caritas working through beneficence.

76. Louis Le Roy, trans., Les Politiques d'Aristote (Paris: Michel de Vascosan, 1568), 852. A second edition of Le Roy's translation (in folio) soon followed (1576). It appeared again in 1599 and in 1600. As for the commentaries, while they are brief and more elementary than others of their kind, Werner Gundersheimer maintains that they must have had a favorable reception since they were included in an English translation of the time. See his chapter on Le Roy's translation of the Politics in The Life and Works of Louis Le Roy (Geneva: Droz, 1966), 47–56.

77. In the third book of De Officiis, he defines *honestum* as "what is worth seeking for its own sake" [propter se esse expetendum]. Trans. Walter Miller (Cam-

bridge: Harvard University Press, 1997), III, 7, 33. The moral good, for Cicero, requires a perfect synthesis of the *utile* and the *honestum*.

78. Aristotle, *Nicomachean Ethics*, trans. Terence Irwin (Indianapolis: Hackett, 1985), X, 1177b, 5–7, 285. For a discussion of the importance Aristotle's *Ethics* assumed in the later *Essais*, see Edilia Traverso, *Montaigne e Aristotele* (Florence: F. Le Monnier, 1974).

79. Aristotle, *Ethicorum Aristotelis* (Paris: Jean Higman and Wolfgang Hopyl, 1496–97), X, VII, 29.

80. *Petri Victori Comentarii in X Libros Aristotelis De Moribus ad Nicomachum* (Florence, 1566), 590; emphasis added.

81. *Aristotelis Ad Nicomachum filium de Moribus, quae Ethica nominantur, libri decem* (Paris: Gabriel Buon, 1576), 132v.

82. Beugnot observes two characteristics defining the discourse of "private" life: "... l'absolution de l'oisiveté qui s'affranchit de tout ce que traînait de négatif avec elle l'*otiositas*, et une réappropriation du temps comme habitat humain." *Le Discours de la retraite au XVIIe siècle* (Paris: Presses Universitaires de France, 1996), 206. See also Marc Fumaroli, Philippe-Joseph Salazar, and Emmanuel Bury, *Le Loisir lettré à L'Age Classique* (Geneva: Droz, 1996).

83. Marcel Conche formulates Montaigne's resistance to finality in the following way: "Montaigne a été prodigieusement libre à l'égard de toutes ces instances qui tendent à nous déposséder de nous-même . . . Par l'activité orientée vers un but, c'est le tout de l'individu qui se subordonne à un terme extérieur. L'insertion de l'individu dans un processus finalisé est asservissement de la liberté; car la liberté véritable n'est pas finalisée, elle est ludique et créatrice." *Montaigne et la philosophie* (Versailles: Editions de Mégare, 1987; reprint, Paris: Presses Universitaires de France, 1996), 21.

84. While Cicero defined the moral good as combining *utilitas* and *honestum*, these terms became polarized in the last quarter of the sixteenth century: *utilitas* belonged to a political and economic discourse while *honestum* belonged to a vanishing nobiliary ideal. The *utile* was, for Montaigne, part of the world of (public and economic) administration—the world of the *robe*—while *honestum* suggested chivalric ideals and a scorn for moral or economic pragmatism. Desan, *Les Commerces de Montaigne*, 227–48.

85. Etienne Pasquier, "Lettre à Monsieur Airault," in *Lettres familières*, 223.

86. Laval, *Desseins des professions nobles et publiques*, 304v.

87. Ibid.

88. On the interrelationship of "books and careers," see the final chapter of Hoffmann's *Montaigne's Career*, 130–55. See also Warren Boutcher's study of the eminently practical uses humanist learning could serve (and was thought to serve) in European courtly political life. "'Who taught thee Rhetoricke to deceive a maid?': Christopher Marlowe's *Hero and Leander*, Juan Boscan's *Leandro*, and Renaissance Vernacular Humanism," *Comparative Literature* (winter 2000): 11–52.

89. L'Hospital's marriage to Marie Morin in 1537 was quite a feat given the fact that his father was in disgrace for having supported Charles Bourbon. Marie Morin's father wrote a letter to the then chancellor Du Bourg suggesting that L'Hospital's knowledge and poetry were almost sufficient motivations for him to accept the marriage. "Monseigneur l'archevêque d'Aix (Filleul) me avoit parlé dudit

même maistre Michel de Lospital, que ne avois congneu sinon par réputation, comme de avoir oy parler de son bon savoir qui estoit tel pour me persuader, sans avoir esgard aux facultés." Quoted in Taillandier, *Nouvelles recherches historiques sur la vie et les ouvrages du Chancelier de L'Hospital*, 11. L'Hospital's Latin verse helped assure him the support and protection of François Olivier, at that time the *premier président* of the Parlement of Paris. As one recent biographer points out, Olivier (who praised L'Hospital as one of the best Latin poets of the time) acquired for him most of his distinctions and helped him launch his political career. Seong-Hak Kim, *Michel de L'Hôpital: The Vision of a Reformist Chancellor during the French Religious Wars*, vol. XXXVI, *Sixteenth Century Essays and Studies* (Kirksville, Mo.: Sixteenth Century Journal Publishers, 1997), 20.

90. Florentin de Thierriat, *Trois Traictez à scavoir 1) De La Noblesse de Race; 2) De la Noblesse Civile; 3) Des Immunitez des Ignobles* (Paris: Lucas Bruneau, 1606), 81. On Thierriat's treatise, see Bitton, *The French Nobility in Crisis*, esp. 49–50, and Huppert, *Les Bourgeois Gentilshommes*, 9–10; 12.

91. Thierriat, *Trois Traictez*, 80.

Chapter 3. Portrait of an Early Modern *Oiseuse*

1. "Lettre à Abel L'Angelier," in *Les Missives*, ed. Larsen, 108.

2. All quotations from Crenne's novel and letters will be from the following editions: *Les Angoysses douloureuses qui procedent d'amours*, ed. Christine de Buzon (Paris: Champion, 1997); and *Les Epistres familières et invectives*, ed. Jerry Nash (Paris: Champion, 1996). To distinguish between the three parts of the novel, and individual personal and invective epistles, respectively, subsequent references will be included within the text and will use the acronyms *AD* I–III, *EF* I–VIII, *EI* I–V followed by the page number.

3. Following the usage adopted by Jerry Nash in his edition to *Les Epistres familières et invectives*, I will use "Hélisenne" to designate the narrator and character in both the *Angoysses douloureuses* and the *Epistres familières et invectives* and "Crenne" for the author of both works.

4. Jean Bouchet, *Les Triumphes de la noble et amoureuse Dame et l'art de honnestement aymer*, in *Le Miroir des femmes*, ed. Luce Guillerm, Jean-Pierre Guillerm, Laurence Hordoir, Marie-Françoise Piéjus (Lille: Presses Universitaires de Lille, 1983), vol. 1, 47.

5. In his *La Nef des dames vertueuses*, Symphorien Champier advises men to marry a woman who is never idle: "On doit prendre une femme diligente et qui ne quert point estre oyseuse et paresseuse. Car ne peult estre que la femme oyseuse ne pense a plusieurs maulx et cogitations illicites ainsi que dit Aristote au vii. des politiques." Quoted in Yandell, *Carpe Corpus*, 87–88.

6. Ruth Kelso, *Doctrine for the Lady of the Renaissance* (Urbana: University of Illinois Press, 1956), 40.

7. "Sainct Paul commande, qui ne laboure ne mange, qui est loy en l'eglise chrestienne. Pour ce est indigne de viande qui consume le jour & sa jeunesse en jeux & voluptez, car c'est vouloir faire Dieu menteur, qui a ordonné que en la sueur de son corps l'on mange son pain; & n'ont pas moins de peché les oyseux, pour tant qu'ilz sont riches que autre qui se exemptent de labeur." Juan Luis

Vives, *Livre de l'institution de la femme chrestienne*, trans. Pierre de Changy (n.d.; reprint, Geneva: Slatkine Reprints, 1970), 59.

8. See Jean-Pierre Guillerm's brief introduction to moral treatises in *Le Miroir des femmes*, vol. 1, 25–27; Kelso, *Doctrine for the Lady of the Renaissance*, 78–135; and Jones, *The Currency of Eros*, 11–35.

9. "A sa contenance bien vi / Que n'estoit pas de grant souci, / Que pou li chaloit de filer . . ." [By her expression, I saw / that she clearly had few worries, / that she cared little for spinning]. Guillaume de Deguilleville, *Pèlerinage de vie humaine*, vv. 6529–31.

10. Ibid., vv. 6595–97.

11. Bouchet, *Les Triumphes de la noble et amoureuse Dame et l'art de honnestement aymer*, in *Le Miroir des femmes*, vol. 1, 18.

12. "Les maryees doivent estre plus rares & tardives a hanter les lieux publicques que les vierges, car elles ont ce que les pucelles semblent chercher." Vives, *Livre de l'institution de la femme chrestienne*, trans. Changy, 211.

13. Bouchet, *Les Triumphes de la noble et amoureuse Dame et l'art de honnestement aymer*, in *Le Miroir des femmes*, vol. 1, 47.

14. ". . . se occupera en telz aucteurs les dimanches & festes, & parfois es autres jours, pour eslever sa pensée en Dieu, comme bonne & devote chrestienne, pour les lyre apres qu'elle aura mis ordre a sa maison & a son faict domestique." Vives, *Livre de l'institution de la femme chrestienne*, trans. Changy, 44.

15. "Plus tost liront les vies des Sainctz & Sainctes, Boece de Consolation, la Vie des Peres, la Fleur des commandemens, & autres escriptures salutaires, esquelles elle aura grant delectation, imprimera son vouloir, & adonnera son desir au service de Dieu." Ibid., 43.

16. "Se je commande aux femmes & filles, par *operations manuelles* ou *sainctes cogitations*, de remercier Dieu de leur estat & benefices, pour y occuper le temps." Ibid., 59; my emphasis.

17. Johanis Cassianus (John Cassian) prescribed manual labor as prevention against acedia. On the anchoritic and cenobitic ideals of manual labor, asceticism, and prayer, see Kuhn, *The Demon of Noontide*, 39–53.

18. For the Renaissance man, "the ideal is self-expansion and realization. He is to develop to the utmost every power that he has, and direct every action with the proud consciousness of his elevation above the crowd not only in position but in worth. All his virtues are turned to insure his pre-eminence, enhance his authority, the essence of Aristotelian magnanimity. For the lady the direct opposite is prescribed. The eminently Christian virtues of chastity, humility, piety, and patience under suffering and wrong, are the necessary virtues." Kelso, *Doctrine for the Lady of the Renaissance*, 36.

19. "Ergo ubi visus eris nostra medicabilis arte, / Fac monitis fugias otia prima meis. / Haec, ut ames, faciunt; haec, quod fecere, tuentur / Haec sunt iucundi causa cibusque mali. / Otia si tollas, periere Cupidinis arcus / Contemptaeque iacent et sine luce faces. / Quam platanus vino gaudet, quam populus unda, / Et quam limosa canna palustris humo, / Tam Venus otia amat; qui finem quaeris amoris, / Cedit amor rebus: res age, tutus eris. / Languor, et immodici sub nullo vindice somni, / Aleaque, et multo tempora quassa mero / Eripiunt omnes animo sine vulnere nervos: / Adfluit incautis insidiosus Amor. / Desidiam puer ille sequi solet, odit agentes: / Da vacuae menti, quo teneatur, opus." *Remedia Amoris*, in

Ovid, vol. II, trans. J. H. Mozley, ed. G. P. Goold (Cambridge: Harvard University Press, 1979), 186–88, vv. 135–50.

20. "L'erreur mortel nous feint, l'Amour un Dieu volage / Cruel, armé de feux, de fleches, de cordage, / Subtil, industrieux, qui s'engendre dans nous, / D'oysiveté, de luxe, en nostre âge plus doux / Lequel si dans son sein, soy-mesme l'on n'alaitte / On rend en peu de jours sa puissance sujette." Jean Aubery, *L'Antidote d'amour, avec un ample discours, contenant la nature & les causes d'iceluy, ensemble les remedes les plus singuliers pour se preserver & guerir des Passions Amoureuses* (Paris: Claude Chappelet, 1599), 3r. Jean Aubery was a physician who studied with André Du Laurens in Montpellier. For a discussion of Aubery's *L'Antidote d'amour*, one of a number of medical treatises on erotic melancholy published at the end of the Renaissance, see Evelyne Berriot-Salvadore, "Les Médecins analystes de la passion," *La Peinture des passions de la Renaissance à l'Age Classique*, Actes du colloque international Saint-Etienne, ed. Bernard Yon (Saint-Etienne: Publications de l'Université de Saint-Etienne, 1995), 258. See also, Kelso, *Doctrine for the Lady of the Renaissance*, 160–63.

21. "Vrayement on ne voit si coustumierement le laboureur ou artisan amoureux, comme le riche & l'oisif: ce n'est pas que les influences d'hazard peslemesle ne respandent leurs forces, aussi bien sur les uns, que sur les autres, mais c'est que ceste cause celeste & universelle ne trouve des dispositions sur les particulieres qui sont le luxe, l'oisiveté, l'aage florissant, la saison printaniere . . ." Aubery, *L'Antidote d'amour*, 86v–87r.

22. Ibid., 128v.

23. Vives, *Livre de l'institution de la femme chrestienne*, trans. Changy, 58.

24. "Mais cette passion qu'on dict estre produite par l'oisiveté au cœur des jeunes hommes, quoy qu'elle s'achemine avec loisir et d'un progrès mesuré, elle represente bien evidemment, à ceux qui ont essayé de s'opposer à son effort, la force de cette conversion et alteration que nostre jugement souffre." Montaigne, *Les Essais*, II, 12, 568–69a.

25. '"Tiercement (dist Rondibilis), par labeur assidu. Car en icelluy est faicte si grande dissolution du corps, que le sang qui est par icelluy espars, pour l'alimentation d'un chascun membre, n'a temps ne loisir, ne faculté de rendre cette resudation seminale et superfluité de la tierce concoction. . . . Comme au contraire disent les philosophes oysiveté estre mere de luxure. Quand l'on demandoit à Ovide quelle cause feut parquoy Ægistus devint adultere, rien plus ne respondoit si non par ce qu'il estoit ocieux. Et qui housteroit oysiveté du monde, bien toust perioient les ars de Cupido. Son arc, sa trousse et ses fleches luy seroient en charge inutile: jamais n'en feriroit persone, car il n'est mie si bon archier qu'il puisse ferir les grues volans par l'aer, et les Cerfz relancez par les boucaiges, comme bien faisoient les Parthes: c'est à dire les humains tracassans et travaillans. Il les demande quoys, assis, couchez et à sejour." Rabelais, *Le Tiers Livre*, 297–99.

26. Georges Bataille, "Kinsey, la pègre et le travail," in *L'Erotisme* (Paris: Minuit, 1957), 165–82.

27. Ronsard, *Œuvres complètes*, vol. 4, 23, v. 4. The reverse applies as well, for work belongs to the distinctly un-erotic universe of his satirical poems. Ronsard will thus represent his stubbornly uncooperative mistress as an old woman engaged in domestic labor—weaving and spinning—as in sonnet XXIV from *Le Se-*

cond livre de sonnets pour Hélène (1578): "Quand vous serez bien vieille, au soir à la chandelle, / Assise aupres du feu, devidant & filant . . ." vv. 1–2, ibid., 265, vol. 17.2. He will also represent himself in sonnet XLIII as the frustrated lover, drenched in sweat ("j'ay la sueur au front . . ." [v. 6]) from serving an indifferent mistress: "Je ne serois marry, si tu comptois ma peine, / De compter tes degrez recomptez tant de fois," ibid., 280–81, vv. 1–2.

28. Verse 1, sonnet XXIII, *Continuation des Amours,* in Ronsard, *Œuvres complètes,* vol. 7, 140.

29. Ibid., vv. 12–14.

30. This motif is also played out in the novella. See Marguerite de Navarre, *L'Heptaméron* (tale 45), ed. Salminen, 369–70.

31. Hélisenne de Crenne, *The Torments of Love,* trans. Lisa Neal and Steven Rendall (Minneapolis: University of Minnesota Press, 1996), 7.

32. Fiammetta attends religious services on a "solemn holiday" in the opening pages of Giovanni Boccaccio's *The Elegy of Lady Fiammetta,* ed. and trans. Mariangela Causa-Steindler and Thomas Mauch (Chicago: University of Chicago Press, 1990), 6.

33. Aubery, *L'Antidote d'amour,* 31r.

34. "Les amants souspirent par intervalles, parc que l'ame estant occupee à la contemplation de son amour, ne se souvient de respirer, de sorte que nature est forcée d'attirer à un coup ce qu'elle eust fait en deux, ou trois auparavant son occupation, ceste respiration s'appelle souspir." Ibid., 31v.

35. For a more detailed catalog of Hélisenne's symptoms, see Philippe de Lajarte, "La Passion amoureuse et sa représentation dans la première partie des *Angoysses douloureuses* d'Hélisenne de Crenne," in *La Peinture des passions de la Renaissance à l'Age Classique,* Actes du colloque international Saint-Etienne, ed. Bernard Yon (Saint-Etienne: Publications de l'Université de Saint-Etienne, 1995), 61–78.

36. Even a hardworking and frugal humanist like Louis Le Roy was forced to recognize this fact. In his history of the arts and sciences, he notes that literary study appeared only after humanity had conquered luxury and idleness. "Donques entre tant de commoditez, croissant l'oysiveté avec l'opulence & ayse, ils s'appliquerent à l'estude des lettres." *De La Vicissitude ou variété des choses en l'univers . . .* (Paris: Pierre l'Huilier, 1575), 27r.

37. In a dedicatory epistle to her brother, Marie de Romieu writes: "Prenez donc en bonne part, mon Frere, ce mien brief discours que je vous envoye, composé assez à la haste, n'ayant pas le loisir, à cause de nostre mesnage, de vacquer (comme vous dedié pour servir aux Muses) à chose si belle et divine que les vers." *Les Premières œuvres poétiques,* ed. André Winandy (Geneva: Droz, 1972), 4. This is also a common theme in the epistles of Madeleine and Catherine des Roches, as Larsen notes. See her introduction, *Les Missives,* 19–20.

38. Hélisenne de Crenne, *A Renaissance Woman: Helisenne's Personal and Invective Letters,* trans. Marianna M. Mustacchi and Paul J. Archambault (Syracuse: Syracuse University Press, 1986), 104.

39. Crenne, *The Torments of Love,* 12–13.

40. ". . . vous pourrez eviter les dangereulx laqs d'amours, en y resistant du commencement, sans continuer en amoureuses pensées. Je vous prie de vouloir eviter ociosité, et vous occupez à quelques honnestes exercices" (*AD* I, 97).

41. Crenne, *The Torments of Love*, 10.

42. "Elle estoit de petite stature, bossue, et boyteuse, et si avoit le visaige fort ridé, les sourcilz larges de deux doigtz . . ." (*AD* I, 121). [She was short of stature, hunchbacked and lame, and her face was also very wrinkled, with eyebrows as wide as two fingers . . ."] ibid., 20.

43. "Jaçoit qu'en une maison s'assemblent plusieurs dames, il est vray que les choses qu'elles traictent entre elles sont fort graves. Je le dis pource qu'elles s'assemblent à manger fruictz, à louer les lignages, à parler des maris, à monstrer leurs ouvrages et coustures, à veoir qui ha la meilleure robbe, à noter les mal vestues, à blandir les belles, à se rire des laides, et murmurer des voisines . . ." *L'Orloge des Princes*, Antonio Guevara, trans. René Bertaut (1540), in *Le Miroir des femmes*, vol. 1, 56–58. Vives, too, has harsh words against gossipers: "Ne pensés pas les festes avoir esté institutees pour jouer, dancer, ou deviser avec voz compaignes & voysines, quant il fault rendre compte de toutes parolles oyseuses. . . ." *Livre de l'institution de la femme chrestienne*, trans. Changy, 44.

44. Denunciations of makeup, clothing, and a general preoccupation with self-adornment are omnipresent. Jean Bouchet, for instance, writes, "Quartement qu'elles [les pucelles] se gardent d'exceder en vestemens, et de farder leurs visages, car ce sont deux choses qui desplaisent à Dieu et au monde. . . ." *Les Triumphes de la noble et amoureuse Dame et l'art de honnestement aymer*, in *Le Miroir des femmes*, vol. 1, 47. Vives's chapter "Des aornemens" encourages married women to "adorn themselves" with virtue, not with clothing, makeup, and jewels: ". . . et sur tout qu'elles ne portassent robes de soye, bagues ne doreures, qui sont instruments de luxure, ains se parer de vertus." *Livre de l'institution de la femme chrestienne*, trans. Changy, 211.

45. Crenne, *The Torments of Love*, 21.

46. Castiglione warns against rapid, abrupt movements, even when the *donna di palazzo* is dancing (III, 8).

47. "l'oisiveté, cause de tous leurs dommages," Béroalde de Verville, "A très vertueuse Dame, Madame Charlotte Adam Dame de la Vallière," in *Misères et grandeur de la femme au XVIe siècle*, ed. Ilana Zinguer (Geneva: Slatkine, 1982), 82.

48. Béroalde de Verville, *Les Avantures de Floride, Histoire Françoise* (Tours: Jamet Mettayer, 1592), 1v.

49. Ibid., 2r–v.

50. Yandell quotes this sixteenth-century proverb from Le Roux de Lincy's collection in *Carpe Corpus*, 88.

51. Especially in chivalric romance, an important intertext in the *Angoysses*, particularly in part 2. On the rhetoric of exemplarity in romance, see Nicole Cazauran, "Entre exemple et recréation," in *Le Roman de chevalerie au temps de la Renaissance*, ed. M. T. Jones-Davies, colloque organisé par le Centre de Recherche sur la Renaissance (Paris: Jean Touzot, 1987).

52. In their critical edition to the *Epistres*, Jean-Philippe Beaulieu and Hannah Fournier contend that some continuity exists between *Les Angoysses* and the *Epistres*. Their introduction pursues the intertextual play between novel and epistles. *Les Epistres familières et invectives de ma dame Helisenne* (Montreal: Presses de l'Université de Montréal, 1995), 13, 24–38.

53. See Constance Jordan, *Renaissance Feminism: Literary Texts and Political Models* (Ithaca: Cornell University Press, 1990), 178–79.

54. Crenne, *A Renaissance Woman*, 59.
55. Berriot-Salvadore, *Les Femmes dans la société française de la Renaissance*, 23.
56. Crenne, *A Renaissance Woman*, 95.
57. Some conduct manuals make this same point. See Kelso, *Doctrine for the Lady of the Renaissance*, 108; cf. St. Jerome, Letter XXII to Eustochium, in *Select Letters of St. Jerome*, ed. and trans. F. A. Wright (New York: Putnam, 1933), esp. 116.
58. See Veblen, *The Theory of the Leisure Class*, 58–61.
59. Crenne, *The Torments of Love*, 21.
60. Ibid.
61. Ibid., 22.
62. ". . . je ne puis faire autre chose que prier les vertueuses Dames d'eslever un peu leurs esprits par-dessus leurs quenoilles et fuseaus . . ." Labé, *Œuvres complètes*, 41–42. Compare to the position of the Dames des Roches, who attempted a reconciliation of work and leisure while preserving the place of the spindle. See Anne R. Larsen, introduction and "Avant Propos," in Madeleine et Catherine des Roches, *Les Œuvres* (Geneva: Droz, 1993), esp. 11, 14, 29.
63. Labé, *Œuvres complètes*, 41.
64. Anne R. Larsen notes that of the some 45 sixteenth-century literary women mentioned in La Croix du Maine's repertory, 27 never published any of their work. "'Un honneste passetems': Strategies of Legitimation in French Renaissance Women's Prefaces," *L'Esprit Créateur* 30, no. 4 (1990): 12–14; see also Ann Rosalind Jones, "Surprising Fame: Renaissance Gender Ideologies and Women's Lyric," in *The Poetics of Gender*, ed. Nancy K. Miller (New York: Columbia University Press, 1986), 74–95.
65. See Rigolot's appendix "Regards sur Louise Labé," Labé, *Œuvres complètes*, 242–52.
66. Crenne, *A Renaissance Woman*, 81.
67. By using *cela*, a deliberately enigmatic demonstrative pronoun, she leaves the reader in doubt as to exactly which text her husband actually read. Nevertheless, all signs point to either one of the last of her personal letters or *Les Angoysses*, both texts being about a woman's illicit passion and written in the first person.
68. Medieval glossators inaugurated the phrase *confessio est regina probationum*. See Peter Brooks, *Troubling Confessions: Speaking Guilt in Law & Literature* (Chicago: University of Chicago Press, 2000), 93.
69. Louise Labé similarly writes that she composed verse as a way to "fuir oysiveté." "Quant à moy tant en escrivant premierement ces jeunesses que en les revoyant depuis, je n'y cherchois autre chose qu'un honneste passetems et moyen de fuir oisiveté . . ." Labé, *Œuvres complètes*, 43. The idleness topos was a common prefatory strategy employed by women. See Larsen, "'Un honneste passetems': Strategies of Legitimation in French Renaissance Women's Prefaces," 14.
70. "Doctrine governing the conduct of women in public held that the resources of the imagination—feigning and fictionalizing—ought to be denied them." Jordan, *Renaissance Feminism*, 178.
71. See Nash, introduction, in Crenne, *Les Epistres familières et invectives*, 15–22.
72. "Writing out of the Double Bind: Female Plot and Hélisenne de Crenne's

Les Angoysses douloureuses qui procedent d'amours," Œuvres et Critiques 19, no. 1 (1994): 61.

73. Crenne, *The Torments of Love*, 28.

74. Ibid.

75. As Gisèle Mathieu-Castellani observes, more than the *énoncés* themselves, it is the modalities of *énonciation* that prove most revealing of the processes that shape women's writing: "la reprise, la répétition, l'imitation, la traduction, peuvent modifier subtilement l'énoncé transposé: dès qu'il est pris en charge dans l'énonciation, de discrets processus d'appropriation se font jour. . . ." *La Quenouille et la lyre*, 169–70.

76. The parallel with Montaigne is all the more suggestive if we recall that for both writers, the text serves in part to exteriorize a mental state, to give a discursive form to interiority, to add a public dimension to idleness, all the more since both essayist and novelist ultimately publish their *otium litteratum*. Moreover, the version of *Les Angoysses douloureuses* that ultimately reached the reader was composed during Hélisenne's sequestration in a tower that prefigures Montaigne's famous tower library. As Martine Debaisieux observes, the *Angoysses* leave an ambivalent image of the writer, at once the prisoner of her jealous husband locked away in a tower awaiting prince charming and an erudite woman withdrawn to a tower to devote herself to writing. "'Des dames du temps jadis': Fatalité culturelle et identité féminine dans *Les Angoysses Douloureuses*," *Symposium* 41, no. 1 (spring 1987): 33.

77. See Nash, introduction, in Crenne, *Les Epistres familières et invectives*, 20.

78. Confession had always been part of the Christian faith, although in varying forms. The practice developed among the desert fathers of the fourth and fifth centuries, the first Christian contemplatives and the first to practice a form of confession. Members of anchorite communities began "confessing" their faults to another solitary. This practice had a therapeutic function: it lessened the burden of the contemplative life with its asceticism, arduous spiritual journey, and constant threat of acedia. See the Groupe de la Bussière, *Pratiques de la confession: Des Pères du désert à Vatican II: Quinze études d'histoire* (Paris: Editions du Cerf, 1983), 25–40.

79. See Thomas Tentler, *Sin and Confession on the Eve of the Reformation* (Princeton: Princeton University Press, 1977), 52; 96–101.

80. See Henry Charles Lea, *A History of Auricular Confession and Indulgences in the Latin Church* (London: Swan Sonnenschein, 1896), 395.

81. A series of bogus hypotheses was made before Marguerite Briet was finally identified as the woman writing under the pen name of Hélisenne de Crenne. See Jerry Nash, "Constructing Hélisenne de Crenne: Reception and Identity," in *"Por le soie amiste": Essays in honor of Norris J. Lacy*, ed. Keith Busby and Catherine M. Jones (Amsterdam: Rodopi, 2000), 371–83.

82. See Leah Chang, who argues that the typography of *Les Angoysses douloureuses* contributes to the same puzzle of authorial identity by both producing and concealing the female authorial figure. *Printing the Muse: Book Production and the Construction of Female Authorship in Renaissance France*. Ph.D. thesis, University of Michigan, 2002, ch. 2, pp. 57–104.

83. See "Telling Secrets: Sacramental Confession and Narrative Authority in

the *Heptameron*," in *Critical Tales: New Studies of the "Heptameron" and Early Modern Culture*, ed. John D. Lyons and Mary B. McKinley (Philadelphia: University of Pennsylvania Press, 1993), 146–47.

84. Debaisieux first observed the parallel. See her discussion of the two scenes in "'Des dames du temps jadis," 37.

85. Jean Gerson explains that the confessor should congratulate confessants who are completely honest. See Tentler, *Sin and Confession on the Eve of the Reformation*, 100.

86. See Tentler's discussion of "the expert confessor"—his knowledge, tact, perseverance, skill, and compassionate demeanor, in ibid., esp. 99–101.

87. For a discussion of the performativity of confessional speech, see Brooks, *Troubling Confessions*, 95.

88. "Il vous fault efforcer d'avoir contrition des offenses que vous avez perpetrez et commis . . . ne povons estre reintegrez en estat de grace, que premierement n'en ayons faict penitence condigne." (*AD* I, 147) ["You must try to feel contrition for the offenses you have perpetrated and committed . . . we cannot return to a state of grace until we have first done appropriate penance." Crenne, *The Torments of Love*, 34–35.]

89. Ibid., 39.

90. Jacopo Caviceo, *Dialogue treselegant intitule le Peregrin*, trans. François Dassy (Paris: Nicolas Couteau for Galliot du pré, 1527), f. XXXVIr.

91. Crenne, *The Torments of Love*, 72.

92. See Buzon's introduction in Crenne, *Les Angoysses douloureuses qui procedent d'amours*, 24.

93. On the dual function of consolation and policing long served by confession, see Tentler, *Sin and Confession on the Eve of the Reformation*, xvi; 3–27.

94. I borrow the notion of a "sacred masterplot that organizes and explains the world" from Peter Brooks, *Reading for the Plot: Design and Intention in Narrative* (Cambridge: Harvard University Press, 1984), 6.

Chapter 4. Leisure as Commodity

1. *The Adventures of Don Quixote*, trans. Tobias Smollett (New York: Farrar, Straus and Giroux, 1986), part 1, chapter 6.

2. As for other early modern forms of serialization, the periodical appeared in France only in 1631 with Renaudot's *Gazette*, although, as Roger Chartier observes, there were antecedents such as the political and historical *occasionnels* published beginning in the late fifteenth century. See his "Pamphlets et gazettes" in *Histoire de l'édition française*, ed. Henri-Jean Martin, Roger Chartier, and Jean-Pierre Vivet, vol. 1 (Paris: Promodis, 1982), 405–25. Joan DeJean argues that Scudéry used serialization to incorporate the events of the Fronde as they developed into the narrative fiction of *Le Grand Cyrus*. As a result, her novel was both a work of fiction and a medium of current events. Joan DeJean, "The Politics of Genre: Madeleine de Scudéry and the Rise of the French Novel," *L'Esprit Créateur* 29, no. 3 (1989): 43–51. For an account of the serialization of English prose romance beginning in the 1580s, see Lori Humphrey Newcomb, *Reading Popular*

Romance in Early Modern England (New York: Columbia University Press, 2002), esp. 21–129.

3. This gesture was commonly associated with the *landorés,* known for their laziness. Rabelais, *Le Tiers Livre,* 23.

4. François Rabelais, *Le Quart Livre,* ed. Gérard Defaux and Robert Marichal (Paris: Librairie Générale Française, 1994), 591.

5. Herberay himself claims to have begun reading romance in order to avoid idleness: "[je] me suis mis (pour eviter la trop pernitieuse oysiveté) à lire plusieurs sortes de livres." *Le Premier Livre d'Amadis de Gaule,* vol. 1, XI. Some translators pretend to have adapted an "old story" in order to avoid idleness, "pour eviter oysiveté mère et nourrice des vices," to quote the prologue to the *Histoire de Giglan filz de messire Gauvain* . . . A condensed version of the prose *Lancelot* printed at the end of the century refers to some common accusations that romance translators were idlers: "plusieurs blasment [les histoires] tant, les appellans songes vains & inutiles forgez par hommes oisifs." *Histoire contenant les grandes prouesses, vaillances, et héroiques faicts d'armes de Lancelot du Lac, Chevalier de la T. R.* (Lyons: Benoist Rigaud, 1591). The prologue to the French translation of *Don Quixote* addresses the reader as "Lecteur oisif," *Le Valeureux Don Quixote,* trans. Cesar Oudrin (Paris: Jean Foüet, 1616).

6. Etienne Jodelle calls romance "la resverie de noz peres" and coins the neologism "fantastiquer" to refer to composing romance. See his epistle prefacing Claude Colet's *Histoire Palladienne. L'Epître au lecteur,* in *Œuvres,* I, ed. Enea Balmas (Paris: Gallimard, 1965), 93; 92.

7. Rabelais had already used the image of the empty bubble to indicate the absence of a higher or deeper meaning. In the preface to *Gargantua,* he suggests that the words and deeds related may turn out to be "belles billevezées." Ed. Defaux, 89.

8. *Le Livre du corps de policie,* ed. Angus Kennedy (Paris: Champion, 1998), 53.

9. See also the prologue to *Guillaume de Palerne,* which speaks of the function of *histoires antiques* in the following terms: "[m]oult valent pour le passetemps de seigneurs/dames & damoiselles en evitant oysivete racine de tous maux. & servent de tres grande recreation & aux vieux et plus anciens oyans parler des choses antiques qui dignes sont de grande veneration." *L'Histoire du noble preux & vaillant chevalier Guillaume de Palerne* (Paris: Nicolas Bonfons, n.d.).

10. Herberay des Essarts, *Le Premier Livre d'Amadis de Gaule,* XII–XIII.

11. Marian Rothstein observes an evolution toward greater reader involvement in Renaissance novels. She argues that *Amadis* called upon the reader to personalize, synthesize, and reconsider throughout the narrative. *Reading in the Renaissance: "Amadis de Gaule" and the Lessons of Memory* (Newark: University of Delaware Press, 1999), 95–114.

12. Prologue, *Pantagruel, Edition critique sur le texte de l'édition publiée à Lyon en 1542 par François Juste,* ed. Floyd Gray (Paris: Champion, 1997), 57. C.f., *Pantagruel* (1532), ed. V.-L. Saulnier (Geneva: Droz, 1965), 4. The *editio princeps* makes no mention of the reader's trade *(mestier),* a term added later and found in the 1542 edition, the last one that Rabelais revised and corrected. This detail suggests an increased emphasis on the importance of idleness for *Panta-*

gruel's inscribed readers. Subsequent references to *Pantagruel* will be from Floyd Gray's edition and will be included within the text.

13. "le genre romanesque [est] le plus sympathique des genres, celui qui s'est donné pour tâche, à force de discrétion et de joyeuse nullité, d'oublier ce que d'autres dégradent en l'appelant l'essentiel. Le divertissement est son chant profond. Changer sans cesse de direction, aller comme au hasard et pour fuir tout but, par un mouvement d'inquiétude qui se transforme en distraction heureuse, telle a été sa première et sa plus sûre justification. Faire du temps humain un jeu et du jeu une occupation libre, dénuée de tout intérêt immédiat et de toute utilité, essentiellement superficielle et capable par ce mouvement de surface d'absorber cependant tout l'être, cela n'est pas peu de chose." Maurice Blanchot, "Le Chant des Sirènes," in *Le Livre à venir* (Paris: Gallimard, 1959), 12.

14. For a discussion of the forms of play at stake in *Pantagruel*, see Raymond La Charité, *Recreation, Reflection, and Re-Creation: Perspectives on Rabelais's "Pantagruel"* (Lexington: French Forum, 1980).

15. See Glending Olson's discussion of medieval theories of recreation, which often associated *delectare* with the narrative surface (both plot and style) and *prodesse* with the spiritual truth hidden within the fiction. *Literature as Recreation in the Later Middle Ages*, 22 passim.

16. Herberay, *Le Premier Livre d'Amadis de Gaule*, vol. 1, XII.

17. Or rather, it is the writer/translator who *works for* the reader. Like an idle lord on his country estate, the reader reaps the fruits of the translator's labor. Herberay presents his adaptation of *Amadis* as "le fruict de mon labeur," XIII. Similarly, the translator of the *Histoire d'Isaie* specifies that putting pen to paper and adapting the *dispositio* and *elocutio* of the story required no small amount of labor "non pas en petit de labeur" (Paris: Jean Bonfons, 1550). The translator of *Meliadus* uses a comparable formula: "ce petit de labeur que jay prins pour mettre ce present volume en la main de tous . . ." *Meliadus de Leonnoys* (Paris: Galliot du Pré, 1528).

18. At its extreme, the tendency to attribute an epistemological function to effort means that "the truth of what is known is determined by the effort put into knowing it." Pieper, *Leisure: The Basis of Culture*, 15.

19. Herberay, *Le Premier Livre d'Amadis de Gaule*, vol. 1, XII.

20. This argument was commonly used by translators. Jacques Gohory's preface to the *Dixiesme Livre d'Amadis de Gaule* encourages Marguerite de France (the addressee) to use *Amadis* as a break from Greek and Latin books: "pour deduyt & recreation apres voz meilleurs livres Grecz & Latins." (Paris: Vincent Sertenas, 1557). The *Proème* to the *Histoire d'Isaie* also identifies romance as an enjoyable (but temporary) break from other books: "il est dedie pour l'augmentation du reliefvement de voz esperitz fatiguez & atenuz des autres livres . . ."

21. All of these arguments are commonplace in the long-standing tradition of literature as recreation. See Olson, *Literature as Recreation in the Later Middle Ages*, 39–89.

22. Rabelais, *Gargantua*, ed. Defaux, 241.

23. Rothstein cautions against applying classical aesthetic norms to Renaissance novels. She studies how incremental repetitions and analogies, sometimes prolonged over hundreds of pages, shaped habits of reading and poetic ideals. *Reading in the Renaissance*, 61–94. I argue below that this aesthetic ideal provided a fertile terrain for experimentation in the serial.

24. Lucien Febvre and Henri-Jean Martin, *L'Apparition du livre* (Paris: Albin Michel, 1958), esp. 162–92.

25. "Or avez-vous, Dame de cueur humain / Vostre Amadis en si petit volume / Que le pourrez porter dedans la main / Plus aysément beaucoup que de coutume." Quoted in Michel Simonin, "La Disgrâce d'Amadis," *Studi Francesi* 28 (1984): 3. On the changing format of *Amadis*, see also Rothstein, *Reading in the Renaissance*, 32–34.

26. Compare to Michel Jeanneret who argues that Renaissance literary productions of all sorts—from novella collections to miscellanies—obey a cumulative or "modular" logic rather than a linear one. The novella serves as a case in point. The allegorical model commonly used to make sense of medieval narratives is replaced in Marguerite de Navarre's *Heptaméron* by opinion and psychology. Plurality and heterogeneity thus supplant a "deeper meaning." See his "Modular Narrative and the Crisis of Interpretation," trans. John D. Lyons, in *Critical Tales: New Studies of the Heptameron and Early Modern Culture*, ed. John D. Lyons and Mary B. McKinley (Philadelphia: University of Pennsylvania Press, 1993): 85–103. It is my contention that the *Amadis* paradigm is more radical insofar as it suspends narrative resolution itself. This distinguishes it from the *Heptaméron* where the individual novellas are formally complete (ending with the resolution of narrative tension) even though the discussions they generate are not. Finally, the new context of serialization distinguishes *Amadis de Gaule* from the *Heptaméron* and novella collections from the first half of the century.

27. Gray, introduction, Rabelais, *Pantagruel*, 22.

28. See Langer, *Divine and Poetic Freedom in the Renaissance*, 103–5. Langer notes that the medieval literary tradition of pointing to a prior cause is emptied of any real significance by Rabelais's way of beginning *Pantagruel*: "Rabelais establishes himself not as a continuer of tradition, but as someone wishing to share the success of a contemporary. . . . Rabelais is not inspired by the *Chroniques*' material, but by its saleability," 104.

29. Olson, *Literature as Recreation in the Later Middle Ages*, 128–63.

30. See the conclusion to Jean Baudrillard's *Le Système des objets: La Consommation des signes* (Paris: Gallimard, 1968), and also Baudrillard's *La Société de consommation*.

31. Jean-Joseph Goux discusses this distinction (moral utility versus economic utility), elaborating on the work of Auguste Walras. "General Economics and Postmodern Capitalism," *Yale French Studies* 78 (1990): 222–24.

32. *Topics* 1.i (100a 18–101a); *Rhetoric* 1.8 (1356b–57a).

33. The preface became the publicity space where sellers addressed potential buyers. For a discussion of how the new status of the book as merchandise shaped liminary discourse, see Philippe Desan, "Préfaces, prologues et avis au lecteur: Stratégies préfacielles à la Renaissance," *What is Literature? France, 1100–1600*, ed. François Cornilliat, Ullrich Langer, and Douglas Kelly (Lexington: French Forum, 1993), 101–22.

34. On 12 July 1540, Herberay gave his publishers Vincent Sertenas and Jean Longis the six-year privilege he had obtained for the first four books of *Amadis*. Annie Parent, *Les Métiers du livre à Paris* (Geneva: Droz, 1974), 106.

35. Ibid., 107.

36. Herberay des Essarts, *Le Quatriesme Livre d'Amadis* (Paris: Jean Longis, 1555).

37. Ibid., sig. Aiiir.

38. Rothstein argues that Oriane and Amadis have a clandestine marriage well before the formal wedding ceremony at the end of book four. She observes that in the France of 1540, clandestine marriage, which consisted of a promise followed by carnal union, was still legitimate. *Reading in the Renaissance*, 129–38.

39. Parent, *Les Métiers du livre à Paris*, 108; 301–2.

40. For a general discussion of the importance of the "end," which confers duration and meaning, see Frank Kermode, *The Sense of an Ending: Studies in the Theory of Fiction* (Oxford: Oxford University Press, 1966).

41. Herberay, *Le Quatriesme Livre d'Amadis*, CXIv; my emphasis.

42. Garci Rodriguez de Montalvo, *Amadís de Gaula*, ed. Juan Manuel Cacho Blecua (Madrid: Catedra, 1987–88), vol. 2, 1765.

43. Herberay des Essarts, *Le Cinquiesme Livre d'Amadis* (Paris: Vincent Sertenas, 1550), CXVIIv; emphasis added.

44. "Mathurin Behu aux Lecteurs," in ibid., sig. Aiiiv.

45. The sixth book opens with a *dizain* addressed to "the Homer of Amadis," which begins: "Quoy que des cinq, voire de ce sixiesme, / France te loue, & son Roy t'en guerdonne, / Cela n'est rien, si n'avons ce septiesme . . ." The poem concludes with the suggestion that Amadis is immortal. "Notre Amadis jamais ne sera vieux." Herberay des Essarts, *Le Sixiesme Livre d'Amadis* . . . (Paris: Estienne Groulleau, 1557). Likewise, the final words address the reader directly, promising the same ample recitation of "faitz & chevaleries" announced by the preceding book. A second clause is also added, assuring the reader that the sequel has "as much grace as any book or *chronique* ever published." CXXVIIIr. Herberay's *Septiesme Livre d'Amadis* (Paris: Jeanne de Marnef, 1546) guarantees the reader as much perfection as the third, fourth, fifth, and sixth. The eighth and last one to be adapted by Herberay claims that the first words will "suddenly incite the listener's desire." The "Discours sur les Livres d'Amadis" by Michel Sevin suggests that the reader will want to read *Amadis* night and day and returns to the theme (previously developed) that (s)he will want to begin again: *"Vouloir aura de le recommencer."* *Le Huitiesme Livre d'Amadis* (Paris: Estienne Groulleau, 1548).

46. See Jean Baudrillard, "il n'y a pas de limites à la consommation. Si elle était ce pour quoi on la prend naïvement: une absorption, une dévoration, on devrait arriver à une saturation. Si elle était relative à l'ordre des besoins, on devrait s'acheminer vers une satisfaction. Or, nous savons qu'il n'en est rien: on veut consommer de plus en plus. Cette compulsion de consommation n'est pas due à quelque fatalité psychologique (qui a bu boira, etc.) ni à une simple contrainte de prestige. Si la consommation semble irrépressible, c'est justement qu'elle est une pratique idéaliste totale qui n'a plus rien à voir (au-delà d'un certain seuil) avec la satisfaction de besoins ni avec le principe de réalité. C'est qu'elle est dynamisée par le projet toujours déçu et sous-entendu dans l'objet." *Le Système des objets*, 238. For a critique of Baudrillard's fascination with this dynamic, the so-called "genius" of capitalism, see Goux, "General Economics and Postmodern Capitalism," 206–24.

47. The *princeps* has disappeared. The first surviving edition was printed in Saragossa in 1508. Montalvo's four books of *Amadis* were printed through 1586, with nineteen editions in all. Daniel Eisenberg, *Castilian Romances of Chivalry in the Sixteenth Century: A Bibliography* (London: Grant & Cutler, 1979).

48. "Prologue de l'Aucteur Espagnol d'Amadis, Traduict en Françoys," Herberay, *Amadis de Gaule*, ed. Hugues Vaganay, vol. I, xvi.

49. Seville, 1510. See Eisenberg, *Castilian Romances of Chivalry*, 43.

50. Eisenberg, *Castilian Romances of Chivalry*, 52.

51. *Le Livre du Nouveau Tristan, Prince de Leonnois, chevalier de la Table Ronde, & d'Yseult, princesse d'Yrlande, Royne de Cornouaille* (Lyons: Benoist Rigaud, 1577), 422v.

52. ". . . le Gentilhomme des Essars, fit revivre, & reflorir, par son Amadis, les vieux Chevaliers de la Grande Bretagne (yssuz neantmoins de nostre province)." *Le Premier Livre de l'Histoire & Ancienne Cronique de Gerard d'Euphrate* (Paris: Estienne Groulleau, 1549).

53. "Il est permis au Traducteur de l'histoire & cronique de Gerard d'Euphrate, contenant 6 livres, la faire imprimer, par tel, ou telz Imprimeurs que bon luy semblera," privilege dated 15 November 1548.

54. Ed. Marie-Madeleine Fontaine (Geneva: Droz, 1996), 199–200.

55. Rothstein estimates the readership of *Amadis* to reach at least half a million by the end of the century. Preface, *Reading in the Renaissance*.

56. Douglas Kelly, "Romance and the Vanity of Chrétien de Troyes," in *Romance: Generic Transformation from Chrétien de Troyes to Cervantes*, ed. Kevin Brownlee and Marina Scordilis Brownlee (Hanover: University Press of New England, 1985): 74–90.

57. Vives, *Livre de l'institution de la femme chrestienne*, trans. Changy, 40.

58. Ibid.

59. Simonin chronicles the reception of *Amadis de Gaule* from its initial success to its "disgrace" in 1560. Rothstein interprets *Amadis*'s fall from grace as the consequence of changing social realities and ideals pertaining to "love and war." See *Reading in the Renaissance*, 129–44.

60. Certain authors "se plaisent par un long discours de faire ostentation de leur bien dire, et monstrer comme ils sçavent Amadi gauliser remplissans une page entière de ce qui se pourroit escrire en deux lignes." Quoted in Simonin, "La Disgrâce d'Amadis," 33.

61. Amyot (trans.), *Histoire Æthiopique de Heliodorus, de nouveau reduite par chapitres pour plus facile intelligence* (Paris: Nicolas Bonfons, 1585), 3v.

62. The image of the *"songes de quelque malade resvant en fievre chaude"* is directly translated from Horace's *Ars Poetica* where it describes a work of art completely lacking harmony ("Velut aegri somnia, uanae," v. 7). This criticism becomes a virtual refrain in the romance polemic. As late as 1591 a condensed version of *Lancelot* begins with a refutation of this accusation: "Car il ne faut point doubter que soubs cette histoire, ou semblables (lesquelles plusieurs blasment tant, les appellans songes vains & inutiles forgez par hommes oisifs) ne soyent comprises, comme soubs des couvertures, plusieurs bons & profitables enseignemens, concernans tant la maniere de bien conserver les uns avec les autres, que les passions d'esprit, pertes d'Estats, & autres accidens, qui arrivent ordinairement aux humains . . ." *Histoire . . . de Lancelot du Lac*. For a discussion of verisimilitude in Amyot's preface, see Marc Fumaroli, "Jacques Amyot and the Clerical Polemic Against the Chivalric Novel," *Renaissance Quarterly* 38 (1985): 22–40.

63. *Epître*, 92–93. André de Rivaudeau similarly complains that otiose romance attracts an enthusiastic public while laborious and useful works are ne-

glected. He contrasts the sleepless nights he spent laboring over a *"bon grand long travail"*—a labor undertaken *"pour servir à la chose publique"*—to "useless" romance: "les Amadis, Tristans, et autres de mesme farine, c'est à dire, ou inutiles, ou indoctes, ou deshonnestes." *Aman* [1566] (Geneva: Droz, 1969), 58.

64. He accuses romancers of writing and publishing "choses vaines" while also accusing the *Amadis* books of being "des instrumens fort propres pour la corruption des mœurs." "Que la lecture des Livres d'Amadis n'est moins pernicieuse aux jeunes gens, que celle des livres de Machiavel aux vieux," *Discours politiques et militaires*, ed. F. E. Sutcliffe (Geneva: Droz, 1967), 161.

65. See Le Goff, *Pour un autre Moyen Age*, 46.

66. "Mais j'ay tousjour creu que la perte & prostitution du temps à chose vaine, & sans fruict, estoit une espece de sacrilege." Laval, *Desseins des professions nobles et publiques*, 304r.

67. In the opinion of "les gens de meilleur estomac"—that is, those who can digest philosophy and history ("la vraye histoire")—reading strictly for the pleasure of romance's "joyeux devis" is "an activity as useless as rolling Diogenes' tub in order to accomplish nothing" ("besongne autant oysive, que de rouller le tonneau de Diogenes pour faire plus que rien"). *L'Onzième Livre d'Amadis de Gaule, Traduit d'Espagnol en Francoys . . .* (Paris: Estienne Groulleau, 1559), sig. aiiijr.

68. Compare to Lori Humphrey Newcomb. Regarding the elite reaction to popular prose romance in England, Newcomb writes, "[t]o defend their exclusivity, they [elite writers] studded their new works with harsh portrayals of older pleasure-reading texts as degraded by market conditions or a too-broad audience. These Jacobean claims for distinction divided the field of cultural production along a line that would later come to define the opposition between literary and popular print cultures." *Reading Popular Romance in Early Modern England*, 78.

69. As in the poem "Quand d'Amadis j'ay veu le premier livre" quoted above. *Le Cinquiesme Livre d'Amadis*, n. p.

70. Baudrillard, *The Consumer Society*, 78.

71. *Don Quijote de la Mancha*, ed. Martin de Riquer (Barcelona: Editorial Juventud, 1971), 325. See also Timothy Hampton's discussion of this passage in light of a nostalgia for an aristocratic world in decline. *Writing from History: The Rhetoric of Exemplarity in Renaissance Literature* (Ithaca: Cornell University Press, 1990), 237–96.

72. ". . . plusieurs jeunes Hommes sont prests de perdre l'Esprit par cette lecture *[Amadis de Gaule]:* Non seulement elle nuyt à leurs estudes, mais elle les destourne encore de faire choix de quelque profession utile, leur faisant croire que la plus belle vie est celle des Chevaliers Errans." Charles Sorel, *De la connoissance des bons livres, ou Examen de Plusieurs Autheurs* (1671), ed. Hervé D. Bechade (Paris: Slatkine, 1981), 96. This judgment is already present in *Francion* and the *Berger Extravagant*. The *Académie* will relegate *Amadis*, *Lancelot*, *Perceforest* to the following definition: "[l]ivres fabuleux qui contiennent des Histoires d'amour et de chevaleries, inventées pour divertir et occuper des fainéants." Quoted in Cazauran, "Les Romans de chevalerie en France: Entre 'exemple' et 'recréation,'" 45.

CHAPTER 5. *"EN PLEINE OYSIVETÉ"*

1. See Tournon, "Vacances intérieures," 559–66.
2. Terence Cave characterizes Montaigne's writing as seeking a plenitude (*res*,

full experience, the real or natural self) while pointing to its own emptiness (*verba*, interpretation, language). "Full experience is always absent; presence is unattainable. All that the *Essais* can do, with their ineradicable self-consciousness, is to posit paradigms of wholeness as features of a discourse which, as it pours itself out, celebrates its own inanity." *The Cornucopian Text: Problems of Writing in the French Renaissance* (Oxford: Clarendon Press, 1979), 321. The other side of the coin, as Mary McKinley points out, is the free play of the signifier, which is never arrested by a signified. "Le langage doit sa prospérité à sa propre insuffisance. Il ne peut jamais prononcer le dernier mot, jamais se reposer dans le silence du sens complet et compris . . ." See her reading of "De la vanité" in *Les Terrains vagues des "Essais": Itinéraires et intertextes* (Paris: Champion, 1996), 105–26.

3. Compare to Michael O'Loughlin, who argues that Montaigne's conception of leisure resolves the age-old opposition of religious contemplation (which situates the end outside of this world) and the civic ideal of the active life. "His characteristic exercise of the contemplative faculty is not to seek the vision of God but to contemplate, as an end in itself, the world once set aside for mere action and not contemplation." *The Garlands of Repose*, 189.

4. See Screech, *Montaigne and Melancholy*. Norton takes idleness to be another name for inertia in *Montaigne and the Introspective Mind*.

5. See Gisèle Mathieu-Castellani, *Montaigne: L'Ecriture de l'essai* (Paris: Presses Universitaires de France, 1988) and Raymond Esclapez, "L'Oisiveté créatrice dans *Les Essais*: Persistance et épanouissement d'un thème," *Bulletin de la Société des Amis de Montaigne*, 33–34 (1993): 25–39.

6. Pierre Villey locates Montaigne's source for "De l'oisiveté" in "L'excellence & les louenges du travail & le dommage qu'engendre oysiveté," in *Les Diverses Leçons de Pierre Messie*, trans. Claude Gruget, 85r-90v. Very similar terms are found in other *compendia*, including Des Caurres, "De l'oisiveté, & maux procedans d'icelle," in *Œuvres morales et diversifiées*; and Pierre de La Primaudaye, "De L'Oisiveté, et Paresse, & du Jeu," in *L'Academie françoise*, 177–82. Compare to Robert Cottrell, who suggests that Plutarch's "Comment il faut ouïr" from *Les Œuvres morales* may have been Montaigne's source for "De l'oisiveté." "L'Image des terres oisives dans 'De l'oisiveté,'" *Bulletin de la Société des Amis de Montaigne* 16 (1975): 63–66.

7. The epideictic genre naturally implies the rhetoric of exemplarity because it is necessary to determine what is praiseworthy in order to pursue virtue—and by extension—imitate the virtuous. For a discussion of the functions of praise and blame along with related theories of the virtues in Renaissance moral philosophy, see Ullrich Langer, *Vertu du discours, discours de la vertu*.

8. ". . . et mes qualitez plus favories: l'oisifveté, la franchise" (III, 9, 969c).

9. Hugo Friedrich begins his study of the *Essais* with a portrait of Montaigne as an idle aristocrat who writes as a way to pass the time. "Les *Essais* de Michel de Montaigne sont de libres considérations d'un gentilhomme français dans l'esprit de l'humanisme finissant du XVIe siècle, rédigées entre sa quarantième et sa soixantième année, publiées par lui-même pour passer le temps dans l'oisiveté de sa vieillesse retirée . . ." *Montaigne*, trans. Robert Rovini (Paris: Gallimard, 1968), 11. See also Jean-Pierre Boon, *Montaigne, gentilhomme et essayiste* (Paris: Editions Universitaires, 1971); and more recently, Desan, *Les Commerces de Montaigne*, 47–81.

10. For a discussion of how the textual productivity of the *Essais* inverts—or negates—Montaigne's studied posture as an idle dilettante, see Tom Conley, "*De Capsula Totoe*: Lecture de Montaigne, 'De trois commerces,'" *L'Esprit Créateur* 28, no. 1 (1988): 18–26. "Montaigne rappelle-t-il les poses stoïques de Sénèque (*Epîtres*, LVI) afin de s'édifier en sa bibliothèque? Il paraît qu'il souligne combien la différence minuscule, ici marquée entre *otii* et *negotio*, devient le travail—ou commerce—est mise en cause, mais moins dans la couche référentielle que dans l'aspect démonique de chaque mot qui choît dans le texte. Le travail se mue en une double opération d'ajouter et de soustraire, par laquelle la production textuelle se manifeste comme une oisiveté au négatif," 24.

11. Reading the *Essais*, he tells us, is not *necessarily* a profitable *lesson* that may be redeemed by the reader. On a more general level, this gesture is emblematic of Montaigne's poetics of the essay. By its very movement, the text undermines any stable product (a meaning or lesson) consumed by the reader. Constructing meanings only to subsequently disrupt them, positing "truths" only to then unveil them as falsehoods, the text frustrates any attempt on the part of the reader to extract a preconstituted and stable *profit*. See Lawrence Kritzman, *Destruction/Découverte: Le Fonctionnement de la rhétorique dans les "Essais" de Montaigne* (Lexington: French Forum, 1980).

12. For a general discussion of Montaigne's definition of the ideal reader, see Terence Cave, "Problems of Reading in the *Essais*," in *Montaigne: Essays in Memory of Richard Sayce*, ed. I. D. McFarlane and Ian MacLean (Oxford: Clarendon Press, 1982), 153–63; and Cathleen Bauschatz, "Montaigne's Conception of Reading in the Context of Renaissance Poetics and Modern Criticism," in *The Reader in the Text*, ed. Susan Suleiman and Inge Crosman (Princeton: Princeton University Press, 1980), 264–91.

13. As in Busbecq's phrase discussed in chapter 2. For whoever masters this difficult art, literary idleness "luy sert d'ornement, & le faict priser, cherir, & bien venir aux compaignies." Laval, *Desseins des professions nobles et publiques*, 304v.

14. From *Huetiana*, Art. VI. Quoted in Alan Boase, *The Fortunes of Montaigne: A History of the Essays in France, 1580–1669* (London: Methuen & Co., 1935), 104.

15. Donald Frame, *Montaigne's "Essais": A Study* (Englewood Cliffs, N.J.: Prentice-Hall, 1969), 16; 75.

16. There are a number of very good studies of the rhetorical structure of "De l'oisiveté," including Carol Clark, *The Web of Metaphor: Studies in the Imagery of Montaigne's "Essais,"* ed. R. C. La Charité and V. A. La Charité (Lexington: French Forum, 1978), 123–29; Georges Van Den Abbeele, *Travel as Metaphor: from Montaigne to Rousseau* (Minneapolis: University of Minnesota Press, 1992), 12–18; and Mathieu-Castellani, *Montaigne: L'Ecriture de l'essai*, 25–32.

17. There was widespread belief that the conjunction of women's semen and menstrual blood resulted in the production of *mola uteri*. In order to produce what Montaigne terms a "generation bonne et naturelle," male semen would also be required. See Ian MacLean, *The Renaissance Notion of Woman: A Study in the Fortunes of Scholasticism and Medical Science in European Intellectual Life* (Cambridge: Cambridge University Press, 1980), 36.

18. "et comme nous voyons que les femmes produisent bien toutes seules, des amas et pieces de chair informes, mais que pour faire une generation bonne et naturelle, il les faut embesoigner d'une autre semence" (I, 8, 32a).

19. See also Richard Regosin, "Montaigne's Monstrous Confessions," *Montaigne Studies* 1 (1989): 73–87; and Terence Cave, "Le Récit montaignien: un voyage sans repentir," in *Montaigne: Espace, voyage, écriture*, Actes du Congrès International de Thessalonique 1992, ed. Zoé Samaras (Paris: Champion, 1995), 125–35.

20. "Si j'avois à revivre, je revivrois comme j'ay vescu" (III, 2, 816c).

21. *Montaigne: L'Ecriture de l'essai*, 25–32.

22. "Toutefois je juge ainsi, qu'à une chose si divine et *si hautaine*, et *surpassant de si loing l'humaine intelligence*, comme est cette verité de laquelle il a pleu à la bonté de Dieu nous esclairer, il est bien besoin qu'il nous preste encore son secours, d'une faveur extraordinaire et privilegée, pour la pouvoir concevoir et loger en nous; et ne croy pas que les moyens purement humains en soyent aucunement capables; et, s'ils l'estoient, tant d'ames rares et excellentes, et si abondamment garnies de forces naturelles és siecles anciens, n'eussent pas failly par leur discours d'arriver à cette connoissance. C'est la foy seule qui embrasse vivement et certainement les hauts mysteres de nostre Religion" (II, 12, 440–41a). Critics have discussed this "fear of high places," including Conche, *Montaigne et la philosophie*, 19; O'Loughlin, *The Garlands of Repose*, 158–62; and Screech, *Montaigne & Melancholy*.

23. See Jean Leclercq, *Otia monastica: Etudes sur le vocabulaire de la contemplation au Moyen Age* (Rome: Herder, 1963). "Et ce qui commence ici-bas dans le sabbat des âmes aura son achèvement lors de la résurrection des corps. Le trépas, le passage de cette vie en l'autre est une mise en vacance: du repos dont on jouissait ici-bas, l'on arrive 'au port de l'éternel repos,'" 82; "La quiétude n'est donc ni une paresse, ni un égoïsme; c'est un désir de Dieu," 83.

24. "Bien heureux sont ceux qui meurent au Seigneur, pource que leurs espritz se reposent de leurs labeurs . . ." (90v). Christian imagery commonly figured the "rest" of the afterlife with the allegory of *homo viator*, a commonplace in both medieval and Renaissance literature: the creature's tiring journey ends only with death when the "wayfarer" finally returns "home" to God. See Gerhart Ladner, "Homo Viator: Mediaeval Ideas on Alienation and Order," *Speculum* 42, no. 2 (1967): 233–59.

25. "The deepest root, then, from which leisure draws its sustenance—and leisure implies the realm of everything that, without being useful, nevertheless belongs to a complete human existence—the deepest root of all this lies in worshipful celebration." Pieper, *Leisure: The Basis of Culture*, 55.

26. See Leclercq, *Otia monastica*, 20. In his survey of the ideal of *quies contemplationis*, Leclercq found this doctrine to be universal in the twelfth century: ". . . sous ces diverses formes, la présence à Dieu doit s'interpréter comme un commencement, une réalisation partielle de la parfaite union à Dieu qui sera celle de l'éternité. Il faut y insister en terminant, car c'est là, dans l'enseignement des spirituels, une donnée constante et unanime . . . Dieu seul est le vrai repos. Toute union avec lui, toute participation à lui est donc, ici-bas, imparfaite; elle n'est qu'une anticipation de ce que sera la béatitude totale dans la vision pour toujours," 122–23.

27. Leclercq quotes Aelred de Rievaulx to similar effect. "Il a montré que la nature humaine tend vers l'union à Dieu comme vers la fin sans laquelle elle n'a point de repos: elle ne trouvera son 'sabbat' que dans cet amour: 'Le sabbat, c'est

le repos de l'âme, la paix du cœur, la tranquillité de l'esprit. Or l'âme humaine, faite pour Dieu, ne trouvera sa vraie quiétude qu'en Dieu: il n'est pour l'homme de vrai sabbat en dehors de Dieu . . .'" *Otia monastica*, 109.

28. Quint characterizes this "new historicism," which tends to make meaning autonomously human, in the following way: "It regards culture as an exclusively human creation, whose meaning is determined by the historical circumstances and individual dispositions of its authors. . . ." *Origin and Originality in Renaissance Literature: Versions of the Source* (New Haven: Yale University Press, 1983), 19. For a nuanced discussion of the problem of positing a human creator as the authority and cause of a literary creation in the *Essais*, see Langer, *Divine and Poetic Freedom*, esp. 110–25.

29. Louis Guyon, *Les Diverses Leçons*, book II (Lyons: Claude Morillon, 1610–25), 253.

30. Ibid.

31. Ibid., 254; Montaigne, 240; Frame, 177.

32. Guyon, 254; Montaigne, 241; Frame, 177.

33. Guyon, 255; Montaigne, 242; Frame, 178.

34. Epicureanism functioned as a "secular" discourse during the Renaissance despite the fact that Epicurus was hardly an atheist. Not only did he practice the religious rituals of his time, but his cosmology included gods: "The Gods exist, the knowledge we have of them is clear proof," *Epistle* III, 123. Quoted in A.-J. Festugière, *Epicure et ses Dieux* (1946; reprint, Paris: Presses Universitaires de France, 1968), 86.

35. Michael Andrew Screech, *Montaigne's Annotated Copy of Lucretius: A Transcription and Study of the Manuscript, Notes, and Pen-marks* (Geneva: Droz, 1998), xix–xx; 91.

36. Pierre Villey counts 149 quotations from *De rerum natura* in the *Essais*. *Les Sources et l'évolution des Essais de Montaigne* (Paris: Hachette, 1933), vol. 1, 189.

37. A highly respected humanist, Dionysius Lambinus also edited Cicero and Plautus. As Screech points out, his edition of Lucretius was well received, winning the support of Charles IX. On earlier editions of *De rerum natura* (including those established by J.-B. Pius, H. Avantius, and Navagero), see Screech, *Montaigne's Annotated Copy of Lucretius*, 17.

38. 1, 44–46, 7. Unless otherwise indicated, all references to Lucretius's text and translations into English will be from the Loeb edition, ed. W. H. D. Rouse and Martin F. Smith (Cambridge: Harvard University Press, 1992).

39. Screech, *Montaigne's Annotated Copy of Lucretius*, 111.

40. Titus Carus Lucretius, *Titi Lucretii Cari "De rerum natura" libri sex.*, ed. Dionysius Lambinus (Paris: Guillaume and Philippe Rouillé, 1564), 9.

41. Insofar as it divorced the *being* of the gods from any *doing* (their nonintervention in human affairs will be my focus below), Epicurean thought constituted a challenge to the fundamental assumptions of Christianity, and, indeed, of most religions. ". . . il est usuel d'associer ainsi l'être des dieux à leur agir." Festugière, *Epicure et ses Dieux*, 73.

42. Specifically, pages 182 (on the gods' nonintervention in human affairs) and 471 (on their peace and tranquillity that mortals cannot disturb). See Screech, *Montaigne's Annotated Copy of Lucretius*, 37–38.

43. It also reveals how much Montaigne's positive reaction diverged from dominant attitudes toward Epicurean leisure. Labeled as "swine" *(pourceaux)* "wallowing" in idleness, Epicureans were frequently under attack during the Renaissance. *To wallow in idleness* became a formula omnipresent in moralist discourse, and from there a generalized idiom. Montaigne activates this sense, only to discredit it in "De la solitude," writing "ne craignons pas en cette solitude nous *croupir* d'oisiveté ennuyeuse" (I, 39, 241a; emphasis added). The topos of the Epicurean "swine" probably came from a misreading of the last verses of Horace's *Epistle* 1, 4. Friedrich, *Montaigne*, 80.

44. Screech, *Montaigne's Annotated Copy of Lucretius*, 273.

45. Lucretius, *De rerum natura*, II, 647–48, 146.

46. Screech, *Montaigne's Annotated Copy of Lucretius*, 117.

47. With verbs of speaking or writing, *prolixe* denotes "at length, in detail." However, without such a verb to limit the meaning, *prolixe* means simply "in large quantity, amply, lavishly." Charlton T. Lewis and Charles Short, *A Latin Dictionary* (Oxford: Clarendon Press, 1879; 1975).

48. I, 39, 247–48a/c.

49. For a discussion of Epicurus's insistence on the importance of separating good desires from bad or "empty" desires *(kenai epithumiai)*, see Martha Nussbaum, *The Therapy of Desire: Theory and Practice in Hellenistic Ethics* (Princeton: Princeton University Press, 1994), 112–13. Marcel Conche studies how this opposition plays out in the *Essais* in *Montaigne et la philosophie*, 89–91.

50. *Epistles* vol. 4 (Cambridge: Harvard University Press, 1996), IX, 13, 50; emphasis added. At about the same time as Montaigne was composing the early essays, his brother-in-law Geoffroy de La Chassaigne, *sieur* de Pressac, was composing the first translation of Seneca's *Epistles* into French. He translated Seneca's ideal of philosophical plenitude with the following phrase *"le sage est contant de soymesme." Epistres de L'Annæe Seneque, philosophe très-excellent* (Paris: Guillaume Chaudière, 1582), 26B.

51. *Epistles*, vol. 5, 72. 8, 102.

52. ". . . j'ay marché aussi avant et le pas qu'il m'a pleu. Cela m'a amolli et rendu *inutile* au service d'autruy, et ne m'a faict bon qu'à moy. Et, pour moy, il n'a esté besoin de forcer ce naturel poisant, *paresseux* et *fay neant*" (II, 17, 643a; emphasis added); "Mais il y devroit avoir quelque coërction des loix contre les escrivains ineptes et *inutiles*, comme il y a contre les vagabons et *faineants*. On banniroit des mains de nostre peuple et moy et cent autres." (III, 9, 946b; emphasis added); "[c]omme nous voyons des terres oysives, si elles sont grasses et fertilles foisonner en cent mille sortes d'herbes sauvages et inutiles" (I, 8, 32a). Montaigne seems to delight in emphasizing the copiousness of these useless weeds *(cent mille sortes)*—or the uselessness of these copious weeds, both concepts being intimately connected.

53. *Nicomachean Ethics*, X, 8, 1178b, 9–32: "For we traditionally suppose that the gods more than anyone are blessed and happy; but what sort of actions ought we to ascribe to them? Just actions? Surely they will appear ridiculous making contracts, returning deposits and so on. . . . However, we all traditionally suppose that they are alive and active, since surely they are not asleep like Endymion. Then if someone is alive, and action is excluded, and production even more, what is left but study? Hence the gods' activity that is superior in blessedness will be an

activity of study. And so the human activity that is most akin to the gods' will, more than any others, have the character of happiness." Ed. and trans. Irwin, 288–89.

54. Regarding Aristotle's ideal of *schole*, Pierre Hadot writes: "le modèle de cette action contemplative, c'est Dieu lui-même et l'univers, qui n'exercent aucune action tournée vers l'extérieur, mais se prennent eux-mêmes pour objets." *Qu'est-ce que la philosophie antique?* (Paris: Gallimard, 1995), 129.

55. ". . . les dieux d'Epicure sont la projection et l'incarnation de l'idéal de vie épicurien. La vie des dieux consiste à jouir de leur propre perfection, du pur plaisir d'exister, sans besoin, sans trouble, dans la plus douce des sociétés." Hadot, *Qu'est-ce que la philosophie antique?* 190.

56. "C'est une nation, diroy je à Platon, en laquelle il n'y a aucune espece de trafique; . . . nulles occupations qu'oysives . . ." (I, 31, 206a).

57. "Je te conseille, en cette pleine et grasse rectraicte, où tu es, de quiter à tes gens ce bas et abject soing du mesnage, et t'adonner à l'estude des lettres, pour en tirer quelque chose qui soit toute tienne" (I, 39, 244a); [I advise you, in this full and prosperous retreat of yours, to leave to your servants the sordid and abject care of the household, and to devote yourself to the study of letters, in order to derive from them something that is all your own] (180).

58. III, 18, 188–89; III, 23–24, 190–91.

59. On the association of walking, writing, and thinking in the *Essais*, see Margaret McGowan, "'Il faut que j'aille de la plume comme des pieds' (III, 9, 991b)," in *La Rhétorique de Montaigne*, ed. Frank Lestringant (Actes du colloque de la Société des Amis de Montaigne, Paris 1984) (Paris: Champion, 1985), 165–73.

60. Hoffmann, *Montaigne's Career*, esp. 11–15.

61. Pieper comments on the passive dimensions of contemplation. "The spiritual knowing power of the human mind, as the ancients understood it, is really two things in one: *ratio* and *intellectus*: all knowing involves both. The path of discursive reasoning is accompanied and penetrated by the *intellectus*' untiring vision, which is not active but passive, or better, *receptive*—a receptively operating power of the intellect." *Leisure: The Basis of Culture*, 11–12.

62. "To see, but not necessarily to be seen. Although the smoke rising from the side chamber's chimney would have signalled to the entire estate that the lord was in his tower, the narrow windows set in walls more than half a meter thick would have made it impossible to know where Montaigne was in the tower. Was he watching the fields outside the chateau where his gardeners, hired hands, and tenant farmers laboured, or was he in the side chamber watching the interior courtyard where the servants worked and lived? Even if he turned away from the windows to read by himself, workers on the estate may very well have remained on their best behavior." Hoffmann, *Montaigne's Career*, 15.

63. III, 18–22, 188–91.

64. Screech, *Montaigne's Annotated Copy of Lucretius*, 125.

65. As Huguet notes, the literal meaning of *tranquillité* during the Renaissance referred to calmness of wind or weather.

66. Compare to David Quint, who argues that Montaigne adopts an ethical position critical of the ideal of Stoic self-mastery in response to the sociopolitical climate of the Wars of Religion. *Montaigne and the Quality of Mercy: Ethical and Political Themes in the Essais* (Princeton: Princeton University Press, 1998).

67. On Seneca's letters as a point of departure for the nascent essay, see Fran-

çois Rigolot, *Les Métamorphoses de Montaigne* (Paris: Presses Universitaires de France, 1988), 79–85.

68. In his dedication to Henri III, La Chassaigne emphasized how well Seneca's lessons were suited to the contemporary nobility, whose beleaguered ranks were in dire need of the constancy taught by Stoic philosophy. "Epistre au Roy," in *Epistres de L'Annæe Seneque, philosophe très-excellent* (Paris: Guillaume Chaudière, 1582). Alain Legros argues that when Montaigne and Geoffroy de La Chassaigne both presented their books to the king in 1580, the intended effect was to present Montaigne as a new Seneca and a would-be counselor to the king. "Montaigne, son livre et son roi," *Studi francesi* 41, no. 2 (1997), 273. See also Jean Balsamo, "Deux gentilshommes 'nécessiteux d'honneur': Montaigne et Pressac," *Montaigne Studies* 13, nos. 1–2 (2001): 141–73.

69. La Chassaigne, *Epistres de l'Annæe Seneque*, 20r.

70. Seneca posits the existence of *two* republics: we are born into the smaller republic (the state) by accident; the other republic is far greater, it is the universe itself, for the Stoics define themselves by their world-citizenship. Moreover, we can serve this greater commonwealth better if we are at leisure: "Huic maiori rei publicae et in otio deservire possumus . . ." (IV. v. 2).

71. The physical principle of atoms' perpetual movement (*De rerum natura*, II, 308–11) is given an ethical value in the form of the necessity of a retreat from the public sphere. See Michel Serres, *La Naissance de la Physique dans le texte de Lucrèce: Fleuves et turbulences* (Paris: Minuit, 1977), 225.

> Retirez-vous de la foire aux honneurs, il y va toujours de la mort et de la cruauté. Suivent les préceptes connus de l'éthique épicurienne. Pourquoi se fonde-t-elle sur une physique, pourquoi requiert-elle une science? Tout simplement parce que la physique est tourbillonnante et qu'elle est une science du trouble. Que cette connaissance exacte de la nature et de l'histoire donne les bonnes leçons. Dès lors, le trouble est tourbillon et le qualitatif quantifiable. De nouveau, la morale est une physique bien entendue. A elle seule nous pouvons poser la question: quel est ce trouble à quoi veut s'arracher la pensée du plaisir? C'est le tourbillon même. Celui qui dévale en croissant la pente du déclin. Celui où le désir engendre le désir par la compensation interposée, où la dégradation se produit elle-même par la recherche d'équilibre interposée.

72. Lucretius, *De rerum natura* II, 1093–99, 180–81.

73. Screech, *Montaigne's Annotated Copy of Lucretius*, 287.

74. Manual labor was not considered, legally speaking, *dérogeance* provided that it was neither performed for another nor motivated by gain. Notwithstanding, there was apparently a popular prejudice against nobles engaging in manual labor, particularly agriculture, which the jurist Loyseau saw the need to dispel: "le labourage ne déroge point à la Noblesse . . ." *Les Œuvres*, 31.

75. In the 1588 edition, Montaigne claims that he has hardly ever had to handle anything but himself: "n'ayant jamais guieres eu en maniement que moy" II, 17, 643 n. 6.

76. "Au niveau conscient Montaigne prend parti pour les valeurs féodales et chevaleresques; or, il est lui-même prisonnier d'un discours qui appartient au monde marchand et ne peut se représenter la noblesse à laquelle il aspire qu'à travers un discours de commerçant." Desan, *Les Commerces de Montaigne*, 87.

77. Charles Beaulieux, *Chronologie du Livre de Raison et des autres œuvres manuscrites de Montaigne* (Bordeaux: E Taffard, 1951), 13.

78. Montaigne recorded births in his family, including his own, the birth of his wife, of their daughters (including those who did not survive), of his grandchildren, of his father, of his wife, of his sisters, of his brothers, and even of his son-in-law, François de la Tour. (The date of his mother's birth [not recorded] is a notable exception.) Jean Marchand, ed., *Le Livre de Raison de Montaigne sur "l'Ephemeris historica" de Beuther* (Paris: Arts Graphiques, 1948).

79. Philippe Desan explores how Montaigne's conception of writing in the *Essais* was shaped by the mode of keeping a *Livre de raison*, premised, as it was, on the centrality of the merchant bookkeeper as a focal point in the record of bills and payments, on a mingling of the personal and the impersonal, on a single unit of measure, and on perpetual open-endedness. See "La Comptabilité de Montaigne," in *L'Imaqinaire économique de la Renaissance* (Mont-de-Marsan: Editions InterUniversitaires, 1993), 175–200.

80. "*Retraict*, conventionnel, c'est un rachapt de la chose vendue, promis & accordé par l'acquereur . . . Est tantost adjectif feminin de Retraict, combien qu'on use plus de ce mot Retirée. Tantost substantif & signifie retour d'où on est parti . . ." Jean Nicot, *Thresor de la Langue Françoise* (Paris: David Douceur, 1606), 567.

81. ". . . les marchants tiennent communement leur meilleure marchandise aux arriere-boutiques . . ." ibid., 47.

82. On the Eyquem-Montaigne cursus, see Desan, *Les Commerces de Montaigne*, 48–81; and Trinquet, *La Jeunesse de Montaigne*.

Bibliography

Primary Sources

Amyot, Jacques. Prologue. *Histoire Æthiopique de Heliodorus, de nouveau reduite par chapitres pour plus facile intelligence*. Paris: Nicolas Bonfons, 1585.

———. *Les Vies des hommes illustres grecs et romains*. Translated by Jacques Amyot. Paris: Michel de Vascosan, 1559.

Aneau, Barthélemy. *L'Imagination poétique*. Lyons: Macé Bonhomme, 1552.

Aristotle. *Nicomachean Ethics*. Translated and edited by Terence Irwin. Indianapolis: Hackett, 1985.

———. *Ethicorum Aristotelis*. Leonardo Bruni. Paris: Jean Higman and Wolfgang Hopyl, 1496–97.

———. *Aristotelis Ad Nicomachum filium de Moribus, quae Ethica nominantur, libri decem*. Joachim Périon. Paris: Gabriel Buon, 1576.

———. *Comentarii in X Libros Aristotelis De Moribus ad Nicomachum*. Pier Vettori. Florence, 1566.

Aubery, Jean. *L'Antidote d'amour, avec un ample discours, contenant la nature & les causes d'iceluy, ensemble les remedes les plus singuliers pour se preserver & guerir des Passions Amoureuses*. Paris: Claude Chappelet, 1599.

Béroalde de Verville. "A très vertueuse Dame, Madame Charlotte Adam Dame de la Vallière." In *Misères et grandeur de la femme au XVIe siècle*, edited by Ilana Zinguer, 81–85. Geneva: Slatkine, 1982.

———. *Les Avantures de Floride, Histoire Françoise*. Tours: Jamet Mettayer, 1592.

Boccaccio, Giovanni. *The Elegy of Lady Fiammetta*. Edited and translated by Mariangela Causa-Steindler and Thomas Mauch. Chicago: University of Chicago Press, 1990.

Bouchet, Jean. *Epistres morales & familieres du Traverseur*. Poitiers: Jacques Bouchet, 1545.

Budé, Guillaume. *Traitté de la venerie*. Translated by Louis Le Roy. Edited by Henri Chevreul. Paris: Auguste Aubry, 1861.

Castiglione, Baldesar. *Le Livre du Courtisan*. Edited and translated by Alain Pons. Paris: Flammarion, 1991.

———. *Le Parfait Courtisan*. Translated by Gabriel Chappuis. Paris: Nicolas Bonfons, 1585.

Caumont, Jean de. *De la vertu de noblesse*. Paris: Jean Charron, 1586.

Caviceo, Jacopo. *Dialogue treselegant intitule le Peregrin.* Translated by François Dassy. Paris: Nicolas Couteau for Galliot du pré, 1527.

Cervantes, Miguel de. *Don Quijote de la Mancha.* Edited by Martin de Riquer. Barcelona: Editorial Juventud, 1971.

———. Translated by Tobias Smollett. New York: Farrar, Straus, and Giroux, 1986.

———. *Le Valeureux Don Quixote.* Translated by Cesar Oudrin. Paris: Jean Foüet, 1616.

Christine de Pizan. *Le Livre du corps de policie.* Edited by Angus Kennedy. Paris: Champion, 1998.

Cicero, Marcus Tullius. *De Officiis.* Cambridge: Harvard University Press, 1997.

Clichtove, Josse. *Le Traicté de la vraye noblesse.* Paris: Jean Longis, 1539.

Crenne, Hélisenne de. *Les Angoysses douloureuses qui procedent d'amours.* Edited by Christine de Buzon. Paris: Champion, 1997.

———. *Les Epistres familieres et invectives de ma dame Helisenne.* Edited by Jean-Philippe Beaulieu and Hannah Fournier. Montreal: Presses de l'Université de Montréal, 1995.

———. *Les Epistres familières et invectives.* Edited by Jerry Nash. Paris: Champion, 1996.

———. *A Renaissance Woman: Helisenne's Personal and Invective Letters.* Translated by Marianna M. Mustacchi and Paul J. Archambault. Syracuse: Syracuse University Press, 1986.

———. *The Torments of Love.* Translated by Lisa Neal and Steven Rendall. Minneapolis: University of Minnesota Press, 1996.

Des Caurres, Jean. *Œuvres morales et diversifiées.* Paris: Guillaume Chaudière, 1575.

Des Roches, Madeleine and Catherine. *Les Missives.* Edited by Anne R. Larsen. Geneva: Droz, 1999.

———. *Les Œuvres.* Edited by Anne R. Larsen. Geneva: Droz, 1993.

Du Bellay, Joachim. "Ample Discours au Roy sur le fait des Quatre Estats du Royaume de France." *Œuvres complètes.* Vol. 4. Edited by Léon Séché. Paris: Revue de la Renaissance, 1913.

———. *Deffence et Illustration de la langue francoyse.* Edited by Henri Chamard. Paris: M. Didier, 1948.

Du Perron, Jacques Davy. *Oraison funèbre sur la mort de Monsieur de Ronsard.* Edited by Michel Simonin. Geneva: Droz, 1985.

Erasmus, Desiderius. *Opera Omnia Desiderii Erasmi Roterodami.* Vol. 2. Amsterdam: Elsevier, 1969.

Estienne, Robert. *Dictionnaire françois-latin.* Paris: Robert Estienne, 1549.

Fasciculus Morum: A Fourteenth-Century Preacher's Handbook. Edited and translated by Siegfried Wenzel. University Park: Pennsylvania State University Press, 1989.

Gohory, Jacques. *Le Dixieme Livre d'Amadis de Gaule.* Paris: Vincent Sertenas, 1557.

———. *L'Onzieme Livre d'Amadis de Gaule.* Paris: Estienne Groulleau, 1559.

———. *Le Treizieme Livre traduit nouvellement d'Espagnol en Francois par JGP*. Paris: Estienne Groulleau, 1571.

Guillaume de Deguilleville. *Pèlerinage de vie humaine*. Edited by J. J. Stürzinger, Roxburghe Club, no. 124. London: J. B. Nichols & Sons, 1893.

Guillaume de Lorris. *Le Roman de la Rose*. Edited by Felix Lecoy. Paris: Champion, 1976.

———. *The Romance of the Rose*. Translated by Frances Horgan. Oxford: Oxford University Press, 1994.

Guyon, Louis. *Les Diverses Leçons*. Lyons: Claude Morillon, 1610–25.

Herberay des Essarts. *Le Premier Livre d'Amadis de Gaule*. Edited by Hugues Vaganay and Yves Giraud. 2 vols. Paris: Nizet, 1986.

———. *Le Quatriesme Livre d'Amadis de Gaule*. Paris: Jean Longis, 1555.

———. *Le Cinquiesme Livre d'Amadis de Gaule*. Paris: Vincent Sertenas, 1550.

———. *Le Sixiesme Livre d'Amadis de Gaule*. Paris: Estienne Groulleau, 1557.

———. *Le Septiesme Livre d'Amadis de Gaule*. Paris: Jeanne de Marnef, 1546.

———. *Le Huitiesme Livre d'Amadis de Gaule*. Paris: Estienne Groulleau, 1548.

L'Histoire de Giglan. Paris: Gilles et Jacques Huguetan freres, 1528.

Histoire d'Isaie. Paris: Jean Bonfons, 1550.

L'Histoire du noble preux & vaillant Chevalier Guillaume de Palerne. Paris: Nicolas Bonfons, n.d.

Histoire Contenant les Grandes Prouesses, Vaillances, et Héroiques faicts d'armes de Lancelot du Lac, Chevalier de la T. R. Lyons: Benoist Rigaud, 1591.

Jerome, St. *Select Letters of St. Jerome*. Edited and translated by F. A. Wright. New York: Putnam, 1933.

Jodelle, Etienne. *Œuvres*. Vol. I. Edited by Enea Balmas. Paris: Gallimard, 1965.

Labé, Louise. *Œuvres complètes*. Edited by François Rigolot. Paris: Flammarion, 1986.

La Chassaigne, Geoffroy de, trans. *Epistres de L'Annæe Seneque, philosophe très-excellent*. Paris: Guillaume Chaudière, 1582.

La Noue, François de. *Discours politiques et militaires*. Edited by F. E. Sutcliffe. Geneva: Droz, 1967.

Lancelot du Lac. Paris: Jean Petit (& Philippe le Noir), 1533.

La Place, Pierre de. *Discours politiques sur la voye d'entrer deuëmment aux estats, & maniere de constamment s'y maintenir & gouverner*. Paris: Robert le Mangnier, 1574.

La Primaudaye, Pierre de. *Academie françoise*. Paris: Guillaume Chaudière, 1581. Reprint, Geneva: Slatkine Reprints, 1972.

Laval, Antoine (Mathé) de. *Desseins des professions nobles et publiques*. Paris: A. L'Angelier, 1605.

Le Roy, Louis. *Enseignements d'Isocrates et Xenophon [. . .] pour bien regner en paix et en guerre*. Paris: Michel de Vascosan, 1568.

———. *Les Politiques d'Aristote*. Translated by Louis Le Roy. Paris: Michel de Vascosan, 1568.

———. *De La Vicissitude ou variété des choses en l'univers.* Paris: Pierre l'Huilier, 1575.

L'Hospital, Michel de. *Poésies complètes du Chancelier Michel de L'Hospital.* Translated and edited by Louis Bandy de Nalèche. Paris: Hachette, 1857.

Loyseau, Charles. *Les Œuvres de Maître Charles Loyseau* (1613). Paris: Michel Bobin et Nicolas le Gras, 1678.

Lucretius, Titus Carus. *Titi Lucretii Cari "De Rerum Natura" Libri sex.* Edited by Dionysius Lambinus. Paris: Guillaume and Philippe Rouillé, 1564.

———. *De rerum natura.* Edited by W. H. D. Rouse and Martin F. Smith. Cambridge: Harvard University Press, 1992.

Marguerite de Navarre. *L'Heptaméron.* Edited by Renja Salminen. Geneva: Droz, 1999.

Maugin, Jean. *Le Livre du Nouveau Tristan, Prince de Leonnois, chevalier de la Table Ronde, & d'Yseult, princesse d'Yrlande, Royne de Cornouaille.* Lyons: Benoist Rigaud, 1577.

Meliadus de Leonnoys. Paris: Galliot du Pré, 1528.

Messie, Pierre (Mexia, Pero). *Les Diverses Leçons de Pierre Messie.* Translated by Claude Gruget. Paris: Estienne Groulleau, 1554.

Le Miroir des femmes. 2 vols. Edited by Luce Guillerm, Jean-Pierre Guillerm, Laurence Hordoir, Marie-Françoise Piéjus. Lille: Presses Universitaires de Lille, 1983.

Montaigne, Michel de. *Les Essais.* Edited by Pierre Villey and V.-L. Saulnier. Paris: Presses Universitaires de France, 1965.

———. *"Essais" de Michel de Montaigne.* Edited by André Tournon. Paris: Imprimerie Nationale, 1998.

———. *The Complete Essays of Montaigne.* Translated by Donald Frame. Stanford: Stanford University Press, 1958.

Montalvo, Garci Rodriguez de. *Amadís de Gaula.* Edited by Juan Manuel Cacho Blecua. Madrid: Catedra, 1987–88.

Muret, Marc-Antoine de. *Commentaires au Premier Livre des "Amours" de Ronsard.* Edited by Jacques Chomarat, Marie-Madeleine Fragonard, and Gisèle Mathieu-Castellani. Geneva: Droz, 1985.

Nicot, Jean. *Thresor de la Langue Françoise.* Paris: D. Douceur, 1606.

Ovid. *Remedia Amoris.* 2nd edition. Translated by J. H. Mozley. Edited by G. P. Goold. Cambridge: Harvard University Press, 1979.

Pasquier, Etienne. *Lettres familières.* Edited by D. Thickett. Geneva: Droz, 1974.

———. *Le Monophile.* Edited by F. H. Balmas. Milan: Cisalpino, 1957.

Pasquier, Nicolas. *Le Gentilhomme.* Paris: Jean Petit, 1611.

Pibrac, Guy du Faur de. *Les Quatrains de Pibrac suivis de ses autres poésies.* Edited by Jules Claretie. Paris: Alphonse Lemerre, 1874.

Plutarch. *Œuvres morales.* Translated by François Fuhrmann. Paris: Les Belles Lettres, 1988.

Le Premier livre de l'histoire & ancienne cronique de Gerard d'Euphrate. Paris: Estienne Groulleau, 1549.

Rabelais, François. *Gargantua.* Edited by Gérard Defaux. Paris: Librairie Générale Française, 1994.

———. *Gargantua*. Edited by Ruth Calder and Michael Andrew Screech. Geneva: Droz, 1970.

———. *Gargantua and Pantagruel*. Translated by J. M. Cohen. London: Penguin, 1955.

———. *Pantagruel, Edition critique sur le texte de l'édition publiée à Lyon en 1542 par François Juste*. Edited by Floyd Gray. Paris: Champion, 1997.

———. *Pantagruel*. Edited by V. -L. Saulnier. Geneva: Droz, 1965.

———. *Le Quart Livre*. Edited by Gérard Defaux and Robert Marichal. Paris: Librairie Générale Française, 1994.

———. *Le Tiers Livre*. Edited by Jean Céard. Paris: Librairie Générale Française, 1995.

Rapin, Nicolas. *Œuvres*. Edited by Jean Brunel and Emile Brethé. Geneva: Droz, 1982.

Rivaudeau, André de. *Aman*. Geneva: Droz, 1969.

Romieu, Marie de. *Les Premières œuvres poétiques*. Edited by André Winandy. Geneva: Droz, 1972.

Ronsard, Pierre de. *Œuvres complètes*. Edited by Paul Laumonier, Isidore Silver and Raymond Lebègue. 20 vols. Paris: Hachette, Didier, Droz, rpt. Nizet, 1914–1983.

Screech, Michael Andrew. *Montaigne's Annotated Copy of Lucretius: A Transcription and Study of the Manuscript, Notes, and Pen-marks*. Geneva: Droz, 1998.

Seneca, Lucius Annaeus. *Epistles*. Vols. 4–5. Cambridge: Harvard University Press, 1996.

Sorel, Charles. *De la connoissance des bons livres, ou Examen de Plusieurs Autheurs* (1671). Edited by Hervé D. Bechade. Geneva: Slatkine, 1981.

Thierriat, Florentin de. *Trois Traictez à scavoir 1) De La Noblesse de Race; 2) De la Noblesse Civile; 3) Des Immunitez des Ignobles*. Paris: Lucas Bruneau, 1606.

Valerius Maximus. *Faits et paroles mémorables*. Translated by C. A. F. Frémion. Paris: C. L. F. Panckoucke, 1835.

Vives, Juan Luis. *Livre de l'institution de la femme chrestienne*. Translated by Pierre de Changy. Geneva: Slatkine Reprints, 1970.

Secondary Sources

André, Jean-Marie. *L'Otium dans la vie morale et intellectuelle romaine*. Paris: Presses Universitaires de France, 1966.

Badel, Pierre-Yves. *Le Roman de la Rose au XIVe siècle: Etude de la réception de l'œuvre*. Geneva: Droz, 1980.

Balsamo, Jean. "Deux gentilshommes 'nécessiteux d'honneur': Montaigne et Pressac." *Montaigne Studies* 13, nos. 1–2 (2001): 141–73.

Bataille, Georges. *L'Erotisme*. Paris: Minuit, 1957.

———. *La Part maudite*. Paris: Minuit, 1967.

———. *Le Procès de Gilles de Rais*. Paris: Pauvert, 1979.

Batany, Jean. "Miniature, allégorie, idéologie: 'Oiseuse' et la mystique monacale récupérée par la 'classe de loisir.'" In *Etudes sur le Roman de la Rose de Guillaume de Lorris*, edited by Jean Dufournet, 7–36. Geneva: Slatkine, 1984.

Baudrillard, Jean. *La Société de consommation: Ses mythes, ses structures*. Paris: SGPP, 1970.

———. *Le Système des objets: La Consommation des signes*. Paris: Gallimard, 1968.

Bauschatz, Cathleen. "Montaigne's conception of Reading in the context of Renaissance Poetics and Modern Criticism." In *The Reader in the Text*, ed. Susan Suleiman and Inge Crosman, 264–91. Princeton: Princeton University Press, 1980.

Beaujour, Michel. *Le Jeu de Rabelais*. Paris: L'Herne, 1969.

Berriot-Salvadore, Evelyne. *Les Femmes dans la société française de la Renaissance*. Geneva: Droz, 1990.

———. "Les Médecins analystes de la passion." In *La Peinture des passions de la Renaissance à l'Age Classique*, Actes du colloque international Saint-Etienne, edited by Bernard Yon. Saint-Etienne: Publications de l'Université de Saint-Etienne, 1995.

Beugnot, Bernard. *Le Discours de la retraite au XVIIe siècle*. Paris: Presses Universitaires de France, 1996.

Bitton, Davis. *The French Nobility in Crisis, 1560–1640*. Stanford: Stanford University Press, 1969.

Blanchot, Maurice. *Le Livre à venir*. Paris: Gallimard, 1959.

Boase, Alan. *The Fortunes of Montaigne: A History of the Essays in France, 1580–1669*. London: Methuen & Co., 1935.

Boon, Jean-Pierre. *Montaigne, gentilhomme et essayiste*. Paris: Editions Universitaires, 1971.

Bossard, Eugène. *Gilles de Rais, Maréchal de France, dit Barbe-Bleue (1404–1440)*. Paris: Champion, 1885.

Bouché, Thérèse. "Les Personnages d'Oiseuse et Déduit dans le *Roman de la Rose* de Guillaume de Lorris." In *Les Loisirs et l'héritage de la culture classique* (Actes du XIIIe Congrès de l'Association Guillaume Budé), edited by Jean-Marie André, Jacqueline Dangel, and Paul Demont, 487–502. Brussels: Latomus, 1996.

Bourdieu, Pierre. *La Distinction*. Paris: Minuit, 1982.

———. *Esquisse d'une théorie de la pratique, précédé de trois études d'ethnologie kabyle*. Geneva: Droz, 1972.

———. *Raisons pratiques*. Paris: Seuil, 1994.

Bourdillon, F. W. *The Early Editions of "The Roman de la Rose."* London: Chiswick Press, 1906.

Boutcher, Warren. "'Who taught thee Rhetoricke to deceive a maid?': Christopher Marlowe's *Hero and Leander*, Juan Boscan's *Leandro*, and Renaissance Vernacular Humanism." *Comparative Literature* (winter 2000): 11–52.

Brooks, Peter. *Reading for the Plot: Design and Intention in Narrative*. Cambridge: Harvard University Press, 1984.

———. *Troubling Confessions: Speaking Guilt in Law & Literature*. Chicago: University of Chicago Press, 2000.

Cave, Terence. *The Cornucopian Text: Problems of Writing in the French Renaissance*. Oxford: Clarendon Press, 1979.

———. "Problems of Reading in the *Essais*." In *Montaigne: Essays in Memory of Richard Sayce*, edited by I. D. McFarlane and Ian MacLean, 153–63. Oxford: Clarendon Press, 1982.

———. "Le Récit montaignien: un voyage sans repentir." In *Montaigne: Espace, voyage, écriture*, Actes du Congrès International de Thessalonique 1992, 125–35. Paris: Champion, 1995.

Cazauran, Nicole. "Entre Exemple et recréation." In *Le Roman de chevalerie au temps de la Renaissance*, edited by M. T. Jones-Davies. Paris: Jean Touzot, 1987.

Chambers, Ross. *Loiterature*. Lincoln: University of Nebraska Press, 1999.

Chang, Leah. *Printing the Muse: Book Production and the Construction of Female Authorship in Renaissance France*. Ph.D. thesis, University of Michigan, 2002.

Châtelain, Jean-Marc. "Heros togatus: Culture cicéronienne et gloire de la robe dans la France d'Henri IV." *Le Journal des Savants* 3–4 (July–December 1991): 263–87.

Choix de Chroniques et Mémoires sur l'Histoire de France. Edited by J. A. C. Buchon. Paris: A. Desrez, 1836.

Clark, Carol. *The Web of Metaphor: Studies in the Imagery of Montaigne's "Essais."* Edited by R. C. La Charité and V. A. La Charité. Lexington: French Forum, 1978.

Conche, Marcel. *Montaigne et la philosophie*. Versailles: Editions de Mégare, 1987. Reprint, Paris: Presses Universitaires de France, 1996.

Conley, Tom. "*De Capsula Totoe*: Lecture de Montaigne, 'De trois commerces.'" *L'Esprit Créateur* 28, no. 1 (1988): 18–26.

Cottrell, Robert. "L'Image des terres oisives dans 'De l'oisiveté.'" *Bulletin de la Société des Amis de Montaigne* 16 (1975): 63–66.

Cremier, Albert. "La Genèse de la notion de noblesse de robe." *Revue d'histoire moderne et contemporaine* 46, no. 1 (January–March 1999): 22–38.

Curtius, Ernst Robert. *European Literature and the Latin Middle Ages*. Translated by Willard R. Trask. London: Routledge & Kegan Paul, 1953.

Dahlberg, Charles. "Love and the Roman de la Rose." *Speculum* 44 (1969): 568–84.

Dare, Byron, George Welton, and William Coe. *Concepts of Leisure in Western Thought*. Dubuque: Kendall/Hunt, 1987.

Debaisieux, Martine. "'Des dames du temps jadis': Fatalité culturelle et identité féminine dans Les Angoysses Douloureuses." *Symposium* 41, no. 1 (spring 1987): 28–41.

DeJean, Joan. "The Politics of Genre: Madeleine de Scudéry and the Rise of the French Novel." *L'Esprit Créateur* 29, no. 3 (1989): 43–51.

Desan, Philippe. *Les Commerces de Montaigne: Le Discours économique des "Essais."* Paris: Nizet, 1992.

———. *L'Imaginaire économique de la Renaissance*. Mont-de-Marsan: Editions InterUniversitaires, 1993.

———. "Préfaces, prologues et avis au lecteur: stratégies préfacielles à la Renaissance." In *What is Literature? France, 1100–1600*, edited by François Cornilliat, Ullrich Langer, and Douglas Kelly, 101–22. Lexington: French Forum, 1993.

Descimon, Robert. "The Birth of the Nobility of the Robe." In *Changing Identities in Early Modern France*, edited by Michael Wolfe. Durham: Duke University Press, 1997.

———. "La Noblesse, 'essence' ou rapport social?" *Revue d'histoire moderne et contemporaine* 46, no. 1 (January–March 1999): 5–21.

Dewald, Jonathan. *The European Nobility, 1400–1800*. Cambridge: Cambridge University Press, 1996.

———. *The Formation of a Provincial Nobility: The Magistrates of the Parliament of Rouen, 1499–1610*. Princeton: Princeton University Press, 1980.

Dictionnaire des Lettres Françaises. Vol. 1 *(Le Seizième Siècle)*. Edited by Georges Grente. Paris: Fayard, 1951.

Dravasa, Etienne. *"Vivre noblement": Recherches sur la dérogeance de noblesse du XIVe au XVIe siècles*. Bordeaux: chez l'auteur, 1965.

Duby, Georges. *Les Trois ordres ou l'imaginaire du féodalisme*. Paris: Gallimard, 1978.

Duport, Danièle. "L'Oisif en ses terres." Paper delivered at "L'Oisiveté au temps de la Renaissance," *Société Internationale de Recherches Interdisciplinaires sur la Renaissance*, Paris, 17 March 2000.

Duval, Edwin. *Design of Rabelais's Tiers Livre de Pantagruel*. Geneva: Droz, 1997.

Eden, Kathy. *Hermeneutics and the Rhetorical Tradition*. New Haven: Yale University Press, 1997.

Eisenberg, Daniel. *Castilian Romances of Chivalry in the Sixteenth Century: A Bibliography*. London: Grant & Cutler, 1979.

Engammare, Max. "Organisation du temps et discipline horaire chez Calvin et à Genève au XVIe siècle." *Bibliothèque de l'Ecole des Chartes* 157 (1999): 341–67.

Esclapez, Raymond. "L'Oisiveté créatrice dans *Les Essais*: Persistance et épanouissement d'un thème." *Bulletin de la Société des Amis de Montaigne* 33–34 (1993): 25–39.

Faral, Edmond. "Guillaume de Digulleville, moine de Chaalis." *Histoire littéraire de la France: Ouvrage commencé par des religieux bénédictins de la congrégation de Saint-Maur* 39 (1962): 1–11.

Febvre, Lucien, and Henri-Jean Martin. *L'Apparition du livre*. Paris: Albin Michel, 1958.

Ferguson, Gary. "Le Chapelet et la plume, ou, quand la religieuse se fait écrivain: le cas du prieuré de Poissy (1562–1621)." *Revue du Seizième Siècle* 19, no. 2 (2001): 83–99.

Festugière, A.-J. *Epicure et ses Dieux*. Paris: Presses Universitaires de France, 1946. Reprint, 1968.

Fleming, John V. *The "Roman de la Rose": A Study in Allegory and Iconography*. Princeton: Princeton University Press, 1969.

Forster, Charles Thornton, and F. H. Blackburne Daniell. *The Life and Letters of Ogier Ghiselin de Busbecq*. 2 vols. London: C. Kegan Paul, 1881.

Frame, Donald. *Montaigne's "Essais": A Study*. Englewood Cliffs, N.J.: Prentice-Hall, 1969.

Friedrich, Hugo. *Montaigne*. Translated by Robert Rovini. Paris: Gallimard, 1968.

Fumaroli, Marc. "Jacques Amyot and the Clerical Polemic Against the Chivalric Novel." *Renaissance Quarterly* 38 (1985): 22–40.

Fumaroli, Marc, Philippe-Joseph Salazar, and Emmanuel Bury. *Le Loisir lettré à L'Age Classique*. Geneva: Droz, 1996.

Gadoffre, Gilbert. *La Révolution culturelle dans la France des Humanistes*. Geneva: Droz, 1997.

Garavini, Fausta. *Monstres et chimères: Montaigne, le texte et le fantasme*. Translated by Isabel Picon. Paris: Champion, 1993.

Glauser, Alfred. *Rabelais créateur*. Paris: Nizet, 1964.

Glidden, Hope H. "*Le Roman de la Rose* and Evangelical Poetics." In *Translation and the Transmission of Culture Between 1300 and 1600*, edited by Jeanette Beer and Kenneth Lloyd-Jones, 143–74. Kalamazoo, Mich.: Western Michigan University Press, 1995.

Gorz, André. *Métamorphoses du travail: Quête du sens*. Paris: Galilée, 1988.

Goux, Jean-Joseph. "General Economics and Postmodern Capitalism." *Yale French Studies* 78 (1990): 206–24.

Gray, Floyd. "Structure and Meaning in the Prologue to the *Tiers Livre*." *L'Esprit Créateur* 3 (1963): 57–62.

Groupe de la Bussière. *Pratiques de la confession: Des Pères du désert à Vatican II: Quinze études d'histoire*. Paris: Editions du Cerf, 1983.

Gundersheimer, Werner. *The Life and Works of Louis Le Roy*. Geneva: Droz, 1966.

Gutton, Jean-Pierre. *La Société et les pauvres en Europe*. Paris: Presses Universitaires de France, 1974.

Hadot, Pierre. *Qu'est-ce que la philosophie antique?* Paris: Gallimard, 1995.

Hampton, Timothy. *Writing from History: The Rhetoric of Exemplarity in Renaissance Literature*. Ithaca: Cornell University Press, 1990.

Hoffmann, George. "Croiser le fer avec le Géographe du Roi: L'Entrevue de Montaigne avec Antoine de Laval aux Etats généraux de Blois en 1588." *Montaigne Studies* 13, nos. 1–2 (2001): 207–22.

———. *Montaigne's Career*. Oxford: Clarendon Press, 1998.

———. "Rites Romains et autres dans l'essai 'Des cannibales.'" In *"D'une fantastique bigarrure": Le Texte composite à la Renaissance: Etudes offertes à André Tournon*, edited by Jean-Raymond Fanlo, 157–66. Paris: Champion, 2000.

Huot, Sylvia. *The "Romance of the Rose" and its Medieval Readers: Interpretation, Reception, Manuscript Transmission*. Cambridge: Cambridge University Press, 1993.

Huppert, George. *Les Bourgeois Gentilshommes*. Chicago: University of Chicago Press, 1977.

———. *The Style of Paris: Renaissance Origins of the French Enlightenment*. Bloomington: Indiana University Press, 1999.

Jeanneret, Michel. "Modular Narrative and the Crisis of Interpretation." Translated by John D. Lyons. In *Critical Tales: New Studies of the Heptameron and Early Modern Culture*, edited by John D. Lyons and Mary B. McKinley, 85–103. Philadelphia: University of Pennsylvania Press, 1993.

Jensen, Kathryn Ann. "Writing out of the Double Bind: Female Plot and Hélisenne de Crenne's *Les Angoysses douloureuses qui procedent d'amours.*" *Œuvres et Critiques* 19, no. 1 (1994): 61–67.

Johnson, Penelope D. *Equal in Monastic Profession: Religious Women in Medieval France*. Chicago: University of Chicago Press, 1991.

Jones, Ann Rosalind. *The Currency of Eros: Women's Love Lyric in Europe, 1540–1620*. Bloomington: Indiana University Press, 1990.

———. "Surprising Fame: Renaissance Gender Ideologies and Women's Lyric." In *The Poetics of Gender*, edited by Nancy K. Miller, 74–95. New York: Columbia University Press, 1986.

Jordan, Constance. *Renaissance Feminism: Literary Texts and Political Models*. Ithaca: Cornell University Press, 1990.

Jouanna, Arlette. *Le Devoir de révolte: La Noblesse française et la gestation de l'Etat moderne (1559–1661)*. Paris: Fayard, 1989.

———. *La France du XVIe siècle, 1483–1598*. Paris: Presses Universitaires de France, 1996.

———. *L'Idée de race en France au XVIème siècle et au début du XVIIème siècle (1498–1614)*. Paris: Champion, 1976.

———. "Le Thème de l'utilité publique dans la polémique anti-nobiliaire en France dans la deuxième moitié du XVIe siècle." In *Théorie et pratique politiques à la Renaissance, XVIIe colloque international de Tours* (De Pétrarque à Descartes 34), 287–99. Paris: Vrin, 1977.

Kelly, Douglas. "Romance and the Vanity of Chrétien de Troyes." In *Romance, Generic Transformation from Chrétien de Troyes to Cervantes*, edited by Kevin Brownlee and Marina Scordilis Brownlee, 74–90. Hanover: University Press of New England, 1985.

Kelso, Ruth. *Doctrine for the Lady of the Renaissance*. Urbana: University of Illinois Press, 1956.

Kermode, Frank. *The Sense of an Ending: Studies in the Theory of Fiction*. Oxford: Oxford University Press, 1966.

Kim, Seong-Hak. *Michel de L'Hôpital: The Vision of a Reformist Chancellor during the French Religious Wars*. Vol. XXXVI, *Sixteenth Century Essays and Studies*. Kirksville, Mo.: Sixteenth Century Journal Publishers, 1997.

Kritzman, Lawrence. *Destruction/Découverte: Le Fonctionnement de la rhétorique dans les "Essais" de Montaigne*. Lexington: French Forum, 1980.

Kuhn, Reinhard. *The Demon of Noontide: Ennui in Western Literature*. Princeton: Princeton University Press, 1976.

La Charité, Raymond. *Recreation, Reflection, and Re-Creation: Perspectives on Rabelais's "Pantagruel."* Lexington: French Forum, 1980.

Ladner, Gerhart. "Homo Viator: Mediaeval Ideas on Alienation and Order." *Speculum* 42, no. 2 (1967): 233–59.

Lafargue, Paul. *Le Droit à la paresse*. Paris: Editions Allia, 2001.

Lajarte, Philippe de. "La Passion amoureuse et sa représentation dans la première partie des *Angoysses douloureuses* d'Hélisenne de Crenne." In *La Peinture des passions de la Renaissance à l'Age Classique*, Actes du colloque international Saint-Etienne, edited by Bernard Yon, 61–78. Saint-Etienne: Publications de l'Université de Saint-Etienne, 1995.

Langer, Ullrich. *Divine and Poetic Freedom in the Renaissance*. Princeton: Princeton University Press, 1990.

———. *Vertu du discours, discours de la vertu: Littérature et philosophie morale au XVIe siècle en France*. Geneva: Droz, 1999.

Larsen, Anne R. "'Un honneste passetems': Strategies of Legitimation in French Renaissance Women's Prefaces." *L'Esprit Créateur* 30, no. 4 (1990): 11–22.

Lea, Henry Charles. *A History of Auricular Confession and Indulgences in the Latin Church*. London: Swan Sonnenschein, 1896.

Lebaube, Alain. *Le Travail: Toujours moins ou autrement*. Paris: Le Monde Editions, 1997.

Leclercq, Jean. *Otia monastica: Etudes sur le vocabulaire de la contemplation au Moyen Age*. Rome: Herder, 1963.

Le Goff, Jacques. *Pour un autre Moyen Age: Temps, travail et culture en Occident*. Paris: Gallimard, 1977.

Legros, Alain. "Montaigne, son livre et son roi." *Studi Francesi* 41, no. 2 (1997): 259–74.

Les Loisirs et l'héritage de la culture classique (Actes du XIIIe Congrès de l'Association Guillaume Budé). Edited by Jean-Marie André, Jacqueline Dangel, and Paul Demont. Brussels: Latomus, 1996.

Lipietz, Alain. *La Société en sablier*. Paris: La Découverte, 1996.

Lofthouse, Marion. "*Le Pèlerinage de Vie Humaine*, by Guillaume de Deguileville." *Bulletin of The John Rylands Library* 19 (1935): 170–215.

Longeon, Claude. *Les Ecrivains foréziens du XVIe siècle: Répertoire bio-bibliographique*. Saint-Etienne: Centre d'Etudes Foréziennes, 1970.

Lyons, John D. *Exemplum: The Rhetoric of Example in Early Modern France and Italy*. Princeton: Princeton University Press, 1989.

MacLean, Ian. *The Renaissance Notion of Woman: A Study in the Fortunes of Scholasticism and Medical Science in European Intellectual Life*. Cambridge: Cambridge University Press, 1980.

Marchand, Jean, ed. *Le Livre de Raison de Montaigne sur "l'Ephemeris historica" de Beuther*. Paris: Arts Graphiques, 1948.

Martin, Henri-Jean, Roger Chartier, and Jean-Pierre Vivet. *Histoire de l'édition française*. Paris: Promodis, 1982.

Mathieu-Castellani, Gisèle. *Montaigne: L'Ecriture de l'essai*. Paris: Presses Universitaires de France, 1988.

———. *La Quenouille et la lyre*. Paris: José Corti, 1998.

McGowan, Margaret. "'Il faut que j'aille de la plume comme des pieds' (III, 9, 991b)." In *La Rhétorique de Montaigne*, edited by Frank Lestringant (Actes du Colloque de la Société des Amis de Montaigne, Paris 1984), 165–73. Paris: Champion, 1985.

McKinley, Mary B. "Telling Secrets: Sacramental Confession and Narrative Authority in the *Heptameron*." In *Critical Tales: New Studies of the "Heptameron" and Early Modern Culture*, edited by John D. Lyons and Mary B. McKinley, 146–71. Philadelphia: University of Pennsylvania Press, 1993.

———. *Les Terrains vagues des "Essais": Itinéraires et intertextes*. Paris: Champion, 1996.

Méda, Dominique. *Le Travail, une valeur en voie de disparition*. Paris: Flammarion, 1998.

Morçay, Raoul. Introduction. *L'Abbaye de Thélème*. Geneva: Droz, 1949.

Mothé, Daniel. *L'Utopie du temps libre*. Paris: Esprit, 1997.

Nash, Jerry. "Constructing Hélisenne de Crenne: Reception and Identity." In *"Por le soie amiste": Essays in honor of Norris J. Lacy*, edited by Keith Busby and Catherine M. Jones. Amsterdam: Rodopi, 2000.

Neuschel, Kristen. *Word of Honor: Interpreting Noble Culture in Sixteenth-Century France*. Ithaca: Cornell University Press, 1989.

Newcomb, Lori Humphrey. *Reading Popular Romance in Early Modern England*. New York: Columbia University Press, 2002.

Norton, Glyn. *Montaigne and the Introspective Mind*. The Hague: Mouton, 1975.

Nussbaum, Martha. *The Therapy of Desire: Theory and Practice in Hellenistic Ethics*. Princeton: Princeton University Press, 1994.

O'Loughlin, Michael. *The Garlands of Repose: The Literary Celebration of Civic and Retired Leisure—The Traditions of Homer and Vergil, Horace and Montaigne*. Chicago: University of Chicago Press, 1978.

Olson, Glending. *Literature as Recreation in the Later Middle Ages*. Ithaca: Cornell University Press, 1982.

Parent, Annie. *Les Métiers du livre à Paris*. Geneva: Droz, 1974.

Pieper, Josef. *Leisure: The Basis of Culture*. Translated by Gerald Malsbary. South Bend: St. Augustine's Press, 1998.

Quint, David. *Montaigne and the Quality of Mercy*. Princeton: Princeton University Press, 1998.

———. *Origin and Originality in Renaissance Literature: Versions of the Source*. New Haven: Yale University Press, 1983.

Randall, Michael. *Building Resemblance: Analogical Imagery in the Early French Renaissance*. Baltimore: Johns Hopkins University Press, 1996.

Regosin, Richard L. *The Matter of My Book: Montaigne's "Essais" as the Book of the Self*. Berkeley: University of California Press, 1977.

———. "Montaigne's Child of the Mind." In *Writing the Renaissance*, edited by R. C. La Charité and V. A. La Charité. Lexington: French Forum, 1992.

———. "Montaigne's Monstrous Confessions." *Montaigne Studies* 1 (1989): 73–87.

Ribard, Jacques. "Introduction à une étude polysémique du *Roman de la Rose* de Guillaume de Lorris." In *Etudes de langue et de littérature du Moyen Age offertes à Félix Lecoy*. Paris: Champion, 1973.

Richman, Michèle. *Reading Georges Bataille: Beyond the Gift*. Baltimore: Johns Hopkins University Press, 1982.

Rigolot, François. *Les Langages de Rabelais*. 1972. Reprinted and revised; Geneva: Droz, 1996.

———. *Les Métamorphoses de Montaigne*. Paris: Presses Universitaires de France, 1988.

Robertson, D. W., Jr. *A Preface to Chaucer*. Princeton: Princeton University Press, 1962.

Robin, Jacques. *Quand le travail quitte la société post-industrielle*. Paris: GRIT, 1993.

Rosanbo, Louis de. "Pierre Pithou, biographie." *Revue du Seizième Siècle* 15 (1928): 279–304.

Rothstein, Marian. *Reading in the Renaissance: "Amadis de Gaule" and the Lessons of Memory*. Newark: University of Delaware Press, 1999.

Saccone, Eduardo. "*Grazia, Sprezzatura,* and *Affettazione* in Castiglione's *Book of the Courtier*." Translated by Susan G. Beecher. *Glyph* 5. Baltimore: Johns Hopkins University Press, 1979.

Schalk, Ellery. *From Valor to Pedigree: Ideas of Nobility in France in the Sixteenth and Seventeenth Centuries*. Princeton: Princeton University Press, 1986.

Screech, Michael Andrew. *Montaigne and Melancholy: The Wisdom of the Essays*. London: Duckworth, 1983. Reprint, Selinsgrove: Susquehanna University Press, 1984.

Serres, Michel. *La Naissance de la Physique dans le texte de Lucrèce: Fleuves et turbulences*. Paris: Minuit, 1977.

Shershow, Scott Cutler. "Of Sinking: Marxism and the 'General' Economy." *Critical Inquiry* 27, no. 3 (2001): 468–92.

Simonin, Michel. "La Disgrâce d'Amadis." *Studi Francesi* 28 (1984): 1–35.

Smith, Pauline. *The Anti-courtier Trend in Sixteenth-Century French Literature*. Geneva: Droz, 1966.

Sombart, Werner. *Luxury and Capitalism*. 1938. Reprint, Ann Arbor: University of Michigan Press, 1967.

Spacks, Patricia Meyer. *Boredom: The Literary History of a State of Mind*. Chicago: University of Chicago Press, 1995.

Stanton, Domna. *The Aristocrat as Art*. New York: Columbia University Press, 1980.

Strubel, Armand. *Le Roman de la Rose*. Paris: Presses Universitaires de France, 1984.

Supple, James. *Arms Versus Letters: The Military and Literary Ideals in the "Essais" of Montaigne*. Oxford: Clarendon Press, 1984.

Taillandier, A. H. *Nouvelles recherches historiques sur la vie et les ouvrages du Chancelier de L'Hospital*. Paris: Librairie de Firmin Didot Frères et Fils, 1861.

Tawney, R. H. *Religion and the Rise of Capitalism*. 1926. Reprint, New York: Harcourt, Brace & Co., 1952.

Tentler, Thomas. *Sin and Confession on the Eve of the Reformation*. Princeton: Princeton University Press, 1977.

Tournon, André. "Vacances intérieures: L'*Essai* du loisir." In *Les Loisirs et l'héritage de la culture classique*. (Actes du XIIIe Congrès de l'Association Guillaume

Budé), edited by Jean-Marie André, Jacqueline Dangel, and Paul Demont, 559–66. Brussels: Latomus, 1996.

Traverso, Edilia. *Montaigne e Aristotele*. Florence: F. Le Monnier, 1974.

Trinquet, Roger. *La Jeunesse de Montaigne*. Paris: Nizet, 1972.

Van Den Abbeele, Georges. *Travel as Metaphor: From Montaigne to Rousseau*. Minneapolis: University of Minnesota Press, 1992.

Veblen, Thorstein. *The Theory of the Leisure Class*. 1899. Reprint, New York: Macmillan Company, 1917.

Velay-Vallantin, Catherine. *L'Histoire des contes*. Paris: Fayard, 1992.

Villey, Pierre. *Les Sources et l'évolution des Essais de Montaigne*. 2 vols. Paris: Hachette, 1933.

Weber, Max. *The Protestant Ethic and the Spirit of Capitalism*. 1930. Reprint, New York: Routledge, 1992.

Wine, Kathleen. *Forgotten Virgo: Humanism and Absolutism in Honoré d'Urfé's "L'Astrée."* Geneva: Droz, 2000.

Wood, James. *The Nobility of the "Election" of Bayeux, 1463–1666*. Princeton: Princeton University Press, 1980.

Wright, Steven. "Deguileville's *Pèlerinage de vie humaine* as 'Contrepartie Edifiante' of the *Roman de la Rose*." *Philological Quarterly* 68, no. 4 (1989): 399–422.

Yandell, Cathy. *Carpe Corpus: Time and Gender in Early Modern France*. Newark: University of Delaware Press, 2000.

Yates, Frances. *The French Academies of the Sixteenth Century*. London: The Warburg Institute, 1947.

Index

allegory: vs. literal reading, 125; representation of desire, 71–72; representation of idleness, 34–43, 122
Amadis de Gaule, 121, 123–25; humanist attitudes toward, 136–42; serialization of, 121, 130–34, 135–36; vs. the Spanish *Amadís de Gaula*, 121, 132, 135, 201n. 47. *See also* Herberay des Essarts, Nicolas de
Amyot, Jacques, 47, 137–38
Aneau, Barthélemy, 62–63, 136
Aristotle, 21, 57, 79, 84; humanist commentaries on, 78–79; on the gods, 156; on rhetoric, 129
Aubery, Jean, 91–92, 95, 192n. 20
Augustine, Saint, 118–19, 125–26, 151
Avantures de Floride. *See* Béroalde de Verville

Badel, Pierre-Yves, 177–78n. 41
Balsamo, Jean, 210n. 68
Bataille, Georges, 16, 31–32, 174–75n. 16, 175nn. 17, 18, 20, 21, and 25, 192n. 26
Batany, Jean, 176n. 31, 177n. 35, 180n. 66
Baudrillard, Jean, 16, 129, 173n. 22, 201n. 46, 203n. 70
Bauschatz, Cathleen, 205n. 12
Beaujour, Michel, 53
Beaulieu, Jean-Philippe, 194n. 52
Beaulieux, Charles, 210n. 77
Béroalde de Verville, 99–100
Berriot-Salvadore, Evelyne, 22, 102
Beugnot, Bernard, 80
Bitton, Davis, 182n. 11, 183n. 15, 190n. 90
Blanchot, Maurice, 125
Boccaccio, Giovanni, 94

Boon, Jean-Pierre, 204n. 9
boredom, 61, 178n. 42
Bosbecq, Augier. *See* Busbecq, Ogier Ghiselin de
Bossard, Eugène, 174nn. 9, 12, 14, and 15
Bouché, Thérèse, 176n. 32, 177nn. 35 and 36
Bouchet, Jean, 26, 87–88, 89–90, 191n. 12, 194n. 44
Bourdieu, Pierre, 16, 32, 83, 175n. 24
Boutcher, Warren, 189n. 88
Briet, Marguerite. *See* Crenne, Hélisenne de
Brooks, Peter, 195n. 68, 197nn. 87 and 94
Budé, Guillaume, 49–52, 56, 68
Busbecq, Ogier Ghiselin de, 60, 69, 81–82, 205n. 13
Buzon, Christine de, 197n. 92

Calvin, John, 19, 54
Cassianus, Johanis, 191n. 17
Caumont, Jean de, 27–28
Cave, Terence, 157, 203n. 2, 205n. 12, 206n. 19
Caviceo, Jacopo, 94, 117
Cazauran, Nicole, 194n. 51
Cervantes, Miguel de, 121, 198n. 5
Chambers, Ross, 127
Champier, Symphorien, 87, 190n. 5
Chang, Leah, 196n. 82
Charles d'Angoulême, 123
Chartier, Roger, 197n. 2
Châtelain, Jean-Marc, 182n. 6
Chrétien de Troyes, 33–34, 134–35
Christine de Pizan, 123
Chroniques gargantuines, 127–30, 141
Cicero, 21, 57, 63, 64, 79, 81, 182n. 6, 187n. 64, 189n. 84

226

Clark, Carol, 205n. 16
Clichtove, Josse, 43–44
Conche, Marcel, 189n. 83, 206n. 22
confession: and contrition, 116, 119; and discursivity, 115–16, 117–18, 119; vs. fiction in *Les Angoysses douloureuses*, 111–13; as proof of guilt, 109, 195n. 68; Renaissance practices of, 113–14; represented in *Les Angoysses douloureuses*, 114–20
Conley, Tom, 205n. 10
Cottrell, Robert, 204n. 6
Cremier, Albert, 182n. 10
Crenne, Hélisenne de: representation of idleness, 96–99, 100–101, 105; use of idleness
commonplace, 93–94. Works: *Les Angoysses douloureuses*, 86–87, 93–99, 100–101, 104–7, 109–20; *Epistles*, 96, 101–3, 109, 111
Curtius, Ernst Robert, 172n. 12

Debaisieux, Martine, 196n. 76, 197n. 84
DeJean, Joan, 197n. 2
Desan, Philippe, 18, 81, 187n. 64, 200n. 33, 210n. 76, 211n. 79
Des Caurres, Jean, 26, 63, 70, 174n. 10, 187n. 66, 204n. 6
Descimon, Robert, 182nn. 10 and 12
Des Roches, Madeleine, 48, 86, 193n. 37, 195n. 62
Dewald, Jonathan, 171n. 1, 182n. 10
Don Quixote. See Cervantes, Miguel de
Dravasa, Etienne, 172n. 14, 183n. 15
Du Bellay, Joachim, 66–67, 182n. 9
Duby, Georges, 33, 175–76n. 27, 176n. 28
Duport, Danièle, 185n. 38
Duval, Edwin, 188n. 75

Eisenberg, Daniel, 201n. 47, 202nn. 49 and 50
Engammare, Max, 172n. 9
enthymeme, syllogism-enthymeme distinction, 129
Epicurus, 156, 158, 160, 207nn. 34 and 41

Erasmus, Desiderius, 56, 62, 146. See also *nemo sibi nascitur*
erotic melancholy, 91–92, 94–96
Esclapez, Raymond, 204n. 5
Essais: "Au Lecteur," 147–48; I, 8 "De l'oisiveté," 70–72, 73–74, 83–84, 148–49, 155, 158, 166; I, 26 "De l'institution des enfans," 145; I, 31 "Des cannibales," 157; I, 35 "D'un default de nos polices," 166–67; I, 39 "De la solitude," 64–65, 145–46, 150, 152–53, 155–56, 162, 166, 168, 183n. 20; II, 10 "Des livres," 162; II, 17 "De la praesumption," 145; III, 3 "De trois commerces," 159–60, 165; III, 9 "De la vanité," 45–48, 64; III, 10 "De mesnager sa volonté," 145, 164, 168
Essarts, Herberay des. See Herberay des Essarts, Nicolas de
exegesis, 125–26

Faral, Edmond, 177nn. 38 and 40, 178–79n. 47
Feast of the Innocents, 93
Febvre, Lucien, 200n. 24
Ferguson, Gary, 172n. 6
Festugière, A.-J., 207nn. 34 and 41
Fiammetta. See Boccaccio, Giovanni
Fournier, Hannah, 194n. 52
Fourth Estate: attitudes toward work, 56–57, 65–66; conceptions of leisure, 59–70, 72–73, 81–85, 146–48; hobbies, 68–69, 82; public service, 61, 62–65; social ascension during the Renaissance, 58–59, 70, 71, 169; use of term, 182n. 9
Frame, Donald, 205n. 15
Friedrich, Hugo, 204n. 9
Fumaroli, Marc, 202n. 62

Gadoffre, Gilbert, 186n. 52
Garavini, Fausta, 171n. 3
Gerard d'Euphrate, 136
Gerson, Jean, 197n. 85
Gilles de Rais, 17, 28–31, 174nn. 7 and 8, 175n. 18
Glidden, Hope, 180n. 64
Gohory, Jacques, 132–33, 140–42,

174n. 4, 199n. 20. See also *Amadis de Gaule*
Gorz, André, 172n. 10, 182n. 8
gossip, 98
Goux, Jean-Joseph, 200n. 31, 201n. 46
Gray, Floyd, 188n. 75, 200n. 27
Guevara, Antonio, 194n. 43
Guillaume de Deguilleville. See *Pèlerinage de vie humaine*
Guillaume de Lorris. See *Roman de la Rose*
Guillerm, Jean-Pierre, 191n. 8
Gundersheimer, Werner, 188n. 76
Gutton, Jean-Pierre, 180n. 59
Guyon, Louis, 152–53

Hadot, Pierre, 209nn. 54 and 55
Hampton, Timothy, 203n. 71
Heptaméron, 101, 174n. 6, 193n. 30
Herberay des Essarts, Nicolas de: contracts with printers, 131, 132; success of, 136–37; use of idleness topos, 15, 198n. 5. See also *Amadis de Gaule*
Hoffmann, George, 18, 65, 159–60, 183nn. 19 and 23, 184–85n. 37, 185n. 40, 186nn. 50, 51, and 62, 189n. 88, 209n. 62
Horace, 70, 138, 186–87n. 62, 202n. 62
Huot, Sylvia, 177n. 40, 178n. 41
Huppert, George, 22, 59, 182nn. 5 and 13, 187n. 63, 190n. 90

idleness: as an aristocratic value, 20, 30–48, 84–85; as an ethical principal, 20–21, 57, 78–81, 84; in moralist literature, 20, 30, 60, 144; in relation to privacy, 15, 24, 62–63, 145–46, 170; as a religious ideal, 23 139–40, 150–53; as a rhetorical commonplace, 19–23, 29, 69–70, 144–46, 172n. 12, 198n. 5; secularization of, 19, 23–24, 88, 90, 139–40, 142, 143, 149–53, 157, 168, 170; as a social code, 15, 17, 59, 61–62; in relation to subjectivity, 15, 62, 65, 143, 170; as symbolic capital, 16, 32, 83, 103, 108, 147–48; synthesis with *neg-otium*, 54, 72–73; women and, 18, 86–87, 89–90, 96–100, 102–9

Jeanneret, Michel, 200n. 26
Jensen, Kathryn Ann, 110
Jodelle, Etienne, 72, 138, 198n. 6
Johnson, Penelope, 172n. 7
Jones, Ann Rosalind, 171n. 1, 195n. 64
Jordan, Constance, 110, 194n. 53
Jouanna, Arlette, 22, 45, 179nn. 52, 54, and 57, 184n. 26, 186n. 60

Kelly, Douglas, 202n. 56
Kelso, Ruth, 90, 191n. 8
Kermode, Frank, 201n. 40
Kim, Seong-Hak, 190n. 89
Kritzman, Lawrence, 205n. 11

Labé, Louise, 15, 107–9, 195n. 69
La Charité, Raymond, 199n. 14
La Chassaigne, Geoffroy de, 162–63, 208n. 50
Ladner, Gerhart, 206n. 24
Lafargue, Paul, 172n. 10
Lajarte, Philippe de, 193n. 35
Lancelot (prose), 134–35, 198n. 5
Langer, Ullrich, 174n. 10, 188n. 75, 200n. 28, 204n. 7
La Noue, François de, 138
La Place, Pierre de, 63–64, 70, 76, 81, 184n. 34
La Primaudaye, Pierre de, 174n. 10, 187n. 66, 204n. 6
Larsen, Anne, 195nn. 62, 64, and 69
Laval, Antoine (Mathé) de, 59–61, 68, 69, 70, 74, 81–82, 148, 183nn. 19, 23, and 24
Lea, Henry Charles, 196n. 80
Lebaube, Alain, 172n. 10, 182n. 8
Leclercq, Jean, 206nn. 23 and 26, 206–7n. 27
Le Goff, Jacques, 178n. 46, 203n. 65
leisure. *See* idleness
leisure class. *See* nobility
Le Roy, Louis, 26, 50, 78–79, 193n. 36
L'Hospital, Michel de, 66, 83, 184n. 35, 185n. 48
Lipietz, Alain, 172n. 10
Longeon, Claude, 183n. 19, 186n. 51

INDEX

lovesickness. *See* erotic melancholy
Loyseau, Charles, 33, 70, 210n. 74
Lucretius: Lambinus's notes to, 154; Montaigne's annotated copy of, 153–55, 163–64; representation of the gods in *De rerum natura*, 154, 155, 158, 160–61, 163–64
Luther, Martin, 54
Lyons, John, 200n. 26

McGowan, Margaret, 209n. 59
McKinley, Mary, 114, 204n. 2
MacLean, Ian, 205n. 17
McLuhan, Marshall, 134
Marchand, Jean, 211n. 78
Marguerite de Navarre. *See Heptaméron*
Martin, Henri-Jean, 200n. 24
Mathieu-Castellani, Gisèle, 150, 171n. 1, 196n. 75, 204n. 5, 205n. 16
Maugin, Jean, 136
Méda, Dominique, 19, 182n. 8
Messie, Pierre, 20, 46, 70, 151, 187n. 66, 204n. 6
Mexia, Pero. *See* Messie, Pierre
Montaigne, Michel de: as a critic of work morality, 56, 80, 145–46; definition of nobility, 44, 59, 62, 71; and modern leisure, 25, 150–52, 169–70; political career, 63, 155, 180n. 59; tower study, 78, 159–61, 163. *See also Essais*
Montalvo, Garci Rodriguez de, 121, 132, 135, 136, 137, 201n. 47
Morçay, Raoul, 181n. 73
Mothé, Daniel, 172n. 10, 182n. 8
Muret, Marc-Antoine de, 187n. 65

Nash, Jerry, 110, 190n. 3, 196nn. 77 and 81
nemo sibi nascitur, 62, 64, 140, 145–46
Neuschel, Kristen, 175n. 23
Newcomb, Lori Humphrey, 197–98n. 2, 203n. 68
Nicot, Jean, 211n. 80
nobility: criticism of, 27, 40, 62–63, 66, 184n. 27; definitions of, 33–34, 44–45; hunting, 49–52; land ownership, 62, 71; as a leisure class, 33, 34–37, 72–73, 84; social function of, 33, 44, 58
Norton, Glyn, 171n. 1, 204n. 4
Nouveau Tristan. *See* Maugin, Jean
Nussbaum, Martha, 208n. 49

oisiveté. *See* idleness
O'Loughlin, Michael, 173n. 16, 204n. 3
Olson, Glending, 22, 125, 199n. 21, 200n. 29
otia monastica, 151, 152; redefinitions of, 48–49, 89–90, 151–52
otium. *See* idleness
otium litteratum (literary idleness): in the Fourth Estate, 69–70, 72–78, 82–83, 146–48; Montaigne's rejection of, 147–48; relation of women to, 90, 107–9
otium sine litteris mors est, 70, 146. *See also* Seneca
Ovidian love psychology, 90–96, 191n. 19

Parent, Annie, 200n. 34, 201n. 39
Pasquier, Etienne, 63, 74–75, 81, 186–87n. 62
Pasquier, Nicolas, 65–66
pastimes: in the Fourth Estate, 68–69; traditional aristocratic conception of, 50, 67, 123, 198n. 9. *See also* recreation
Pèlerinage de vie humaine: allegorical representation of idleness in, 37–43, 178nn. 44 and 46; manuscripts and editions of, 177n. 40, 178–79n. 47
Peregrino. *See* Caviceo, Jacopo
Pibrac, Guy du Faur de, 21, 56, 60, 69–70
Pieper, Josef, 23, 151, 173n. 23, 199n. 18, 209n. 61
Pizan, Christine de. *See* Christine de Pizan
Plutarch, 46–48
Pons, Alain, 185n. 44

Quint, David, 151–52, 209n. 66

Rabelais, François: *Gargantua*, 48–49, 52–55, 126–27, 198n. 7; *Pantagruel*, 124–25, 127–30, 198n. 12; *Quart*

Livre, 120–22; *Tiers Livre*, 75–77, 91–92, 140–41
Rais, Gilles de. *See* Gilles de Rais
Ramus, Petrus, 56
Randall, Michael, 180 n. 64
Rapin, Nicolas, 60, 186–87 n. 62, 187–88 n. 68
recreation: as a justification for reading romance, 122–25; late medieval theories of, 123–25; Rabelais's use of the topos, 128
Regosin, Richard, 206 n. 19
Ribard, Jacques, 177 n. 35
Rigolot, François, 53, 195 n. 65, 209–10 n. 67
Rivaudeau, André de, 202–3 n. 63
Robe. *See* Fourth Estate
Robertson, D. W., 176–77 n. 35
Robin, Jacques, 182 n. 8
Roman de la Rose: allegorical personification of idleness in, 20, 23, 34–37, 53, 73, 96; popularity during the Renaissance, 48–49; woodcut illustration, 20, 35, 172 n. 15
Romieu, Marie de, 193 n. 37
Ronsard, Pierre de, 15, 70, 92–93, 192–93 n. 27
Rosanbo, Louis de, 182 n. 3, 185 n. 48
Rothstein, Marian, 136–37, 198 n. 11, 199 n. 23, 200 n. 25, 201 n. 38, 202 n. 59

Saccone, Eduardo, 66
salary, invention of, 139
Schalk, Ellery, 44, 171 n. 1
Screech, Michael Andrew, 154, 171 n. 3, 204 n. 4, 206 n. 22, 207 nn. 37, 39, and 42
Seneca, 21, 70, 146, 156, 162, 163–64, 210 n. 70; French translation of *Epistles*, 162–63, 208 n. 50
sentimental romance, 116–20
serialization: 197 n. 2; as commodification of leisure, 18, 139, 142; following the *Amadis* model, 134–36; humanist attitudes toward, 127–30, 136–42; medieval antecedents, 134–35; role of desire, 132–34, 141–42. *See also Amadis de Gaule*

Serres, Michel, 210 n. 71
Shershow, Scott Cutler, 175 n. 25
Simonin, Michel, 200 n. 25, 202 n. 59
Socrates, 169
Sombart, Werner, 178 n. 43
Sorel, Charles, 142
Spacks, Patricia Meyer, 183 n. 22
sprezzatura, 16, 66, 185 nn. 42 and 44
Stanton, Domna, 177 n. 36
Strubel, Armand, 176–77 n. 35
Supple, James, 44, 58, 171 n. 1

Tabourot des Accords, Etienne, 137
Tentler, Thomas, 196 n. 79, 197 nn. 86 and 93
Thierriat, Florentin de, 83–85
Thomas Aquinas, Saint, 151
Tiraqueau, André, 59
Tournon, André, 171 n. 3, 183 n. 16, 203 n. 1
Trinquet, Roger, 187 n. 64, 211 n. 82

Urfé, Honoré d', 53

Valerius Maximus, 29–30
Van Den Abbeele, Georges, 205 n. 16
Veblen, Thorstein, 16, 31, 36, 55, 103–4
Velay-Vallantin, Catherine, 174 n. 7
Villey, Pierre, 149, 204 n. 6, 207 n. 36
Vives, Juan Luis, 87, 89–90, 91, 137, 190–91 n. 7, 191 nn. 12, 14, and 16, 194 n. 43

Weber, Max, 19
Wine, Kathleen, 181 n. 74
Wood, James, 179 n. 52, 182 n. 10
work: in relation to *derogeance*, 43, 47, 59, 84, 164–65, 182–83 n. 14; moral imperative for women, 87–90; *négoces*, 33, 34, 58–59, 61, 71, 166–69; requirement of exegesis, 125–26; responsibility of the Third Estate, 33, 43; value for the Fourth Estate, 53–54, 56–57, 65–67
Wright, Steven, 178 nn. 41 and 44

Yandell, Cathy, 18, 182 n. 7